CHILDREN'S FASHIONS
1900–1950
AS PICTURED IN
SEARS CATALOGS

Edited by
JOANNE OLIAN
Curator Emeritus, Costume Collection
Museum of the City of New York

DOVER PUBLICATIONS, INC.
Mineola, New York

For Amy Rose

Bibliographical Note

This Dover edition, first published in 2003, is a new selection of patterns from
Sears, Roebuck & Co. catalogs published between 1902–1950.
The catalog images within this book are reprinted by arrangement with Sears,
Roebuck & Co. and are protected under copyright. No duplication is permitted.

Library of Congress Cataloging-in-Publication Data

Children's fashions, 1900–1950, as pictured in Sears catalogs / edited by JoAnne
Olian.
     p. cm.
  "A new selection of patterns from Sears, Roebuck & Co. catalogs published
between 1902–1950"—T.p. verso.
  ISBN 0-486-42325-5 (pbk.)
    1. Children's clothing—United States—History—20th century—Pictorial
works. 2. Costume—United States—History—20th century—Pictorial works.
3. Sears, Roebuck and Company—Catalogs. I. Olian, JoAnne. II. Sears,
Roebuck and Company.

GT615.C55 2003
391'.3'097309041—dc21

                                          2003043842

Manufactured in the United States of America
Dover Publications, Inc., 31 East 2nd Street, Mineola, N.Y. 11501

Introduction

"What is the use of a book without pictures?" asked Alice. Had Sears been available in Lewis Carroll's Victorian England, she would undoubtedly have pored eagerly over the pages of each catalog the moment it arrived. If a history of American childhood were to be compiled, it could do no better than to be composed of illustrations from the pages of Sears. The ultimate picture book, it also served as a school book in many a farm community.

> In rural schoolhouses children were drilled in reading and spelling from the catalogue. They practiced arithmetic by filling out orders and adding up items. They tried their hand at drawing by copying the catalogue models, and acquired geography by studying the postal-zone maps. In schoolrooms that had no other encyclopedia, a Ward's or Sears' catalogue handily served the purpose; it was illustrated, it told you what something was made of and what it was good for, how long it would last, and even what it cost. Many a mother in a household with few children's books pacified her child with the pictures in the catalogue. When the new book arrived, the pictures in the old catalogue were indelibly fixed in the memory of girls who cut them up for paper dolls."[1]

The pages of Sears are to American clothing what Norman Rockwell's paintings are to American art. Both convey an idealized image of an optimistic middle class in which happy families went about their lives and domesticity ruled the day. Emblematic of this philosophy was the editorial in Sears Fall 1936 Golden Jubilee catalog: "Father and Son! The greatest combination on earth! . . . Nothing can lick a Dad and his boy—when they hitch themselves up in double harness and pull—TOGETHER. And exactly the same thing goes for a Mother and her daughter."

Much can be learned by observing a society's attitude toward its children, who are the visible manifestation of a family's aspirations. In turn-of-the-century America, in what Thorstein Veblen identified as "vicarious consumption," parental pride was manifested by dressing one's children as well as possible, even if it entailed sacrifice, so that they might bear witness to the family's well-being. While everyday garb might have been fashioned from the canvas of the covered wagon that had carried them across the plains, in photographs, pioneer children pose solemnly in their starched Sunday best beside the family sod house or before an ornate studio backdrop, poignant testimony to their parents' pride and hopes. Hence, it is not surprising to find considerable space devoted to juvenile apparel in the pages of Sears.

"Not until the late nineteenth century was it common in the United States to think of 'children' as a distinct class of the nation's population, meriting and requiring special treatment.

For most of modern history, the social and psychological meaning of childhood was vague; a child was, for all practical purposes, simply a small adult. The change in American thinking appeared only as 'children' became a minority of the population,"[2] transformed into mouths instead of productive hands.

In earlier times, children lacked the freedom enjoyed by modern-day youngsters. Restrictive clothing made them look like miniature adults, which indeed they were. One of the first influences on modern-day thinking toward children was Jean-Jacques Rousseau, who dealt extensively with their education and physical well-being in *Emile,* written in 1762. Rousseau recommended that "The limbs of the growing child be free to move easily; there should be nothing tight, nothing fitting closely to the body, no belts of any kind. The French style of dress, uncomfortable and unhealthy for a man is especially bad for children. The best plan is to keep children in frocks for as long as possible, and then to provide them with loose clothing, without trying to define the shape, which is only another way of deforming it. Their defects of body and mind may be traced to the same source, the desire to make men of them before their time." While Rousseau's pedagogic philosophy was to prove an important influence on education, less attention was paid to his theories of dress. For the next hundred years mothers continued to dress their children as small adults, in the most picturesque fashion possible, with little regard to comfort or freedom, prompting such observers as Elizabeth Cady Stanton, a pioneer in the nineteenth-century women's rights movement, to remark, "The most casual observer could see how many pleasures young girls were continually sacrificing to their dress. In walking, running, rowing, skating, dancing, going up and down stairs, climbing trees and fences, the airy fabrics and flowing skirts were a continual impediment and vexation."

Despite improvements in standards of health and falling child mortality rates, families were having fewer babies, and the resultant decline in the proportion of children from over half to about one third of the population made them more visible and their particular needs more easily recognized. "Child Study" became an important movement, spawning such proponents as Arnold Gesell of Yale, and later the beloved Dr. Benjamin Spock.

This focus on children as separate entities with special needs resonated in the area of their clothing. A time-tested truth is that children want to look like each other. To be dressed differently is to be conspicuous and open to ridicule. One of Sears' virtues was that it provided a safe haven of middle-of-the-road style. Emily Post, a leading authority on etiquette, well aware of the importance of conformity in dress, advised: "Children should be allowed to dress like their friends. Nothing makes a child, especially a boy, more self-conscious than to look 'strange' to the children he plays with.

In other words the mother who dresses a boy—or even a girl—in noticeably different clothes, may make the child not merely temporarily unhappy but can very easily set him so far apart, as to warp his whole future life." Proof of Mrs. Post's admonition was widespread during the Great Depression, as evidenced by one seven-year-old child of an out-of-work father who could still recall, years later, "sneaking to 6AM mass so that her friends would not see her wearing ugly dresses and shoes provided by the welfare bureau."[3]

In the early years of the twentieth century, suitable dress was considered essential at every level of society, a far cry from eighteenth-century reformer John Wesley's tenet that the fairer the garb, the less pious the wearer. Ready-made, mass-produced clothing and mass distribution blurred class distinctions and enabled the immigrants who were arriving in unprecedented numbers between 1880 and 1920, to blend in with the American-born population. "Greenhorn" and "hayseed" were epithets that could be avoided simply by dressing like everyone else. Chain stores and mail-order catalogs expanded the horizons of rural and small-town America. Sears and Montgomery Ward published in German and Swedish as well as English, permitting farmers in the remotest reaches of the American plains, wherever Rural Free Delivery was available, to be as up-to-date in their appearance as any big-city dwellers. Such resplendence was not to be squandered, however. A homesteader's child might treasure a pair of store-bought "dress" shoes, but as one of them remembered, "Of course, you never wore them around home. You only wore them when you went somewhere." Similarly, two sisters in Helena, Montana owned white kid gloves, saved for special occasions; as one of them recalled, "If we fell down we had to remember to fall on our elbows instead of our hands so that we wouldn't spoil our gloves."[4]

Advertisements featuring "Pictures of handsomely attired people admiring an equally handsome, streamlined car inspired a 'desire to appear at one's best' and brought home to Americans on 'every farm, in every hamlet, town and city, the significance and personal value of the well-dressed look.'. . . Americans of all walks of life—farmer's wives and immigrant factory workers, business men and boulevardiers—paid increasingly close attention to the clothes on their backs."[5] Etiquette manuals and magazines were filled with the importance of correct dress and how to achieve it. Appropriate clothing for every occasion was an essential component; school clothes were unthinkable for parties and the same was true of everyday coats, shoes, and the obligatory hat, mandating an extensive wardrobe at every level of society.

Sadly, poverty created an entire sub-class of children to whom fashion did not apply. While laws passed early in the century limited the hours a child was permitted to work to a maximum of sixty-six per week and prohibited night work, and regulations concerning compulsory education were established, factories relied heavily on child labor. Youthful urban wage-earners such as newsboys, who were responsible for fifty percent of newspapers' circulation until 1920, toiled every spare minute. The families of these children were dependent on their wages, and clothing, other than basic necessities, was beyond their reach.

Americans were nothing if not thrifty, and many women, as evidenced by the variety of fabrics and trimmings offered by such publications as Sears, spent long hours bent over the home sewing machine, turning out more or less accurate approximations of store-bought apparel. Sears encouraged such endeavors by sponsoring a dressmaking contest with a grand prize of one thousand dollars, a princely sum in 1935, with a special category for youngsters under fourteen. If any article of clothing were to be store-bought it would have been Sunday best, and Sears stood ready to outfit the whole family from newborn to nonagenarian. In order to protect the "good" clothes, serviceable denim overalls for "dad's helper" (1922, page 43), playsuits, rompers, and aprons appeared in every issue.

Thrift was emphasized in Sears' ads as much as fashion, especially in the early thirties during the height of the Depression, when page after page declared "drastic price revisions." Hand-me-downs were one way to economize; some ready-made children's clothing undoubtedly did double-duty on younger siblings, while it was not unusual for a boy to wear a suit cut down from one of his father's, or a girl to have a complete dress from the fabric of her mother's skirt. Another form of recycling was described by Louisa May Alcott in *An Old-Fashioned Girl,* when Polly showed her newly-poor cousins how to turn a faded outfit so that its wrong side could become the right side of a new one. All sorts of subterfuges were resorted to in the service of being well-dressed, which was synonymous with respectability and success.

Ever aware of its customer demographics, in 1935 Sears sponsored a 4-H county progress contest, awards going to "those counties making the greatest progress in the development of their own communities—agriculturally, socially and economically," announcing the winner in the Fall/Winter 1935–36 catalog and building a clubhouse for the lucky chapter in St. Louis County, Minnesota. Clearly, although the fashions might come from New York or Hollywood, they were beamed at the farmer's daughter—as well as his son.

Children's clothing, like that of adults, reflects the prevailing aesthetic of its time, and the basic silhouette is a scaled-down version of a grown-up one. Loose or tight garments, short or long skirts, bright or subdued colors, all are miniatures of the current mode. A perfect case in point are the 1902 girls' dresses on page 3, which, aside from higher hemlines, echo the matronly S-curved monobosom silhouette of their mothers' apparel. Since it was mother who chose the clothing, styles were geared to her taste; therefore it is no surprise that children's garb was an echo of their mothers'.

A glance through Sears' pages is more than a mere history of children's clothes, it is a chronicle of the personalities and events that shaped their lives. Naval uniforms have been beloved by children since 1846 when Queen Victoria's five-year-old son, Edward, Prince of Wales, sat for his portrait by Winterhalter in a sailor suit, continuing in popularity through the Spanish-American war when tropical white uniforms first made their appearance on board ship and in the playground. Theodore Roosevelt won the Nobel Peace Prize in 1905 for his role in mediating the Russo-Japanese war, and the resultant publicity popularized the high-necked Russian suits and dresses seen for the next several years. When Roosevelt dispatched a fleet of battleships on a round-the-world cruise, the fashion for nautical attire received renewed impetus. Sailor suits and dresses appeared in everyday and dressed-up versions from cotton to velvet in sizes from one to sixteen, the middy being the unofficial schoolgirl and sports uniform. World War I popularized boys' military-style ulsters with army-style hats; military influence was also apparent in girls'

dresses and boys' suits. Jodhpurs, worn by the United States cavalry in 1916 on an airplane mission to Mexico, became the Army aviators' uniform in World War I. Hero-worshipping boys, in homage to Charles Lindbergh, who flew solo across the Atlantic to Paris in 1927 in his monoplane, *The Spirit of St. Louis,* wore jodhpurs with sheepskin jackets and leather helmets with goggles. Aviator outfits even appeared as playsuits, along with space suits, complete with ray guns, à la science-fiction comic-strip hero Buck Rogers (1935, page 77). Cowboy and Indian outfits enjoyed perennial popularity in playsuits for both sexes. Testimony to the popularity of America's national pastime and heroes such as Ty Cobb, Babe Ruth, and "Dizzy" Dean, baseball uniforms were featured in every issue prior to World War II.

Hollywood was a major influence. Sears peppered its pages with Judy Garland fashions, Jane Withers accessories, Sonja Henie winter sportswear, along with clothing featuring Disney characters such as Mickey Mouse who made his debut in 1928. The 1935 catalog featured a full page of Shirley Temple fashions including an eponymous doll (page 79). Her puff-sleeved dresses barely reached her knees: white socks and black patent Mary Janes completed the look. With her bouncy ringlets and dimpled smile, she embodied the ideal of childish pulchritude mothers aspired to for their little girls. In the *New York Daily News* annual Beautiful Child contest, the finalists in the Sunday rotogravure section bore a striking resemblance to the child star, as did the models in the pages of mid-thirties Sears catalogs.

Nancy Drew, the "fearless teenage sleuth who motored about in a blue roadster solving crimes" in over 30 novels starting in 1930, "personified the all-American girl for generations of readers. She had . . . an athletic boyfriend named Ned, a doting widowed father and the ability to survive being beaten, choked and tossed into car trunks; escape spiders and snakes—and then retire at night in her own four-poster bed in a golden bedroom."[6] This intrepid blond, blue-eyed teenager, whose adventures were devoured by every little girl of the era, had considerable influence on the grown-up looking preteen clothing of the 1930s. Nancy Drew was the twentieth-century incarnation of the the girls whose "happy audacity" Alexis de Tocqueville admired on his 1835 visit to America. "Before she has completely left childhood behind, she already thinks for herself, speaks freely and acts on her own. All doings of the world are ever plain for her to see. Seldom does an American girl, whatever her age, suffer from shyness or childish ignorance."

> The all-American girl has been a persistent image of our culture ever since. Even though she doesn't have any current pop culture embodiment as powerful as Katharine Hepburn, or Judy Garland, or even Doris Day, she is still starring in countless books written for preteenage girls. And amazingly, after more than half a century, cute, feisty Betty is still doing battle in the newspaper comic pages with glamorous, pampered Veronica for that dubious prize, Archie.[7]

In the early years of the century tots' garb was undifferentiated as to gender with smocks and tailored frocks geared to little boys who by then wore dresses only briefly as infants, and ceased wearing them at all by 1920. Creepers began to be shown early on and were worn by both sexes as soon as they could crawl. Creepers differed from rompers in the manner in which they buttoned to allow for changing diapers. The advent of rubber diaper covers made this new garment possible. By the age of three boys were wearing tapered knee pants (1902, page 6) which were replaced by knickerbocker pants before 1910, except for little boys' suits with bloomers or "straight pants," looser and somewhat shorter than the knee pants of 1900. Knickers were worn from the age of six or seven in grammar school, while shorts were worn by preschoolers. Graduation from short to long trousers in adolescence was a significant rite of passage. Sears promoted them under their Ucanttear brand in 1916: "When 'Willie' Becomes 'William' . . . That first long pants suit! How proud a boy feels on such an eventful day! What matter though other boys chuckle with glee at his transformation! It marks an epoch from youth to manhood—from the playground to bright visions of a business career. And mothers and fathers are glad, not only because they are proud of their manly son, but because they know he will take better care of his clothes." Although knickers were still seen occasionally in Sears catalogs as late as 1945, after the thirties they were gradually superseded by long trousers.

Appropriateness was the byword that governed dress, applying equally to age and occasion. The littlest girls wore Empire-waisted dresses, while children under fourteen wore dresses with waistlines more or less at the natural waist, and skirts, while a little longer with each year, never touched the floor. When they were deemed old enough to put up their hair at about sixteen years of age, hems fell correspondingly, akin to boys' long trousers.

The sailor suit, the pleated Norfolk jacket suit with a belt, and the Russian suit vied in popularity with the Buster Brown suit, based on the cartoon character, who wore a double-breasted, hip-length jacket with a low belt, a shirt with a flat, round collar and a floppy bow, with short pants worn with a round straw hat over his short hair and bangs, much like the ones on page 14 (1912).

Girls wore, in addition to navy serge or white sailor dresses, plaids, checks, navy, deep reds, and browns for winter; and white lawn or dotted swiss trimmed with lace and embroidery in warm weather, all made with deep hems. Blue serge was worn by boys and girls in nautical outfits and knicker suits. Fake fur coats such as "nearmink, bearskin and caracul cloth," with matching muffs, kept little girls cozy while plaid wool mackinaws for boys changed little, sharing popularity with leather jackets from the twenties.

In the twenties the automobile became the means for a family vacation. Production of cars, from eight million in 1920, increased to 23 million by 1930. At the same time, the tractor transformed agriculture. The number of tractors jumped from 250,000 in 1929 to 920,00 in 1930, creating more leisure for the farmer, hence sportswear for both sexes filled more pages in Sears. For boys it appeared mainly in the guise of outing suits and overalls; girls wore knickers and middies. In the thirties, like the starlets in movie magazines who were dressed California style, girls began to wear slacks and pajamas which could do double duty for beach, sleeping, or just lounging.

Each illustration depicted much more than merely garments, it pictured the prevailing hairstyle and footwear as well. At the turn of the century, Sears boasted that its dresses were "serviceable" and "recommended by sanitary officers of

public schools." Demure, shy little girls and earnest little boys embody the principles outlined in *Home and Health,* 1907:

What a Little Girl Should be Taught

That her dress should be plain, and should not be the chief subject of her thoughts or conversation.
That she should wear only such style of clothing as will cover her person modestly.
That she should dress for health and comfort as well as for appearance.

What a Little Boy Should be Taught

To be strong and brave—to be a little man.
To be neat and orderly in his habits and appearance.

From 1900 to the 1920s, descriptions were transformed from "serviceable" to "snappy," promoting such items as "collegiate" outfits or "Rakuna" imitation raccoon coats. Boys appeared to be in the act of cheering enthusiastically while girls looked a lot like baby flappers in short smock dresses. Both had rosy cheeks presumably acquired by spending time engaged in outdoor activities.

In the thirties, girls (and their mothers) in Sears looked older and more feminine in their fitted frocks and longer flaring skirts than they did in the previous decade. Pretty dresses and sports separates were very much Hollywood-influenced, even to the stars' name endorsements and the "Little Women" frocks inspired by the film, any one of which would have suited Nancy Drew "to a T." Boys, portrayed in increasingly confident and dashing attitudes, tended to dress more and more like the aviators, sports figures, and leading men who were their heroes.

The contemporary sportswear explosion began in the late thirties and continued throughout the forties and fifties with the combined influence of California and the innovative college shops in department stores which sold casual, boy-inspired campus apparel for girls. Playsuits, slack suits, shorts, pinafores, dirndl skirts worn with peasant blouses; loafer jackets and polo shirts for boys; with denim dungarees for both sexes starting at size 1, appeared increasingly, becoming much more important in the wardrobe than conventional suits or dresses. Photographed on professional models, they convey the picture of health, poise, and ease of movement.

Sears' clothing pages are a graphic record of the enormous changes that took place as a result of the democratization of fashion. From advancements in the sewing machine to the techniques and sophisticated machinery of mass production and distribution, the contrast between 1900 and 1950 was light years more dramatic than that of any other equivalent period in history. Taken for granted were good quality clothes at all price levels, a combination that was to make Sears, Roebuck and Company the nations' largest retailer by the mid-twentieth century. In 1938, Vogue commented, "But, you say, these are commonplaces. And so they are, the commonplaces of mass production and mass distribution, the ordinary week-day tale of great businesses that cater to the great mass of American women; of a nation that has grown strong because it has believed that commonplace needs were important. Perhaps the founding fathers would be surprised if they should wake to-day, to see our literal interpretation of their theories, to see a democracy of government achieve also the only democracy of fashion in the world. They might be surprised, but we do not believe that they would be displeased.

JoAnne Olian
Sands Point, New York

[1] Daniel J. Boorstin, *The Americans: The Democratic Experience,* Vintage Books, a division of Random House, New York, 1973.
[2] Boorstin, *op.cit.*
[3] Paul S. Boyer et al, *The Enduring Vision: A History of the American,* D.C.Y. Heath and Co., Lexington, Mass., 1990.
[4] Linda Peavy and Ursula Smith, *Frontier Children,* University of Oklahoma Press, Norman, Oklahoma, 1999.
[5] Jenna Weissman Joselit, *A Perfect Fit,* Henry Holt and Company, New York, 2001.
[6] *The New York Times,* 5/30/02.
[7] Thomas Hine, *The Rise and Fall of the American Teen-Ager,* Avon Books, Inc., New York, 1999.

CHILDREN'S DRESSES.

When ordering Children's Dresses, state age.

No 7519
59 ¢

No 7520
75 ¢

No 7522
98 ¢

No 7528
$1.25

No 7529
$1.50

No 7527
$1.98

No 7524
$1.39

No 7526
$1.75

No 7530
$2.00

No 4600
$3.25

No 4601
$3.50

No. 7519. GINGHAM DRESS, pink, sky, and navy, lace trimmed, sizes 2, 3, 4 and 5 years,
....**59c**

No. 7520. GINGHAM DRESS, pink, sky, and navy, trimmed with edging of hemstitched lawn, sizes 2, 3, 4 and 5 years..............**75c**

No. 7523. DRESS, similar style to No. 7520, made of fine quality pink and blue gingham, trimmed with fine tucks and hemstitched lawn, sizes 2, 3, 4 and 5 years **1.25**

No. 7522. GINGHAM DRESS, pink, sky, and navy, tucked yoke, sizes 2, 3, 4 and 5 years,
....**98c**

No. 7524. DRESS made of plain chambray,

colors pink, blue, and red, tucked yoke, with fancy braid trimming, sizes 2, 3, 4 and 5 years,
....**1.39**

No. 7526. DRESS, made of plain chambray. colors pink, blue, and red, trimmed with white pique and fancy braid, sizes 2, 3, 4 and 5 years.............................**1.75**

No. 7527. LONG-WAISTED DRESS, of fine gingham, colors pink, blue, navy, and red, trimmed with embroidery insertion and elaborate tucking, sizes 2, 3, 4 and 5 years,
....**1.98**

No. 7528. GINGHAM DRESS, in pink and blue, trimmed with lace, sizes 6, 8, 10, 12 and 14 years **1.25**

No. 7529. GINGHAM DRESS, in pink, navy and light blue, trimmed with fancy braid, sizes 6, 8, 10, 12 and 14 years **1.50**

No. 7530. DRESS made of gingham and chambray combination, colors pink, sky, and navy, trimmed with fancy braid, sizes 6, 8, 10, 12 and 14 years **2.00**

No. 4600. SAILOR SUIT, made of navy blue all-wool serge, lined throughout, trimmed with soutache braid, kilted skirt, sizes 20, 22, 24 and 26 inches long **3.25**

No. 4601. DRESS, made of navy blue all-wool serge, lined throughout, trimmed with straps of silk, sizes 26, 28, 30, 33 and 36 inches long,
....**3.50**

Our prices are always the lowest at which "Honest Goods" can be made.

No. 17T393
$3.98

No. 17T394
$5.50

No. 17T389
$2.98

No. 17T391
$2.98

No. 17T385
$1.75

No. 17T386
$2.35

No. 17T390
$3.98

No. 17T387
$2.50

No. 17T392
$3.25

No. 17T388 $2.65

GIRLS' LONG COATS OR AUTOMOBILE JACKETS.

SPECIALTIES IN CHILDREN'S COATS.

Positively the very best styles shown; made of honest material and superior workmanship. All desirable goods that will wear and look well.

Regular sizes are, years	4	6	8	10	12	14
Numbers below the age designate number of inches around the bust	22	24	26	28	30	31

When ordering please state catalogue number, color, age and number of inches around the bust.

CHILDREN'S REEFER JACKETS.

No. 17T885 CHILD'S REEFER JACKET. MADE OF GOOD QUALITY MELTON CLOTH. Double breasted front, coat shaped collar and lapels, box back. Lined throughout with spun grass lining. Embroidered with soutache braid. Colors, blue with red embroidery and red with blue embroidery.
Price................... (If by mail postage, extra, 35 cents)..................**$1.75**

No. 17T886 CHILD'S REEFER JACKET. MADE OF GOOD QUALITY BEAVER. Double breasted front. Loose back. Trimmed with soutache braid on the collar, on shoulder cape and around the sleeves. Facing in front of same material. Colors, blue with white trimming or castor with brown trimming.
Price................... (If by mail, postage extra, 38 cents)..................**$2.35**

No. 17T887 CHILD'S REEFER JACKET MADE OF GOOD QUALITY HEAVY WEIGHT MELTON. Double breasted front, coat shaped collar and lapels; patch pockets; bound around collar and lapels with satin folds and silk cord. Similar trimming around sleeves. Colors, blue or red. Price....(If by mail, postage extra, 35 cents)....**$2.50**

No. 17T888 VERY NOBBY CHILD'S REEFER JACKET. MADE OF ALL WOOL BEAVER CLOTH. Double breasted front, loose back. Silk cord trimming on sleeves, on collar and on shoulder cape which is also inlaid with black velvet. Facing in front of same material. Best value for the money. Colors, blue or red.
Price................... (If by mail, postage extra, 38 cents)..................**$2.65**

No. 17T889 CHILD'S VERY STYLISH REEFER JACKET, MADE OF ALL WOOL KERSEY. Double breasted front, loose back, square shoulder cape and stylish cuffs. Shoulder cape is trimmed with satin folds and strap trimming of the same material. Satin fold trimming around the cuffs as well as on the collar. Colors, blue with black trimming or castor with brown trimming. Price..................**$2.98**
If by mail, postage extra, 41 cents.

No. 17T890 CHILD'S REEFER JACKET OR BOX COAT. VERY PRETTY. MADE OF ALL WOOL KERSEY. Double breasted front, loose back coat, shaped collar and lapels, velvet collar and cuffs. Facing in front of same material. Lined half way with mercerized sateen. Colors, red or castor. Price..................**$3.98**
If by mail, postage extra, 38 cents.

CHILDREN'S LONG COATS.

THIS TABLE SHOWS THE RELATIVE LENGTH TO AGE AND BUST MEASURES.

Age, years	4	6	8	10	12	14
Bust, inches	22	24	26	28	30	31
Length, inches	32	34	36	38	40	42

We don't make any changes if the young lady is large for her age. Please state so and give bust measurements.

No. 17T891 CHILD'S LONG COAT OR RAGLAN. MADE OF GOOD QUALITY WOOL MIXED MELTON. Double breasted front, velvet collar. Piping of velvet around the lapels in front and on sleeves showing the cuff effect; on side pockets, on yoke in front and on pointed yoke in back. Facing in front of same material. Colors, oxford gray with an invisible fancy plaid. Very serviceable.
Price................... (If by mail, postage extra, 58 cents)..................**$2.98**

No. 17T892 CHILD'S NEW MARKET OR RAGLAN COAT. MADE OF GOOD QUALITY HEAVY WEIGHT MELTON. Double breasted front, buttoning up to the neck. Storm collar. Facing in front of same material. Loose back neatly trimmed with an inch wide velvet strip on pointed yoke in front, in back as well as on sleeves. Very attractive and stylish. Colors, blue only.
Price................... (If by mail postage, extra, 58 cents)..................**$3.25**

No. 17T893 CHILD'S NEW MARKET OR RAGLAN. MADE IN THE VERY NEWEST GIBSON STYLE DOUBLE BREASTED FRONT, half tight back, bound around the collar and cuffs with black braid and trimmed on yoke in front across shoulders and on the shoulder pleat with the same trimming. Colors, blue or red.
Price................... (If by mail, postage extra, 60 cents)..................**$3.98**

No. 17T894 VERY NOBBY CHILD'S LONG COAT OR RAGLAN. MADE OF GOOD QUALITY ALL WOOL BEAVER IN THE NEWEST GIBSON STYLE. Neatly trimmed with satin folds in front around the pockets, on sleeves and in back as well as on the collar. Facing in front of same material. Loose back. Colors, blue or red.
Price................... (If by mail, postage extra, 60 cents)..................**$5.50**

No. 38T2304
$2.25

No. 38T2306
$2.48

No. 38T2303
$1.75

No. 38T2302
$1.48

No. 38T2307
$2.75

No. 38T2309
$2.98

No. 38T2305
$1.98

No. 38T2301
$1.19

No. 38T2308
$2.89

No. 38T2310
$3.25

No. 38T2311
$3.48

GIRLS' LINED DRESSES.

SIZES 4 TO 14 YEARS. When ordering please state age, height, weight and number of inches around bust. When necessary to make a dress to order, we will charge 20 per cent extra for material and labor.

Scale of sizes, showing proportion of bust and length to the age of child:

Age	4	6	8	10	12	14
Bust	24	27	28	29	30	31
Skirt length	18	20	22	24	26	28

No. 38T2301 EXTRA GOOD VALUE GIRLS' DRESS. Made of novelty plaid material, has a V-shape yoke made of cashmere trimmed with braid and pearl buttons, shoulder capes extending to back and trimmed with one row of braid to match, satin ribbon bow, waistband and cuffs made of cashmere and trimmed with braid, lined with cambric, wide hem. Colors, blue or red predominating.
Price................(If by mail, postage extra, 21 cents)............**$1.19**

No. 38T2302 GIRLS' DRESS. Made of novelty plaid, has a round yoke made of cashmere trimmed with tucks and three small pearl buttons, has a ruffle all around yoke extending to back, which is trimmed with three rows of cord. Waistband and cuffs made of cashmere, standing collar, waistband and cuffs trimmed with three rows of soutache to match. Lined throughout with cambric, wide hem at bottom. Colors, combination of plaids, blue or red predominating. Price.....(If by mail, postage extra, 21 cents)... **$1.48**

No. 38T2303 VERY PRETTY GIRLS' DRESS. Made of all wool novelty plaid material, front made of cashmere trimmed with tucks and small pearl buttons, bolero effect, shoulder capes trimmed with cashmere and two rows of braid. Cashmere standing collar, waistband and cuffs trimmed with two rows of braid to match. Lined throughout with cambric, wide hem at bottom. Colors, blue, red or green predominating.
Price.................(If by mail, postage extra, 22 cents)............... **$1.75**

No. 38T2304 VERY STYLISH GIRLS' DRESS. Made of all wool cashmere, V shaped yoke trimmed with tucks and small pearl buttons, has shoulder capes trimmed with one row of silk gimp. Standing collar, waistband and cuffs trimmed with three rows silk gimp to match. Lined throughout with cambric, wide hem at bottom. Colors, navy blue or brown. Price ....(If by mail, postage extra, 22 cents)....... **$2.25**

No. 38T2305 VERY STYLISH GIRLS' DRESS BLOUSE EFFECT. Made of novelty plaid material, V-shaped yoke made of velvet trimmed with two rows of silk gimp, shoulder capes also trimmed with two rows of silk gimp. Standing velvet collar and cuffs with trimmings to match, velvet tie, lined throughout with cambric, wide hem at bottom. Combination of plaids blue or red predominating.
Price.................(If by mail, postage extra, 30 cents)............ **$1.98**

No. 38T2306 VERY PRETTY DRESS. Made of all wool cashmere, round yoke trimmed in front with tucks, has shoulder capes extending to back and trimmed with silk and two rows of braid. Standing collar, waistband and cuffs trimmed with braid to match, satin ribbon bow at yoke, lined throughout with cambric, wide hem at bottom. Colors, navy blue or red Price .....(If by mail, postage extra, 22 cents)..........**$2.48**

No. 38T2307 GIRLS' DRESS. Made of all wool flannel, very pretty round yoke trimmed with three plaits and six rows of cord, shoulder capes extending to back trimmed with three rows of cord and small pearl buttons. Standing collar, waistband and cuffs trimmed with cord to match. Lined throughout with cambric, wide hem at bottom. Colors, navy blue or red. Price.......(If by mail, postage extra, 21 cents) **$2.75**

No. 38T2308 VERY STYLISH GIRLS' DRESS. Made of all wool cashmere, trimmed in front with tucks and pearl buttons, bolero effect vest trimmed with four rows of cord and one row of gimp, large shoulder capes extending to back, which are trimmed with four rows of cord and gimp to match. Standing collar, waistband and cuffs trimmed with similar trimmings. Gored skirt, dress lined throughout with cambric, wide hem. Color, blue or brown. Price ....(If by mail, postage extra, 24 cents)..... **$2.89**

No. 38T2309 VERY PRETTY GIRLS' DRESS. Made of all wool flannel, beautifully trimmed in front with silk cord, gimp and small pearl buttons, has wide shoulder capes with trimmings to match, has standing collar, waistband and cuffs trimmed with gimp and cord to match. Gored skirt, dress lined throughout with cambric, wide hem. Colors, navy blue or red. Price ....(If by mail, postage extra, 22 cents)......... **$2.98**

No. 38T2310 A HANDSOME GIRLS' DRESS. Made of all wool cashmere; bolero effect, trimmed with metal buttons and three rows of silk cord. Silk front trimmed with numerous rows of tucks, has large shoulder capes extending to back, trimmed with three rows of silk cord. Standing collar, waistband and cuffs trimmed with cord to match, gored skirt, dress lined throughout with cambric, wide hem. Color, blue or brown. Price....... (If by mail, postage extra, 21 cents)......... **$3.25**

No. 38T2311 AN EXCEEDINGLY PRETTY GIRLS' DRESS. Made of all wool cashmere; front trimmed with numerous rows of tucks, three rows of silk straps extending around back of yoke, trimmed with pearl ornaments. Revers extending from waist to shoulder, which are trimmed with two rows of gimp. Standing collar, waistband and cuffs trimmed with one row of silk and two rows of gimp to match. Gored skirt, dress lined throughout with cambric, wide hem at bottom. Colors, royal blue or red. Price..(Postage extra, 19 cents)... **$3.48**

4   [1902]

Child's Dress, $1.69

No. 38T1218
Child's Dress, made of high grade lawn. Swiss embroidery around the collar. Insertion in front, which forms a pleasing effect, and double ruffle of fine Swiss embroidery in front, and one ruffle right from the shoulders to the back, and Swiss insertion around the sleeves as well as ruffles. Two rows of triple tucking in back to the waist. A very desirable style and neat. Ages, 6 months, 1, 2 and 3 years.
Price, each.. ..$1.69
If by mail, postage extra, 7 cents.

CHILDREN'S APRONS.

For children, ages, from 4 to 12 Years.

Gingham Apron, 23 Cents.
No. 38T1226 Girls' Apron, made of good quality gingham in blue or brown and white checks as per illustration. Fancy slashed collar and cuffs trimmed with white lace. Yoke in front and back. Opens in the back and tied with 3-inch strings. Price, each 23c
If by mail, postage extra, 9 cents.

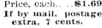

Mention age. sizes, from 4 to 12 years.

No. 38T1230 Girls' Lawn Apron, yoke trimmed with three rows of embroidery, shoulder strap edged with narrow lace. Very good value. Color, white only.
Price, each............27c
If by mail, postage extra, 6 cents.

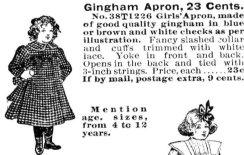

No. 38T1234 Very neat Girls' Lawn Apron, yoke trimmed with two rows of fine embroidery, flounce over shoulders which is hemstitched, wide hem at bottom. Exceptionally good value. Color, white only.
Price, each...........38c
If by mail, postage extra, 7 cents.

48 Cents Buys This Prettily Embroidered Apron.

No. 38T1236 Very pretty Girls' Lawn Apron, yoke made of two rows of fine embroidery, ruffle of fine embroidery, extending from waist to shoulder, wide hem at bottom. Color, white only.
Price, each................48c
If by mail, postage extra, 7 cents.

BE SURE AND GIVE SIZE DESIRED.

No. 38T1240 Girls' Apron, made of good quality of lawn, yoke in front and back, with insertion of embroidery, also insertion over shoulders, with lawn ruffle, which is hemstitched; wide hem at bottom. A regular 75-cent apron. Color, white only.
Price, each 55c
If by mail, postage extra, 7 cents.

Children's White Lawn Aprons.

No. 38T1244 A beautiful Girls' Apron, made of fine white lawn, with insertion of lace all around body with six rows of fine tucks, lace edging around neck and shoulder ruffles, wide hem at bottom. Extra good value.
Price, each.............69c
If by mail, postage extra, 7 cents.

GIVE AGE DESIRED.
Sizes, 4 to 12 years.

No. 38T1248 Very neat Girls' Apron, made of good quality white lawn, eight rows of tucks (each hemstitched), in front, shoulder strap with two wide embroidery insertions and wide lawn ruffle, deep hem at bottom. Exceptionally good value.
Price, each..............82c
If by mail, postage extra, 7 cents.

INFANTS' OUTFITS.

We call special attention to our two Infants' Outfit sets as described on this page. They consist of 24 pieces in each set and you will find that if you bought the pieces separately, the total cost of either set would be nearly double our price.

Infant's Outfit, Consisting of 24 Pieces, for $5.95.

These sets have been carefully selected with a view of offering a complete outfit at the very lowest price, such as you would pay nearly twice as much for elsewhere. In these sets you will find, as described below, everything that baby needs to wear, thus doing away with the making of different selections of the so many different articles for the baby's wardrobe.

1 Very dainty long Cambric Robe, embroidery down front and around bottom.
1 Muslin Day Slip, square yoke made of fine embroidery insertion, wide hem at bottom.
2 Muslin Night Slips, fancy yoke of embroidery and herringbone braid.
1 Domet Flannel Wrapper, embroidered around collar and epaulets over shoulders.
1 Cambric Long Skirt, with three fine tucks around bottom.
1 Cambric Long Skirt, with two clusters of tucks (3 tucks in a cluster,) Hamburg embroidery around bottom.
1 Long Skirt, made of fleeced canton flannel.
1 Long Canton Skirt, fleeced, stitched around bottom with silk.
1 All Wool Flannel Shawl, beautifully embroidered with silk on corner.
3 Bibs, honey comb pattern, edged all around with lace.
2 Rubber Diapers (white).
1 Silk Bonnet, beautifully embroidered with silk.
2 Pair All Wool Knit Bootees, very closely knitted with fine all wool zephyr.
1 All Wool Knitted Sacque, trimmed with tassels.
1 Flannel Sacque, stitched all around collar, down front and cuffs with silk.
2 Bands, made of cantor flannel.
2 Pinning Blankets or Barrior Coats, made of cream color canton flannel.
No. 38T1262 Price for complete outfit, 24 pieces............................$5.95
If by mail, postage extra, 58 cents.

Ball's Celebrated Waist for Children, 38 Cents.

38c

No. 18T4952 Dr. Ball's Child's Corset Waist will train your child's figure while young. The Dr. Ball's Waist is easy, comfortable and perfect fitting, patent tape fastened buttons and taped buttonholes. White or drab. Sizes, 18 to 28. Always give waist measure.
Price, each..38c
If by mail, postage extra, 10 cents.

Misses' Strip Corset 40 Cents.

No. 18T4954 Misses' Strip Corset, made of good quality corset jeans. This corset has a decidedly advantageous feature, being soft and pliable, which makes it most healthful for growing children. Colors, drab or white. Sizes, 18 to 26. Always give waist measure.
Price, each..40c
If by mail, postage extra, 12 cents.

40c

The Coronet Jackson Waists for Misses are the Best, 55 Cts.

No. 18T4956 Coronet Misses' Waist. We supply a long felt and needed want by the ambitious miss just blooming into womanhood, when her figure begins to take on the matronly form which this garment so beautifully displays; made of sateen, white or drab. Sizes, 18 to 28. Always give waist measure.
Price, each..55c
If by mail, postage extra, 12 cents.

55c

Dr. Ball's Elastic Corsets for Growing Girls, 75 Cents.

No. 18T4958 Dr. Ball's Perfect Fitting Misses' Corset, an ideal corset for growing girls, shaped on scientific principles, made of fine, heavy drill, laced and elastic gored hook, shoulder straps and clasp front, lace edging. A perfect corset. White or drab. Sizes, 18 to 26. Always give waist measure.
Price, each..75c
If by mail, postage extra, 12 cents.

75c

No. 38T1570 Poke Bonnet, made of fine quality mercerized faille, with cape of same material. The band on top of cape is wired so as to preserve the shape. Heavy lace ruching at top. Wide faille strings. Lined throughout. A very stylish and serviceable bonnet. Colors, cardinal, navy blue or brown. Sizes, 13 to 17.
Price, each............74c
If by mail, postage extra, 10 cents.

No. 38T1572 Very Pretty Child's Bonnet, made of silk faille, two ruffles around front, edged with silk baby ribbon, satin ribbon bows on side, ruche in face, lined with cambric, wide silk ties. Colors, navy blue, pale blue or cardinal. Sizes, 13 to 17.
Price............98c
If by mail, postage extra, 8 cents.

No. 38T1574 Exceedingly Pretty Child's Poke Bonnet, made of silk faille, ruffled all around bonnet, ruche in front and chiffon around face and top, wide cape. Lined with sateen and interlined with wadding, wide silk faille strings. Colors, navy blue or cardinal. Sizes, 13 to 17. Price...$1.19
If by mail, postage extra, 8 cents.

TAM O'SHANTERS.

No. 38T1614 Our New College Shape Tam O'Shanter, made of fine quality ribbed flannel. This tam is made of navy blue. Around the brim is a medium wide row of white felt, finished with a row of fancy trimming braid, with a gold thread running through; on top of crown a new, original design, made of white felt; in center of crown is a white felt covered button, over which hangs a silk tassel. The cap is lined, and a very dressy and splendid value. Price, each 39c
If by mail, postage extra, 15 cents.

No. 38T1618 This Pretty College Shape Tam O'Shanter is made of fine quality black velvette; around the curved band are three rows of silk soutache trimming, and over top of crown it is finished with a fancy braided design, and silk tassel; lined throughout; very stylish and one of the prettiest tams made.
Price, each.......48c
If by mail, postage extra, 15c

No. 38T1622 Circular Tam O'Shanter. Trimmed with two rows hercules braid on top and silk pompon; has one row of hercules braid on band; made of pressed flannel, lined throughout; very neat and serviceable. Colors, navy blue or cardinal. Price...25c
If by mail, postage extra, 12 cents.

No. 38T1626 This stylish Circular Tam O'Shanter is made of fine quality black velvette with a row of 1-inch faille silk ribbon around brim, completed with a little bow of same material. For a rich and dressy tam for either a boy or girl, this is an excellent number; lined throughout. Sizes, 6¼ to 6⅞. Price....47c
If by mail, postage extra, 12 cents.

No. 38T1628 Circular Shape Tam O'Shanter. New, original design, making a pretty, elaborate appearance. The top of crown is trimmed with two rows of soutache braid, and is finished with brass buttons as shown in illustration. Two rows of gold soutache around brim; made of fine quality all wool flannel. Can be ordered in cardinal or navy blue. Price..........49c
If by mail, postage extra, 12 cents.

No. 38T1630 Circular Shape Tam O'Shanter. It is a combination tam, made of all good quality flannel; the center design on top of crown is good quality Astrakhan cloth, finished with a covered flannel button in center; the brim is made of the same quality Astrakhan cloth, which can be pulled down over the ears; lined throughout. Can be ordered in combination of colors as follows: Red flannel with black Astrakhan, or navy blue flannel with black Astrakhan. Price..52c
If by mail, postage extra, 11 cents.

CHILD'S CAPS AND TOQUES.

No. 38T1642 Child's Cap, made of good quality pressed flannel, white fancy band around peak of cap, and fancy design on top of crown of soutache braid; the cap is lined and well made. Colors, cardinal or navy blue. Price........24c
If by mail, postage extra, 10 cents.

No. 38T1643 This is a very neat little cap, made of all wool flannel, fancy ornamental design on crown of silk braid, as shown in illustration. Black velvet rim and peak, black velvet covered button on top of crown, satin lined. A very neat and dressy little cap. Colors, cardinal or navy blue. Price, 41c
If by mail, postage extra, 12c

No. 38T1644 This is a very stylish and dressy little cap for boys. Made of good quality velvette; the rim is made of a fancy mixture of cloth, with a double row of silk cord around front; satin lined. Colors, black only.
Price 49c
If by mail, postage extra, 12 cents.

No. 38T1645 Child's Toque. Turkish design. Made of nice quality flannel; very ornamental in design; around the crown are two bands of fancy braid, and over the flowing end of the crown seven rows of band trimming as shown in illustration. Silk tassel on end of cap; cap is lined, and a very excellent value. Colors, cardinal or navy. Price, each (If by mail, postage extra, 8 cents) 23c

No. 38T1646 Child's Toque. Oriental design, combination design, made of good quality black velvette and all wool cardinal flannel; with two rows of gold silk soutache braid around brim, while the crown has braided rows of gold soutache braid with gold spikes on ends. (See illustration.) Long silk tassel on end; this is a very original and pretty design.
Price, each...........48c
If by mail, postage extra, 8 cents.

IF YOU ARE INTERESTED IN

BOYS' AND CHILDREN'S CLOTHING,

send for our free Cloth Sample Book of Boys' and Children's Clothing, containing cloth samples of everything shown in this department. We sell boys' and children's clothing at about one-half the prices usually charged and can save you a great deal of money on these goods.

INFANTS' KNIT BOOTEES.

WE SHOW A COMPLETE LINE of these dainty and comfortable articles for infants.
NOTE OUR PRICES AND QUALITIES CAREFULLY.

No. 38T1652 Infants' Bootees, hand crocheted, made of all wool zephyr. Colors, solid white, pink and white, or blue and white. Price, per pair....9c
If by mail, postage extra, per pair, 2c.

No. 38T1656 Infants' Bootees, closely hand crocheted, made of good quality zephyr. Colors, solid white, pink and white, or blue and white. Price, per pair....15c
If by mail, postage extra, per pair, 2 cents.

No. 38T1660 Infants' Bootees, closely hand crocheted, neat design, made of fine zephyr. Colors, solid white, pink and white, or blue and white. Price, per pair..............20c
If by mail, postage extra, per pair 2 cents.

No. 38T1664 A very neat all wool Ribbed Bootee, very closely knitted, trimmed with small tassels at ankle. Colors, solid white, pink and white, or blue and white. Price, per pair.................25c
If by mail, postage extra, per pair, 2 cents.

No. 38T1668 Infants' High Bootees, made of all wool zephyr, closely crocheted, turned over top finished with silk. Colors, solid white, pink and white, or light blue and white. Price, per pair.....................30c
If by mail, postage extra, per pair, 2 cents.

No. 38T1672 Infants' High Bootees, made of silkatine; it looks like silk, but wears better. Closely crocheted and very pretty. Colors, solid cream, pink and cream, or light blue and cream. Price, per pair....................35c
If by mail, postage extra, per pair, 2 cents.

No. 38T1676 A Very Pretty Bootee made of very fine closely knitted Saxony yarn; trimmed with baby ribbon, ribbon at ankles; excellent value. Colors, solid white, pink and white, or blue and white. Price, per pair.....................40c
If by mail, postage extra, per pair, 2 cents.

No. 38T1680 Infants' High Bootees, hand crocheted of extra good quality zephyr with silk fancy work, turned over top; very good quality for the money. Colors, solid white, pink and white, or light blue and white. Price, per pair.....................48c
If by mail, postage extra, per pair, 2 cents.

Infants' Knitted Slippers.

No. 38T1684 Infants' Knitted Slippers, with lamb's wool sole, very pretty, made of all wool yarn. Colors, solid white, white and blue, or white and pink. Price, per pair...............30c
If by mail, postage extra, per pair, 4 cents.

Infants' Knit Sacques.

No. 38T1696 Infants' Sacque, made of all wool Shetland yarn. Colors, solid cream, pink and cream, or light blue and cream.
Price, each.....19c
If by mail, postage extra, each, 3 cents.

No. 38T1702 Infants' Sacque, closely hand crocheted, made of all wool zephyr, tassels in front, very neat design. Colors, solid white, pink and white, or light blue and white.
Price, each...32c
If by mail, postage extra, each, 4 cents.

Fancy Green and Brown Mixed Cheviot in Two-Piece Knee Pants Suit, $3.50.

This closely woven all wool cheviot is a very desirable fabric for boys' clothing and you will surely be pleased if you send us your order for a suit of this material. The color is a pretty brown and green mixture with a hairline overplaid in red. We are not exaggerating when we say that it is as good, if not better, than any $5.00 suit shown in retail clothing stores. The coat is cut in double breasted style like illustration, is double stitched all around, thoroughly well tailored and neatly trimmed. Pants are made with double seat and knees, the usual number of pockets and patent buttons on fly and waistband.

No. 40T802 Price for boys' two-piece knee pants suit, ages 8 to 15 years..... **$3.50**

BOYS' VESTEE AND NORFOLK SUITS.

Boys' Vestee and Norfolk Suits are made up as described under each number. Vestee suits are made in sizes for boys from 3 to 8 years of age, and Norfolk suits from 4 to 10. No other sizes can be furnished in each style. In ordering, it will only be necessary to state age of boy and whether large or small for age.

Heavy Weight Brown Mixed Cassimere Vestee Suit, $1.50.

The suit is made from heavy weight union cassimere, excellent wearing material although not all wool. Cut as shown in illustration, vest of same material with a fancy dickey to match. Pants are made with double seat and knees, double sewed and taped through crotch, elastic waistband and three buttons at knee.

No. 40T850 Price for boys' vestee suit, ages 3 to 8 years $1.50

Dark Mixed Cheviot Vestee Suit, $2.00.

Made from a good weight dark brown and gray mixed cheviot, woven in a neat herringbone pattern. We made arrangements for obtaining a large quantity of this material because we feel sure that it will be a heavy seller, as it is just the thing for a splendid wearing every day suit and we put the price at the lowest possible figure. The suit is made in imitation double breasted style, with round corners, double breasted vest and fancy shield. Pants have double seat and knees, closed front, buckle and buttons at bottom.

No. 40T852 Price for boys' vestee suit, ages 3 to 8 years.................$2.00

Bauendahl's Chinchilla Reefer, $3.50.

We can recommend this navy blue chinchilla reefer as a strictly all wool warm and dressy garment. We invite you to compare it with the cheap grades of this material which are usually offered at about our price and you will appreciate its exceptional value. The coat is lined with dark plaid wool lining, which makes it a very warm garment. It is made double breasted with large storm collar, two ulster and two lower pockets, and has extra buttons on inside facings to replace any which may become lost or broken. You will find the coat a perfect garment in every respect.

No. 40T918 Price for boys' reefer coat, ages, 9 to 15 years (no smaller or larger sizes)..**$3.50**

Boys' Short Top Coat, $4.50.

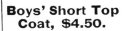

This is a very stylish and popular garment. It is a short box fly front coat as shown in illustration. We have them in blue, brown or tan beaver. State color preferred. The coats are made with a velvet collar to match material, have two lower and a cash pocket with flaps and the latest style turn up cuffs. You will find our price much lower than garments in this style are usually offered at and feel sure that you will be more than pleased if you get one of these coats.

No. 40T920 Price for boys' short top coat, ages 10 to 16 years (no other sizes can be furnished)........**$4.50**

Boys' Cape Overcoat in Dark Mixed Cassimere, $2.50.

We have this number in several shades, some in a dark brown and some in a green mixed heavy weight cassimere, materials especially well adapted for cape overcoats which will give splendid satisfaction. The coats are lined with a good quality of Italian body lining, are thoroughly well sewed and have a large detachable cape.

No. 40T922 Price for boys' cape overcoat, ages 4 to 12 years.. ....**$2.50**

Boys' Blue Beaver Cape Overcoat, $3.50.

This coat is made from an extra good quality of Rareton mills blue beaver cloth and makes a very dressy and warm garment. It is made in double breasted style with a large detachable cape, well lined and tailored. It has large ulster pockets, two lower pockets and is double stitched all round. A very desirable garment in every respect at a price much below that at which garments of this material usually sell.

No. 40T924 Price for boys' cape overcoat, ages 4 to 12 years...**$3.50**

Little Men's Raglan Coat, $4.50.

This handsome little garment is made exactly like opposite illustration. A strictly up to date little men's coat in the popular raglan style with Kitchener yoke and upright pockets. The material we use for it is all wool, a pretty dark green and black mixture and makes a garment of which any boy will be proud. The coat is made fly front with a handsome velvet collar, turned up cuffs and is well lined and tailored throughout.

No. 40T926 Price for little men's raglan coats, ages 6 to 10 years.**$4.50**

BOYS' WAISTS AND BLOUSES.

In our Boys' Waist Department we show a line of garments which you will find of better material and better made than goods of this kind usually are. We do not think it pays our customers to buy real cheap garments of this kind as they are practically valueless and we do not carry a cheap grade on that account. In ordering waists or blouses it will only be necessary to state age of boy and whether large or small for age. Only such sizes as are quoted under each number can be furnished.

Boys' Domet Flannel Blouse.

Made as shown in illustration on the left, in a fine quality of striped domet flannel in a variety of shades. Large sailor collar, double cuffs and trimmed with pearl buttons and thoroughly well sewed. You will find this a most excellent garment for the price.

No. 40T950 Price for boys' blouse, ages 3 to 10 years, **40c**

Boys' Domet Flannel Waist.

We furnish this waist in neat check patterns in medium shades. It is made, as shown in illustration on the right, with turn down collar, one outside pocket, double cuffs and double stitched seams. The material is a good wearing quality of domet flannel

No. 40T952 Price for boys' waist, ages 4 to 14 years, **40c**

No. 40T950

No. 40T952

Boys' Military Blouse, $1.25.

This handsome little blouse is made exactly like opposite illustration in a very fine all wool gray flannel, trimmed with two straps of dark blue flannel and a dark blue military collar. The garment has one outside pocket, broad double cuffs and is thoroughly well sewed throughout. This is a very popular style and at our price is an exceptionally good value.

No. 40T962 Price for boys' military blouse, ages 3 to 10 years..........$1.25

Fancy Blue Tricot Flannel Blouse, $1.25.

This blouse is made of a very pretty shade of light blue, all wool, tricot flannel. Large sailor collar, neatly trimmed with three rows of white braid, fly front and double cuffs. Non-shrinkable collar band. It makes a very desirable garment which is sure to give satisfaction.

No. 40T964 Price for boys' blouse, ages 3 to 10 years..$1.25

BOYS' WASH WAISTS.

Boys' 25 Cent Wash Waist.

Made from a good quality of heavy percale in neat striped patterns. Small collar, single box plait and double cuffs. An excellent garment for the price.

No. 40T970 Price for boys' waist, ages 4 to 14 years...................................25c

Extra Quality Wash Percale Waist, 45c.

This waist is made from an extra good quality of wash percale in a variety of shades. State your preference. Made with three box plaits in front and back, open cuffs and detachable mothers' friend waistband. A very durable and dressy waist.

No. 40T972 Price for boys' waist, ages 4 to 12 years.........45c

Box Plaited Waist Without Collar, 50c.

Made of fine wash percale in neat striped patterns or in plain white. The garment is made to wear with a collar, has box plaits in front and open cuffs, and patent adjustable waistband. It is a very popular style of garment.

No. 40T974 Price for boys' waist, ages 4 to 12 years................50c

White Lawn Blouse Waist 50c.

Made from fine quality of white lawn, neatly embroidered, large sailor collar, double cuffs, and well finished throughout. Exactly as illustrated.

No. 40T976 Price for boys' blouse, ages 3 to 8 years..........50c

Boys' White Laundered Shirt Waist, 60c.

This waist is made from a fine quality of white lawn muslin. Three box plaits front and back, open cuffs and collar attached to waist. It is provided with patent detachable waistband.

No. 40T978 Price for boys' waist, ages 4 to 12 years..............60c

Boys' Fancy Blouse Waist, 75c.

Made from a fine quality of linen lawn, with a large pique sailor collar and box plait down front and cuffs of same material. A very handsome and very popular garment which is sure to give satisfaction.

No. 40T980 Price for boys' waist, ages 3 to 8 years... ....75c

Boys' Striped Percale Waist, 75 Cents.

Made from a very fine wash percale, in neat striped patterns. State color preferred. This garment is double sewed throughout, extra well stayed at shoulders, and is trimmed with pearl buttons. Collar and cuffs are attached to waist. You will find this an excellent waist for the price.

No. 40T982 Price for boys' waist, ages 4 to 14 years 75c

Boys' Military Waist, 85 Cents.

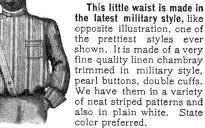

This little waist is made in the latest military style, like opposite illustration, one of the prettiest styles ever shown. It is made of a very fine quality linen chambray trimmed in military style, pearl buttons, double cuffs. We have them in a variety of neat striped patterns and also in plain white. State color preferred.

No. 40T984 Price for boys' waist, ages 3 to 10 years.......... ....85c

Our 40-Cent Boys' Turban.

No. 33T2734 Boys' Turban, made of fine quality of heavy oxford cheviot, with wide pull down band and silk binding. Fancy silk lined. Color, oxford gray only. A very dressy looking cap and one that retails for 75 cents. Sizes, 6⅞ to 7⅛ only.
Price, each.....................................40c
If by mail, postage extra, each, 11 cents.

BOYS' OR YOUTHS' PLUSH CAPS.

SPECIAL NOTICE.—We sell no pieced plush caps of any kind, but all are cut from whole cloth. We warrant every one to be perfect in workmanship, and the best value you have seen for the price. Sizes, 6⅜, 6½, 6⅝, 6¾, 6⅞, 7 and 7⅛.

No. 33T2740 Boys' Fine Silk Plush Caps, Brighton style, full width pull down band and silk lined. Sizes, 6⅜ to 7⅛ only.
Price, each..........50c
If by mail, postage extra, each, 10 cents.

No. 33T2746 Boy's Fine Silk Plush Turban Caps, with handsome satin lining throughout; wide pull down band to protect the ears. Finely made and finished. Sizes, 6⅜ to 7⅛ only.
Price, each.......50c
If by mail, postage extra, each, 10 cents.

Boys' Plush Brighton, 75 Cents.

No. 33T2750 Boys' Silk Plush Brighton Style Caps, made of extra quality fine silk plush, with fine satin lining. Regular retail price. $1.00. Sizes, 6⅜ to 7⅛. Price, each.....75c
If by mail, postage extra, each, 10 cents.

No. 33T2756 Boys' Extra Fine Silk Plush Academy Cap. Latest style, six-piece top with fine heavy satin lining, and pull down band to protect the ears. This is an exceptionally fine winter cap. Good, heavy weight; very fine and dressy in appearance. Sizes, 6⅜ to 7⅛ only.
Price, each....................75c
If by mail, postage extra, each, 10 cents.

No. 33T2760 Boys' Extra Quality Fine Silk Plush Caps, in golf style with pull down band. Fine satin lining and it usually retails at $1.00. A very dressy style. Sizes, 6⅜ to 7⅛ only.
Price, each....................75c
If by mail, postage extra, each, 10 cents.
Don't forget to give size when you order a cap.

WARM CAPS FOR LITTLE PEOPLE.

Sizes, 6⅛, 6¼, 6⅜, 6½, 6⅝ and 6¾ only. A line of warm caps made especially for children from two years to about ten years of age. If you do not know size see illustration showing how to measure on first page of this department.

Junior Caps.

No. 33T2800 Junior Caps made of good quality wool cloth in golf yacht style with silk ornament on front. Navy blue only. Sizes, 6¼ to 6¾ only. Price, each....................23c
If by mail, postage extra, each, 6 cents.

No. 33T2804 Junior Caps, made of fancy plaid cassimere cloth, all wool in medium plaid medium dark colors, pretty ornament in front with bow. Wide band to pull down over ears. Sizes, 6¼ to 6¾ only. Price, each.......35c
If by mail, postage extra, each, 8 cents.

No. 33T2806 Junior Caps, made from corded velveteen, with a wide pull down over the ears, which can be buttoned over the top. Fine, heavy mercerized lining. A very stylish cap for small boys. Colors, navy blue or red. Sizes, 6¼ to 6¾. Price, each....................40c
If by mail, postage extra, each, 8 cents.

No. 33T2814 Junior Caps in new style and combination. Navy blue broadcloth, with beaver plush band, closed with bow in front and ornamented with star; silk lined. This is another of the new good things for this season. Sizes, 6¼ to 6¾ only. Price, each....................45c
If by mail, postage extra, each, 8 cents.

CHILDREN'S CLOTH, SILK AND WASH COATS.

FOR 6 TO 14 YEAR OLD GIRLS. WHEN ORDERING GIVE CATALOGUE NUMBER, COLOR WANTED, BUST MEASURE AND AGE OF CHILD.

No. 17E7366 NOBBY CHILD'S REEFER. Made of white washable duck. Box back, double breasted front. Neat sleeves, fancy cuffs. Belt in back. Facing of same material. Color, white with blue trimming around neck, cuffs and pocket flaps. For other color same style see next description. Give age of child. Price....$1.35

No. 17E7367 Same style as No. 17E7366 in alice blue color with white trimming. When ordering give child's age and bust measure Price................$1.35 If by mail, postage extra, either garment, 30c.

No. 17E7368 NEAT CHILD'S REEFER. Made of good quality washable German linen. Loose back, double breasted front. Large sailor collar, neatly trimmed with fancy braid. Similar trimming on cuffs. Belt in back. Facing of same material. Color, white with light blue sailor collar, cuffs and pocket flaps. For other color same style see next description. Always give child's age and bust measure. Price....$1.48

No. 17E7369 Same style as No. 17E7368. Made of blue washable material with white trimming. Don't forget to state child's age and bust measure. Price................$1.48 If by mail, postage extra, either garment, 30 cents.

No. 17E7370 SPLENDID CHILD'S REEFER. Made of good quality washable linen. Loose back and double breasted front. Large sailor collar, neatly trimmed. Fancy cuffs. Belt in back. Facing of same material. Color, white with blue trimming. For other color see next description. When ordering state age of child. Price, $1.75

No. 17E7371 Same style as No. 17E7370. Color, light blue with white trimming. Be sure to give child's age and bust measure when you order. Price..........$1.75 If by mail, postage extra, either garment, 24 cents.

No.17E7372 SPLENDID VALUE IN CHILD'S REEFER. Made of all linen crash. Loose back, double breasted front. Large sailor collar, neatly trimmed with braid. Fancy cuffs and pocket flaps. Pearl buttons in front. Belt in back. Color, linen colored, tan with blue sailor collar, cuffs and pocket flaps. Trimmed with braid. When you order don't forget to state child's age and bust measure. Price................$1.98 If by mail, postage extra, 30 cents.

No. 17E7374 NOBBY CHILD'S THREE QUARTER COAT. Made of good quality washable material. Loose back and front. From 26 to 30 inches long according to size. Double breasted front. Collarless effect. Neat trimming around the collar, cuffs and pocket flaps. Color all white with blue, and white trimming around collar, cuffs, pocket flaps and buttons. When you order always state child's age and bust measure. For other color see next description. Price................$1.48

No. 17E7375 Same style as No. 17E7374. Color, all blue with white trimming. State age of child. Price..................$1.48 If by mail, postage extra, either garment, 24 cents.

No. 17E7376 THIS UP TO DATE CHILD'S THREE-QUARTER COAT is made of high grade washable madras cloth. Loose back and double breasted front. Large sailor collar finished with silk star, neatly trimmed. Similar trimming on cuffs. Fancy bow in front. Color, blue with white trimming. When ordering don't fail to state age and bust measure of child. Price.......$1.75 If by mail, postage extra, 24 cents.

No. 17E7379 CHILD'S REEFER JACKET. Made of all wool ladies' cloth, circular cape, double breasted front, loose back finished with a belt. Trimmings of white soutache, with fancy lace braid around the cape. Puff sleeves, fancy turnover cuffs. Facing of same material. Color, blue. For other color see next description. Always give age of child when ordering. Price....$1.48

No. 17E7380 Same style as No. 17E7379. Color, brown. State age of child and bust measure. Price..........................$1.48 If by mail, postage extra, either garment, 20 cents.

No. 17E7381 CHILD'S LONG REEFER COAT. Made of all wool ladies' cloth, double breasted front, box back, finished with a fancy belt. Imitation collar, shoulder capes and straps over shoulders. Puff sleeves, fancy turnover cuffs. Patch pockets. Fancy metal buttons. Trimmings of fancy silk braid around the capes and cuffs, and embroidered silk eagle on sleeve. Lined throughout with sateen. Color, blue. For other color see next description. Be sure to give age of child. Price, $1.75

No. 17E7382 Same style as No. 17E7381. Color, brown. When ordering give age and bust measure of child. Price......................$1.75 If by mail, postage extra, either garment, 20 cents.

No. 17E7383 CHILD'S LONG REEFER COAT. Made of all wool covert cloth, collarless effect, double breasted front, box back finished with belt. Stylish sleeves finished with puff, turnover cuffs. Nice gilt button trimmings. Facing in front of same material. Very neat. Color, castor only. When you order give age and bust measure of child. Price....$2.75 If by mail, postage extra, 20 cents.

No. 17E7384 CHILD'S LONG REEFER COAT. Made of all wool covert cloth, collarless effect, double breasted front, loose back made with box and side plaits, finished with fancy belt. Stylish puff sleeves, fancy turnover cuffs. Fancy metal buttons. Facing of same material. Trimmings of brown leather colored broadcloth around the neck. Color, castor only, with trimmings as described. Always give age of child and bust measure. Price..........................$3.35 If by mail, postage extra, 20 cents.

No. 17E7385 CHILD'S THREE-QUARTER TOP COAT. Made of fine all silk peau de soie, double breasted front, loose back finished with fancy belt. Shoulder capes. Pearl buttons. Trimmings of fancy white braid around collar, capes, belt and cuffs. Full puff sleeves. Lined throughout with light blue sateen. Color, black only with white trimming. Don't forget age and bust measure of the child. Price.........$3.50 If by mail, postage extra, 30 cents.

No. 17E7386 CHILD'S THREE-QUARTER COAT. Made of fine all silk peau de soie, double breasted front, loose back with fancy belt. Large circular collar, fancy sleeves with puff, turnover cuffs. Pearl buttons. Trimmings of cream colored lace medallions around collar and white silk stitching. Lined throughout with light blue sateen. Very pretty garment. Color, black only. Be sure to state age and bust measure of child. Price..................$3.95 If by mail, postage extra, 30 cents.

GIRLS' WHITE LAWN DRESSES.

TRIMMED WITH LACE.

98c

No. 38E5105 Girls' Dress, made of good quality white lawn, has round yoke trimmed with five clusters of numerous pin tucks, a neat wide bertha edged with valenciennes lace. Full blouse, newest style sleeves. Skirt made full with deep hem. White only. Ages, 6 to 14 years. Price...... **98c**
If by mail, postage extra, 20 cents.

$1.15

VERY NEAT TRIMMED LAWN DRESS.

No. 38E5107 This Dress is made of white sheer lawn, has round yoke with numerous rows of neat pin tucks, wide bertha edged with embroidery and trimmed with two lace medallions. Back trimmed with two box plaits. Newest fashion sleeves. Full blouse. Skirt made nice and full with deep hem. Ages, 6 to 14 years. White only. **$1.15**
If by mail, postage extra, 21 cents.

STYLISH WHITE LAWN DRESS.

No. 38E5109 A very stylish white Lawn Dress, round yoke with five insertions of neat pattern valenciennes lace. Has fancy pointed bertha with insertion of valenciennes lace, and edge to match. Back trimmed with six wide tucks. Collar and new wide cuffs trimmed with valenciennes lace to match. Newest fashion sleeves. Skirt made full with deep hem at bottom. Ages, 6 to 14 years. White only. Price... **$1.48**
If by mail, postage extra, 21 cents.

Very stylish and neatly trimmed dresses, suitable for confirmation parties and other occasions. Ages, 6 to 14 years. State age and bust measure when ordering.

$1.69

HANDSOME WHITE LAWN DRESS.

No. 38E5112 Girls' Dress, made of good quality white lawn. Fancy pointed tucked yoke with three medallions. 5-inch embroidery ruffle extending to back of yoke, which is trimmed with six tucks. Collar and cuffs are trimmed with embroidery. White lawn belt. Skirt made full with deep hem at bottom. Ages, 6 to 14 years. Color, white only. Price... **$1.69**
If by mail, postage extra, 22 cents.

$1.75

NEWEST EMBROIDERY TRIMMED DRESS.

No. 38E5115 This Handsome Dress is made of white sheer lawn, round tucked yoke with insertion of hemstitched embroidery. Yoke followed with embroidery ruffle in the very newest button effect. Cuffs trimmed with insertion of embroidery to match. Back trimmed with six fine tucks. Newest fashion sleeves, skirt made nice and full with deep hem. Ages, 6 to 14 years. White only. Price...... **$1.75**
If by mail, postage extra, 21 cents.

$1.89

VERY PRETTY DESIGNED DRESS

No. 38E5119 Very Neatly Designed Dress, made of good quality white lawn, has round yoke solidly tucked, with insertion of neat valenciennes lace. The wide bertha is trimmed with insertion and edged also with lawn ruffle which is trimmed with lace to match. Back is trimmed with six wide tucks. Collar and wide cuffs are trimmed with neat valenciennes lace to correspond. Newest fashion sleeves. Skirt made generously full with deep hem. Ages, 6 to 14 years. White only. Price................. **$1.89**
If by mail, postage extra, 20 cents.

BEAUTIFULLY TRIMMED LAWN DRESS.

$1.98

No. 38E5123 This Dress is made of good quality white lawn, has a very neat tucked yoke trimmed with insertions of neat hemstitched embroidery. The wide bertha is edged with embroidery and set in with lace medallions. Back is trimmed with six wide tucks. Collar and new wide cuffs edged with embroidery and edge to match. Newest fashion sleeves. Skirt made nice and full with deep hem. For girls, ages, 6 to 14 years. White only. Price..... **$1.98**
If by mail, postage extra, 20 cents.

$2.25

DRESS TRIMMED WITH LACE AND EMBROIDERY.

No. 38E5127 This Dainty Dress is made of fine quality white linon, has fancy round yoke made of embroidery and insertions of neat valenciennes lace, followed with wide ruffle of fine embroidery which is trimmed with three neat tucks. Yoke ornamented with narrow ribbon rosette. Back trimmed with six wide tucks. Collar and cuffs trimmed with embroidery to correspond. Newest fashion sleeves. Skirt trimmed with three wide tucks made nice and full with deep hem. White only. Ages, 6 to 14 years. Price...... **$2.25**
If by mail, postage extra, 22 cents.

$2.98

VERY STYLISH DRESS.

No. 38E5131 This Beautiful Dress is made of finest quality white sheer French lawn, yoke front and back alike of neat tucks with insertions of valenciennes lace. Fancy wide bertha trimmed with tucks, valenciennes lace and edge to match. Back trimmed with six wide tucks. The new wide cuffs are solidly tucked with insertion of valenciennes lace and edge to match. Collar trimmed with lace to correspond. Newest fashion sleeves. Skirt is trimmed with three wide tucks and insertion of valenciennes lace to match, made nice and full with deep hem. A very pretty dress for girls, ages, 6 to 14 years. White only. Price................. **$2.98**
If by mail, postage extra, 22 cents.

$3.50

MAGNIFICENT WHITE LAWN DRESS.

No. 38E5135 An Exceedingly Fine Dress, made of fine French lawn; fancy yoke, trimmed with tucks and very neat pattern of embroidery insertion. Yoke in back, trimmed to correspond and has wide embroidered ruffle extending to back of dress. New wide cuffs, trimmed with tucks and hemstitched embroidery insertion with edge of valenciennes lace. Collar trimmed to match. Skirt is very neatly trimmed with numerous pin tucks and insertions of fine embroidery to match, made nice and full with deep hem. An exceptionally fine dress for girls, ages, 6 to 14 years. White only. Price, **$3.50**
If by mail, postage extra, 23 cents.

$3.98

If by mail, postage extra, 23 cents.

EXTRA FINE WHITE LAWN DRESS.

No. 38E5139 This Nobby Dress is made of the finest quality white sheer lawn, has a very pretty sailor collar effect of neat embroidery and insertions with fine satin ribbon tie. V shaped yoke trimmed with numerous rows of tucks. Back trimmed with 6 wide tucks. Collar and cuffs edged with embroidery to match. A very pretty skirt trimmed with two clusters of numerous pin tucks, edged with neat pattern of neat embroidery, and made nice and full. A very stylish dress for girls, ages, 6 to 14 years. White only. Price...... **$3.98**

$4.35

A CHARMING WHITE LAWN DRESS.

No. 38E5143 An Exceedingly Fine Dress, made of white sheer organdy, has a neat drop bertha, which is neatly tucked and trimmed with insertions of valenciennes lace and edge to correspond. The new cap sleeves neatly tucked with insertion of valenciennes lace and edge to match. Full blouse front, neatly trimmed with tucks and satin ribbon sash. Skirt made generously full, with two clusters (5 in each cluster) of fine tucks wich deep hem at bottom. The ⅜-length sleeves trimmed with insertion, valenciennes lace and edge to match. Very neatly trimmed. Dress for girls, ages, 6 to 14 years. White only. Price.... **$4.35**

$1.95

DON'T FAIL TO GIVE AGE AND BUST MEASURE WHEN ORDERING.

DRESS OF DOTTED SWISS.

No. 38E5150 This Dress is made of fine dotted Swiss, fancy pointed yoke trimmed with numerous tucks and insertion of hemstitched embroidery. The wide bertha is trimmed with hemstitched embroidery and edge to match. Collar and new wide cuffs are also edged with embroidery. Newest fashion sleeves. Skirt made nice and full with deep hem. For girls, ages, 6 to 14 years. Price..................... **$1.95**
If by mail, postage extra, 23 cents.

If by mail, postage extra, 19 cents.

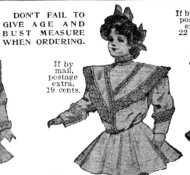

LACE TRIMMED DOTTED SWISS DRESS.

No. 38E5154 This Dress is made of good quality dotted Swiss, full blouse front trimmed with insertion of neat valenciennes lace. Has new Gibson effect which is trimmed with insertion of valenciennes lace and edge to match. Back trimmed with tucks and insertion to correspond. Collar and sleeves trimmed with insertion and lace edge. Skirt made nice and full with deep hem. A very neatly trimmed dress. For girls, ages, 6 to 14 years. White only. Price................. **$2.39**

$4.95

If by mail, postage extra, 22 cents.

Ages, 6 to 14 years Give age and bust measure.

GIRLS' POINT D'ESPRIT DRESS, $4.95.

No. 38E5158 An Extra High Grade Dress; made of fine point d'esprit. Underdress is made of fine organdy, the yoke is neatly trimmed with rows of narrow satin ribbon and insertion of valenciennes lace forming a square, ornamented with a silk ribbon rosette, the wide bertha is trimmed with three rows of narrow silk ribbon and edged with fine valenciennes lace. Yoke in back trimmed with tucks. Collar, cuffs and waistband trimmed with ribbon to match, very full skirt trimmed with three rows of narrow satin ribbon. An exceptionally fine dress for girls. Ages, 6 to 14 years. Color, white only. Price.................... **$4.95**

HERE WE OFFER OUR VERY FINEST OVERCOATS AND REEFER TOP COATS FOR LITTLE FELLOWS

In buying clothing for little boys like in buying all other things it is always advisable to buy the better qualities because they give so much more satisfaction. These overcoats and reefer top coats are of the very best quality and our prices for them are no more than the prices charged elsewhere for inferior qualities. Each garment is furnished only in sizes mentioned in description. When ordering, give boy's age and tell us whether he is large or small for his age.

$4.00 BLACK ASTRAKHAN CLOTH OVERCOATS FOR LITTLE FELLOWS

Something which is always stylish and always in great demand. Our sales on these garments are increasing every season, which shows that the great values which we offer in these coats are appreciated by our customers. Made exactly as illustrated. Collar and sleeves are trimmed with black cloth and front with eight neat appearing buttons. Lined with black Italian cloth, made with deep inside facings, two outside pockets with flaps. Say how old the boy is when ordering.

Goods No. 40L6866

Price for little fellows' overcoats, sizes 3 to 8 years only. **$4.00**

$4.25 BEAUTIFUL DARK BROWN KERSEY OVERCOATS.

Something in the very latest and most popular shade in a very plain style as illustrated which is greatly in demand at present. Double breasted front with large box plait in center. Ivory buttons, two outside pockets with flaps. Fancy imitation cuffs and broad velvet collar to match material. A very attractive durable coat, trimmed and tailored in the best possible manner. Sizes, 3 to 8 years only. Be sure to give age of boy, and state if he is large or small for his age.

Goods No. 40L6868 Price for little fellows' overcoats, sizes 3 to 8 years only.......... **$4.25**

$5.75 THE MOST EXTRAORDINARY VALUE IN LITTLE FELLOWS' BEARSKIN COATS.

A very stylish little coat which buttons with loops and olives, has two outside pockets with flaps and 6-in. slits on the sides. Lined throughout with fine Venetian cloth and perfectly tailored in every respect. Illustration is an exact representation of coat. Material is so called bearskin, a very popular fabric for little fellows' coats. Color, a mixture of gray and brown in a curly effect. Be sure to state age of boy.

Goods No. 40L6869 Price for little fellows' overcoats, sizes 3 to 8 years only............... **$5.75**

$4.98 ONE OF THE HANDSOMEST WINTER COATS WE HAVE EVER BEEN ABLE TO OFFER FOR THE PRICE.

Material, all wool chinchilla cloth. Color, a handsome medium gray mixture. One of the most desirable, dressy and durable coats it is possible to produce. Made as illustrated with fly front and velvet collar to match. Two outside pockets with flaps, and front trimmed with three fancy corded clusters and loops. A neatly trimmed and perfectly tailored coat in every respect. Sizes 3 to 8 years only. Be sure to state age of boy.

Goods No. 40L6870

Price for little fellows' overcoats, sizes 3 to 8 years... **$4.98**

$6.00 FOR OUR FUR TRIMMED OVERCOATS.

Made of fine dark navy blue kersey cloth in good weight. Collar and cuffs are trimmed with black electric seal, a handsome appearing fur. Front is ornamented with black silk loops and clusters. The coat buttons with a fly, has two outside pockets with flaps, deep inside facings, and it is lined with a very fine black Italian cloth. If you like fur trimmed coats, you will not find anything anywhere for the price at which we offer this coat. Give age of boy.

Goods No. 40L6871 Price for little fellows' overcoats, sizes 3 to 8 years of age only..... **$6.00**

$1.49 SOMETHING OF UNUSUAL VALUE IN LITTLE FELLOWS' REEFER COATS.

Material, blue cotton chinchilla cloth. Made as illustrated, with two outside pockets with flaps, double breasted appearing front, trimmed with six metal buttons. Velvet collar. Lined with good black twill lining. A comfortable everyday coat for the little fellows at a price heretofore unheard of for coats in this material. State boy's age.

Goods No. 40L6872

Price for little fellows' reefer coats, sizes 3 to 8 years only.... **$1.49**

$3.25 EXTRAORDINARY VALUE IN ALL WOOL RED CHINCHILLA REEFER COATS.

Made of bright red all wool chinchilla cloth in button to the neck reefer style. Double breasted with a handsome inlaid velvet collar. Trimmed with black braid and black silk soutache. Venetian lined, two outside pockets with flaps, broad inside facings. If you like something real stylish and cute, you will surely be pleased with the handsome coat we offer under this number. Be sure to state age of boy.

Goods No. 40L6874

Price for little fellows' reefer coats, sizes 3 to 8 yrs., **$3.25**

$2.68 DARK NAVY BLUE REEFER TOP COATS FOR BOYS FROM 4 TO 12 YEARS OF AGE.

Exceptionally well made stylish garments, lined throughout with red flannel. Made with deep inside facings and bottom facings. Stylish broad lapels, velvet collar, three outside pockets, fancy cuffs on sleeves. On left arm is a silk emblem which is put on so that it can be removed if desired. Material, medium weight dark navy blue cheviot cloth. How old is the boy?

Goods No. 40L6876

Price for boys' reefer coats, sizes 4 to 12 years only...... **$2.68**

$2.75 FOR HEAVY WEIGHT DARK OXFORD GRAY REEFER TOP COATS.

Material, heavy weight dark oxford melton cloth in a diagonal weave. A well made coat, exactly as shown in illustration, with a velvet collar, three outside pockets, lap seams fancy cuffs on sleeves, silk emblem on left arm, and lined throughout with all wool red flannel. If you want your boy to have a stylish warm winter coat, order this number. Give age of boy.

Goods No. 40L6878

Price for boys' reefer coats, sizes 4 to 12 years of age only **$2.75**

$3.75 FOR OUR FINEST AND MOST STYLISH FANCY REEFER COATS.

Color, beautiful medium gray cheviot with a striped effect in black. Stylish cut reefer coats, double breasted style and good length. Handsome broad lapels, three outside pockets, a fine velvet collar, stylish imitation cuffs piped with black velvet, six ivory buttons in front and three on each sleeve. The coats are lined throughout with all wool red flannel, are made with bottom facings, emblem on left arm, and slits on the sides. Give boy's age.

Goods No. 40L6880

Price for reefer top coats, for boys from 4 to 12 years only **$3.75**

BUY YOUR LITTLE BOY AND LITTLE GIRL ONE OF THESE "PLAY IN THE MUD" SUITS.

Just the thing for little tots to play in. Comfortable, sanitary and healthy and allows them freedom. Easy to slip over better garments and easy to take off. We manufacture them ourselves and our prices are less than what wholesale dealers and jobbers ask for similar garments in wholesale quantities. Mothers will find these garments to be money savers, as by dressing the little children with them you will save their better clothing. Made from extra strong washable materials in styles illustrated below. We furnish them only in sizes to fit little boys and little girls from 2 to 7 years of age. Mention child's age when ordering.

45c NEAT PLAY SUITS FOR LITTLE FELLOWS, MADE WITH STRAIGHT PANTS. MATERIAL, STRONG AMOSKEAG CHEVIOT, BLUISH GRAY PINCHECK EFFECT.

Style B80

Style B81

Collar, top of pocket, waist line and cuffs are trimmed with blue material, which sets off the garment nicely. We sell these garments all the year around, and the continuous increase in sales shows their great usefulness is appreciated by mothers. If you once get into the habit of dressing your little children with them, you will never be without them. Sizes, 2 to 7 years only. Order by age.

Goods No. 40L6962

Price for little fellows' play suits, sizes 2 to 7 years, in style B80, as illustrated........................ **45c**

45c PLAY IN THE MUD SUITS WITH BLOOMER PANTS.

Made of the same material as No. 40L6962, but in style B81, as illustrated, with bloomer pants. Can be worn by either boys or girls. Color, bluish gray. A one-piece garment with neckband in place of collar. Yoke, belt and cuffs trimmed in blue. Very substantially made, and great money savers, as they will save a whole lot of the children's better clothing. Just the thing for the little fellows to play in around the house in the winter time. Sizes, 2 to 7 years. Order by age only.

Goods No. 40L6964

Price, for little tots' play suits, sizes 2 to 7 years, in style B81.. **45c**

98c MILITARY KHAKI PLAY SUITS WITH LONG PANTS, STYLE B-82. A VERY CUTE LITTLE SUIT.

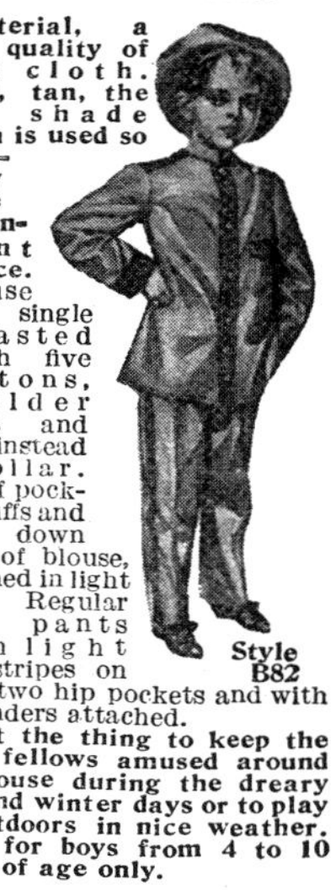

Style B82

Material, a good quality of khaki cloth. Color, tan, the same shade which is used so extensively in the government service. Blouse cut single breasted with five buttons, shoulder straps and band instead of collar. Top of pockets, cuffs and plait down front of blouse, trimmed in light blue. Regular long pants with light blue stripes on sides, two hip pockets and with suspenders attached.

Just the thing to keep the little fellows amused around the house during the dreary fall and winter days or to play in outdoors in nice weather. Sizes for boys from 4 to 10 years of age only.

Goods No. 40L6966

Price, for little fellows' military play suits, sizes 4 to 10 years only, style B82, **98c**

DON'T OVERLOOK THESE BOYS' WASHABLE WAISTS AND BLOUSES.

We offer but a few staple garments made from reliable washable fabrics suitable for all year around wear. Every garment is guaranteed to be cut full and roomy and not skimpy like many that are found on the market today. They come only in the sizes mentioned in each description. When ordering give boy's age.

23c FOR WASHABLE BLOUSES IN NEAT STRIPED EFFECTS.

Made in blouse style with turn down collar, one plait down front, double cuff and well stayed shoulders. Good washable material in medium and dark shades. Sizes 4 to 13 years. Be sure to state age of boy.

Goods No. 40L6971

Price for blouses for boys from 4 to 13 years of age only.............. **23c**

Postage extra, 8 cents.

25c FOR LITTLE FELLOWS' MILITARY BLOUSES.

A very practical and popular style. Made of a good quality of washable striped chambray in a variety of neat patterns. Full cut, well made garments at the very lowest possible price. Sizes 3 to 8 years only. Order by age.

Goods No. 40L6972

Price for little fellows' military blouses from 3 to 8 years of age only. **25c**

Postage extra, 8 cents.

25c WASHABLE WAISTS FOR BOYS, WITH MOTHERS' FRIEND BELTS.

A variety of neatly striped patterns from odds and ends. All good washable fabrics. Made with a box plait down front, ivory buttons, small turn down collar, double cuffs, and with a mothers' friend belt attached. Be sure to state age of boy.

Goods No. 40L6973

Price for washable waist for boys from 4 to 13 years of age only...... **25c**

If by mail, postage extra, 8c.

45c FOR BLACK SATEEN BLOUSES.

Very desirable garments for all year around wear. Made of a good quality of fast black washable sateen. Full size, turn down collar, double cuffs, well stayed shoulders, pearl buttons. Sizes 6 to 15 years only. Order by age.

Goods No. 40L6974

Price for blouses for boys from 6 to 15 years of age only........... **45c**

Postage extra, 9 cents.

45c EXTRA WELL MADE FULL CUT BLOUSES WITHOUT COLLAR.

A great variety of handsome striped patterns particularly selected in the darkest patterns possible, made with one plait down front, outside breast pocket, open cuffs, and with a band instead of collar to which a collar of any kind can be attached. Sizes 6 to 15 years. Be sure to state age.

Goods No. 40L6975

Price for blouses for boys from 6 to 15 years of age only.............. **45c**

If by mail, postage extra, 9c.

45c OUR BOYS' FINEST WASHABLE BLOUSES.

We bought up a lot of blouses of the best makes at less than the regular market price and we offer them all at one price. They are as well made as any blouse in the market. A variety of neat patterns in chambrays and madras. Made with collar attached, box plait down front, outside breast pocket.

Goods No. 40L6976

Price for blouse for boys from 6 to 15 years of age. (Postage, 9 cents).. **45c**

MISSES' AND CHILDREN'S STYLISH SHOES AND SLIPPERS

No. 15L308

$1.00

PER PAIR

DON'T FAIL TO STATE SIZE.

A high class style never before seen in misses' or children's shoes. Vici kid stock, with patent leather tip and medium broad toe last. Slightly extended soles of best quality and low heel. Very handsome. Sizes and half sizes, 8 to 2. Widths, D, E and EE. Weight averages 19 ounces.

LITTLE CINDERELLA.

No. 15L423

$1.00

PER PAIR

DON'T FAIL TO STATE SIZE.

A nice Sunday shoe for the girls at a ridiculously low price. The vamp is cut from chrome tanned patent leather, while the top is of dongola. The soles are very durable and the shoe is one we recommend for satisfactory wear. Sizes and half sizes, 8 to 2. Full widths only. Weight averages 22 ounces.

BOX CALF WINNER.

No. 15L335

$1.00

PER PAIR

DON'T FAIL TO STATE SIZE.

You will appreciate the value contained in this Misses' and Children's Best Grade Box Calf Shoe, as it is made with plump out soles, low heel and guaranteed leather counter and inner soles. Sizes and half sizes, 8 to 2. Widths, D, E and EE. Weight, 20 ounces.

LITTLE EMPRESS.

No. 15L390

89c

PER PAIR

DON'T FAIL TO STATE SIZE.

A very stylish and durable light weight school shoe, made from a plump grade of kid stock with durable soles. Cut on the Blucher pattern and has a neatly perforated patent tip. Sizes and half sizes, 8 to 2. Widths, full. Weight averages 22 ounces.

VICTORIA OXFORD.

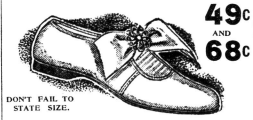

No. 15L313

$1.15

PER PAIR

DON'T FAIL TO STATE SIZE.

An entirely new design for Misses' and Children's Low Shoes, made of chrome patent leather, with a fine, smooth dull calf quarter. A very serviceable shoe, especially adapted for summer wear. Full widths only. Sizes and half sizes, 8½ to 2. Weight, 17 to 22 ounces.

SEROCO HEALTH SHOE.

No. 15L640

$1.00

PER PAIR

DON'T FAIL TO STATE SIZE.

Children's Vici Kid Stock, fleece lined, low heel, and just the proper shoe for winter wear. Sizes and half sizes, 9 to 2. Full widths. Weight, 16 ounces.

PATENT SANDAL.

49c AND 68c

DON'T FAIL TO STATE SIZE.

Beats the world and seems almost impossible to furnish a sandal so stylish at the price we mention. Patent leather vamp, genuine cabretta quarter, spring heel, light turned sole, kid quarter lining and bow strap. Widths, full. Weight averages 12 ounces.

No. 15L464 Misses' sizes, 8½ to 2. Price, per pair..................................68c

No. 15L466 Children's sizes, 5 to 8. Price, per pair..................................49c

WHITE KID SANDAL.

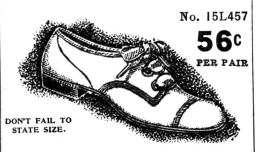

49c AND 68c

DON'T FAIL TO STATE SIZE.

These sandals are made of the very best quality white kid stock, spring heel, fancy bow at instep and genuine light turned sole. Our one profit plan enables us to quote them to you at this unheard of price. The correct thing for graduating exercises, confirmation or party wear. Widths, full. Weight averages 14 ounces.

No. 15L468 Misses' sizes, 8½ to 2. Price, per pair..................................68c

No. 15L470 Children's sizes, 5 to 8. Price, per pair..................................49c

VICTORIA SANDAL.

74c AND 94c

DON'T FAIL TO STATE SIZE.

Just as stylish as any Ladies' Sandal, and why should they not be? All patent leather, spring heel, three straps, hand turned soles and suitable for dress wear. Widths, full. Weight averages 15 to 20 ounces.

No. 15L305 Girls' sizes, 8½ to 2. Price, per pair..................................94c

No. 15L309 Children's sizes, 5 to 8. Price, per pair..................................74c

EXTRA QUALITY.

No. 15L413

$1.00

PER PAIR

DON'T FAIL TO STATE SIZE.

An extra value made in the Blucher style of serviceable dongola kid with patent leather perforated tip and low heel. Has light but durable sole and can be worn for week day and Sunday wear. At $1.00 is truly a wonderful example of our great shoe values. Sizes and half sizes, 8 to 2. Widths, C, D, E and EE. Average weight, 16 ounces.

WHITE CANVAS OXFORD.

No. 15L457

56c

PER PAIR

DON'T FAIL TO STATE SIZE.

Neatest and latest thing in summer foot wear is the White Canvas Blucher Cut Oxford with large eyelets and large laces. Misses' sizes, 8½ to 2. Widths, full. Weight averages 14 ounces.

UNEQUALED VALUE.

No. 15L434

74c

PER PAIR

DON'T FAIL TO STATE SIZE.

An up to date Blucher Oxford, reliable counter and inner sole, low heel, one-half double sole, fair stitched, patent leather tip. Misses' sizes, 8½ to 2. Weight averages 18 ounces.

DRESSES ═══ TO FIT AGES 6 TO 14 YEARS

MAIL SHIPMENTS. We advise you to include orders for these dresses with orders for other goods to be shipped by freight or express, but should you desire to have any dress shipped by mail be sure to send postage extra, 1 cent an ounce   Shipping weight of the dresses on this page averages 28 ounces each.

$2.19 TWO-PIECE SAILOR SUITS.

This serviceable and very popular style is made of a good quality navy blue cloth of good weight and smooth finish. The wide sailor collar and yoke are trimmed with narrow braid. Wide plaited skirt is made with attached cambric waist, with dickey front. Knot tie of red mercerized poplin gives the necessary touch of color. Taking it altogether, this is a splendid dress for all seasons of the year and is priced remarkably low. Color, navy blue. Ages, 6 to 14 years. Be sure to mention age desired.
No. 38R7590
Price, each.........$2.19

$3.89 BEST WORSTED SERGE.

Two-Piece Sailor Suit of extra fine quality navy blue wool serge. Woven from finest worsted yarns. The round sailor collar and neck band are trimmed with numerous rows of silk braid and finished with a red sailor knot tie. The wide plaited skirt is combined with cambric waist that has dickey front, which is neatly trimmed with a silk embroidered emblem. The sleeves are gathered in narrow plaits and finished with braid trimmed cuffs. Silk embroidered emblem on left sleeve. Color, blue. Ages, 6 to 14 years. Don't forget to state age.
No. 38R7594
Price, each.........$3.89

$1.74 GALATEA CLOTH. WASHABLE.

Recommended by sanitary officers of public schools. This exceedingly handsome and cleverly designed dress is made of splendid galatea cloth, a very fine and closely woven fabric in good weight. Front of dress is made with panel of cloth with the stripes running crosswise, giving the dress the long one-piece front; also trimmed down front with narrow strappings and narrow red piping. The collar, belt and cuffs are neatly trimmed with red piping to match. Color, navy blue with white stripes. Ages, 6 to 14 years. What age shall we send you?
No. 38R7647
Price, each.........$1.74

$1.75 SHEPHERD CHECK. WASHABLE.

This dress is made in a simple yet charming design. Best quality galatea cloth, very fine, and yet of sufficient weight for winter wear. Front is tastefully trimmed with narrow red piping, with large buttons to match. Trimmed pocket on the right side. Collar, belt and cuffs neatly piped with red. Extra wide kilted skirt with deep hem. Buttons in back from collar to hem, making it easy to launder. School authorities recommend them. Color, the popular black and white shepherd checks. Ages, 6 to 14 years. State age desired.
No. 38R7648
Price, each.........$1.75

$1.48 FINEST PERCALE. WASHABLE.

Very neat and serviceable dress, made of blue and white striped percale of the finest quality. Wide band on front of waist, with collar and cuffs made of plain navy blue percale, piped around edges with plain white material. Wide plaits running to shoulders. Wide plaited skirt with deep hem. This dress is buttoned from collar to hem, making it an easy matter to press plaits. A dress that will give everlasting service. Color, blue and white stripes. Ages, 6 to 14 years. State age, please.
No. 38R7649
Price, each.........$1.48

$1.59 BEARSKIN
Three-Quarter Length Bearskin Coat at a Price that Cannot be Equaled.
Made of good quality bearskin cloth. Double breasted effect, with six pearl buttons on front. Storm collar. Lined throughout with selected sateen. Sizes, to fit ages 2 to 6 years. Three-quarter length.
No. 38R8076 Color, White.
No. 38R8078 Color, Gray.
Price, each.........$1.59
Bearskin Bonnet to match.
No. 38R8325 Color, White.
No. 38R8326 Color, Gray.
Price, each.........39c

$3.50 CHINCHILLA
Red Chinchilla Coat of Extra Quality and Weight.
Splendidly made and finished. Wide double breast, smartly trimmed with fancy buttons. High storm collar. Lined throughout with good quality mercerized sateen. Sizes, to fit ages 2 to 6 years.
No. 38R8123 Color, Red.
Price, each.........$3.50
Suitable Bearskin Bonnet to wear with this coat.
No. 38R8324 Only in White.
Price, each.........75c

$3.75 PONYSKIN
Made of very fine bearskin cloth in the ponyskin pattern. Double breasted with fly front, trimmed with silk ornaments. Storm collar. Lined throughout with heavy quilted sateen. Sizes, to fit ages 2 to 6 years.
No. 38R8100 Color, White.
No. 38R8101 Color, Gray.
Price, each.........$3.75
Ponyskin Bonnet to match.
No. 38R8328 Color, White.
No. 38R8329 Color, Gray.
Price, each.........79c

$3.25 SPECIAL
Novelty Cord All Wool Cloth Coat.
Especially trimmed and very handsomely finished at collar and cuffs with fancy braid. Very stylish and neat in its appearance. Lined with good quality mercerized sateen. Sizes, to fit ages 2 to 6 years.
No. 38R8119 Color, Red.
No. 38R8120 Color, Brown.
Price, each.........$3.25
Suitable Curly Bearskin Bonnet to wear with this coat.
No. 38R8330 Only in White.
Price, each.........89c

$1.98 POPULAR
Full Size Bearskin Coat, an Unequaled Value at Our Price.
Selected quality bearskin cloth. Double breasted, with large pearl buttons. Storm collar, turnback cuffs. Lined with good quality sateen. Sizes, to fit ages 2 to 6 years.
No. 38R8080 Color, White.
No. 38R8081 Color, Gray.
Price, each.........$1.98
Bearskin Bonnet to match.
No. 38R8331 Color, White.
No. 38R8332 Color, Gray.
Price, each.........39c

YOUNG GIRLS' AND CHILDREN'S COATS

$2.98 No. 40R659
STYLISH DOU-BLE BREASTED SUIT WITH KNICKERBOCKER PANTS, IN SOFT FINISHED MATERIAL.
Pattern, dark stone gray with stripes in black and light gray. As illustrated, with three outside pockets, cuff effect on sleeves. Derby back with false plaits and buttons at end of side seams. Perfectly tailored, interlined, padded, and well stayed. Bar tacks on all pockets, bottom facings, and good button stands on coats. Knickerbocker pants, double stitched and taped seams, suspender buttons, and strap and buckle at knee. Extra buttons and patch piece free. SIZES, 8 to 16 years. Mention age of boy.

$3.65 No. 40R661
SPECIAL VALUE IN A KNICKERBOCKER SUIT WITH EXTRA PAIR STRAIGHT PANTS.
Material, soft finish Union cassimere. Pattern, dark navy blue with a faint stripe effect in black, green and dark maroon. Suits in this material and style always sell extremely well and we have endeavored to give the greatest possible value. Our Ucanttear brand has no equal for quality of material or workmanship. Buy it once and you won't buy any other brand. This is proven by the enormous increase in our sales of boys' clothing. SIZES, 8 to 16 years. Give age of boy.

$3.45 No. 40R663
DRESSY WORSTED FINISH SUIT IN ONE OF THE SEASON'S NEWEST EFFECTS.
Material, worsted front with a cotton chain in the back. Pattern, black with neat stripes formed by alternating gray, red, and black threads. Notice the beautiful shape of lapels, the stylish flap on pockets, cuff effect on sleeves, etc. Double breasted style with slit in back. Seams, double stitched and taped. Bottom facings, good button stands, well padded, interlined, and lined with extra strong Italian. Pants, full cut knickerbocker style with side pockets, hip pocket, suspender buttons, strap and buckle at knee. SIZES, 8 to 16 years. Give age of boy.

$2.75 No. 40R665
EXTRA DURABLE SCHOOL SUIT WITH KNICKERBOCKER PANTS.
Material, strong cheviot cloth. Pattern, medium gray and green mixture with a faint stripe effect. Exactly as illustrated, with stylish long lapels, fancy flaps on all pockets, pretty cuff effect on sleeves, false plaits at side seams, known as a Derby back. Substantially tailored and well trimmed suit at a price which we know cannot be duplicated elsewhere. Extra buttons and a patch piece free. SIZES, 8 to 16 years. Mention age of boy.

$2.60 No. 40R667
ONE OF THE NEWEST MODELS OF THE SEASON IN A DOUBLE BREASTED SUIT WITH REGULAR PANTS.
Material, medium weight wool filled cheviot. Pattern, latest olive brown stripe effect. Stylish long roll lapels, fancy shaped flaps on all pockets, neat cuff effect on sleeves, derby back, French seams, canvas fronts, well padded shoulders, bottom facings. Pants, regular style with three buttons at knee, suspender buttons, side pockets, and hip pockets. SIZES, 8 to 16 years. Give age of boy when ordering.

$3.25 No. 40R669
AN ALL WOOL KNICKERBOCKER SUIT IN A FANCY MODEL.
Pattern, handsome dark gray stripe effect with colorings in light gray, green, and orange. Material, all wool medium weight cheviot. New style with fancy shaped lapels, neat flaps and buttons on all pockets, stylish cuffs, shaped with a slit in back. Knickerbocker pants with side pockets, hip pocket, belt loops, suspender buttons, and strap and buckle at the knee. Well lined and perfectly tailored garments. SIZES, 8 to 16 years. Mention age of boy.

Ucanttear Brand Suits for Little Fellows

No. 40K292
$1.75 LITTLE MANLY STYLE SUIT. Made of medium weight strong cotton cheviot. Pretty gray stripe effect. Coat has silk handkerchief effect in breast pocket and imitation side vents. Full cut bloomer pants with side pockets and one hip pocket. Double stitched and taped seams. Canvas interlining. SIZES—5 to 9 years. State boy's age.

No. 40K294
$1.95 NEAT SINGLE BREASTED BUTTON TO THE NECK STYLE SUIT. Made of splendid wearing cotton fabric in medium brown. Strongly tailored. Coat has silk handkerchief effect in breast pocket and twill lining. Full cut bloomer pants with side pockets, one hip pocket, elastic bottoms and double stitched and taped seams. SIZES—4 to 8 years. Mention boy's age.

No. 40K296
$2.00 PRETTY DARK GRAY SUIT. Made of soft finish wool and cotton mixed fabric. Blouse has sailor collar with neck opening piped in white, detachable silk embroidered shield, cuffs made to button and fly front. Bloomer pants. SIZES—5 to 9 years. Mention boy's age.

No. 40K290
$1.50 BUTTON TO THE NECK STYLE SUIT. Made of good weight soft finish cotton fabric in brown and gray mixture. Coat has silk handkerchief effect in breast pocket and bottom facings. Bloomer pants. All seams double stitched and taped. SIZES—4 to 8 years. State boy's age.

No. 40K300
$2.25 NORFOLK STYLE SUIT. Made of hard finish strong cotton fabric in brown and gray mixture. Coat cut with yoke and has twill lining and bottom facings. Knickerbocker pants have side pockets, one hip pocket, and strap and buckle at knee. SIZES—5 to 9 years. Mention boy's age.

No. 40K298
$2.25 FANCY NAVY BLUE SUIT. Made of good weight soft finish wool and cotton mixed fabric. Front of coat has inlaid plait trimmed with soutache, silk handkerchief effect in breast pocket, and derby back. Full cut bloomer pants with elastic bottoms, side pockets and one hip pocket. SIZES—4 to 8 years. State boy's age.

No. 40K308
$2.75 LITTLE FELLOWS' DOUBLE BREASTED SUIT. Made of wide diagonal weave cotton worsted. A splendid quality. Coat has yoke effect, fancy plaits trimmed with brown tape, derby back and fancy cuff effect. Knickerbocker pants have side pockets, hip pockets, and strap and buckle at knee. SIZES—5 to 9 years. State boy's age.

40K290

40K298

40K292

40K294

40K296

40K300

40K302

40K304

40K306

No. 40K302
$1.95 POPULAR ETON BLOUSE SUIT. Made of soft finish good weight wool and cotton mixed fabric, in neat dark blue pattern. Blouse trimmed with silk embroidered emblem, cuffs made to button and elastic bottom. Knickerbocker pants with side pockets, one hip pocket, and strap and buckle at knee. SIZES—5 to 9 years. State boy's age.

No. 40K304
$2.65 NEW STYLE AND FABRIC IN LITTLE FELLOWS' SUIT. Made of wide diagonal weave cotton worsted in olive brown. Button to neck coat with turndown collar, leather lined belt, slash pockets, fancy cuff effect, ivory buttons, and twill lining to match. Bloomer pants with side pockets, one hip pocket and elastic bottoms. SIZES—4 to 8 years. State boy's age.

No. 40K306
$2.50 NOBBY SINGLE BREASTED PATCH POCKET STYLE SUIT. Made of good weight wool and cotton mixed cassimere in a blue and brown mixture. Breast pocket has silk handkerchief effect. Derby back. Knickerbocker knee pants have side pockets, one hip pocket, and strap and buckle at knee. SIZES—5 to 9 years. Mention boy's age.

Illustrations show garments in their actual styles and colors. Note descriptions for sizes. When ordering state boy's age and whether he is large, small or of average size. Average shipping weight of suits, each, 2¼ pounds.

Ucanttear Brand Suits and Overcoats for Little Fellows

No. 40K332
$3.85 DOUBLE BREASTED NORFOLK EFFECT SUIT. Strictly pure wool worsted, handsome brown pattern. Yoke effect, plaits trimmed with braid to match, slash pockets and derby back. Full lined knickerbocker pants, strap and buckle at knee, hip pocket and side pockets. SIZES—5 to 9 years. Mention boy's age.

No. 40K682
40c RAH RAH HAT in brown color to match above suit. SIZES—6¼. 6⅜, 6½, 6⅝ and 6¾. State size.

No. 40K334
$4.75 LATEST HIGH COLLAR BLOUSE STYLE SUIT in strictly pure wool cassimere. Beautiful gray pattern, as illustrated. Blouse buttons on the side. Silk emblem on left sleeve, silk tie, and plaited cuffs made to button. Knickerbocker pants. Elastic bottoms. SIZES—5 to 9 years. State boy's age.

No. 40K682
40c RAH RAH HAT in gray color to match above suit. SIZES—6¼. 6⅜, 6½, 6⅝ and 6¾. State size.

No. 40K336
$4.50 SAILOR COLLAR BLOUSE SUIT of latest diagonal weave pure wool brown worsted. Neck opening piped in white, detachable silk embroidered shield, silk handkerchief effect in breast pocket, and fancy cuffs made to button. Full lined knickerbocker pants with strap and buckle at knee. SIZES—5 to 9 years.

No. 40K682
40c RAH RAH HAT in brown color to match above suit. SIZES—6¼, 6⅜, 6½, 6⅝ and 6¾. State size.

No. 40K330
$3.75 ALL WOOL WORSTED NAVY BLUE SERGE SUIT. Blouse has fancy trimmed sailor collar, silk embroidered white shield, silk tie and plaited cuffs made to button. Full lined knickerbocker pants with side pockets, one hip pocket, strap and buckle at knee, and taped seams. SIZES—5 to 9 years. State boy's age.

No. 40K686
42c CAP in material to match above suit. Navy style. SIZES—6¼, 6⅜, 6½, 6⅝ and 6¾. State size.

No. 40K430
$1.50 LITTLE FELLOWS' BUTTON TO NECK STYLE OVERCOAT. Exceptional value. Full cut garment of good weight wool and cotton mixed melton. Embroidered emblem in front. Velvet collar, metal buttons, and belt in back. SIZES—3 to 8 years. State boy's age.

No. 40K338
$4.75 MILITARY COLLAR STYLE SUIT in medium gray mixture pure wool cassimere. Trimmed with fancy braid and soutache, as illustrated. Leather belt, bloomer pants. Very pretty and comfortable. SIZES—2½ to 6 years. State boy's age.

No. 40K682
40c RAH RAH HAT in gray color to match above suit. SIZES—6¼, 6⅜, 6½, 6⅝ and 6¾. State size.

No. 40K438
$2.65 PRACTICAL CONVERTIBLE COLLAR STYLE OVERCOAT of good weight wool and cotton mixed Union cassimere. Can be worn in the regular way, as illustrated, or with collar buttoned up to the neck. Cut in semi-raglan effect with belt back and long slit. Italian lining to match. SIZES—5 to 9 years. State boy's age.

No. 40K432
$1.75 NEAT APPEARING INEXPENSIVE OVERCOAT of strong wool and cotton fabric in fancy blue and gray mixture. Silk embroidered emblem in front, belt in back, cuff effect on sleeves, and twill lining. SIZES—3 to 8 years. State boy's age.

No. 40K434
$2.35 NATTY DARK BROWN AND GRAY MIXTURE OVERCOAT. Buttons on the side as illustrated, with breast pocket, two lower pockets, ticket pocket on sleeves and belt in back. Material is wool and cotton mixed cassimere. SIZES—3 to 8 years. State boy's age.

No. 40K436
$2.25 LITTLE FELLOWS' OVERCOAT in latest bluish gray effect. Pretty and inexpensive. Material is a good weight wool and cotton mixed cassimere. Has velvet collar, belt in back, cuff effect on sleeves, buttons on the side, and wool lining. SIZES—3 to 8 years. State boy's age.

Girls' Fashionable Dresses

31K1834

31K1836

31K1828

31K1830

31K1832

31K1824

31K1820

31K1838

31K1822

GIRLS' SAILOR DRESS. Extra fine heavy quality pure wool serge. Sailor collar of red broadcloth. Collar, cuffs and belt trimmed with black and white silk soutache. Buttons in back. Full plaited skirt. Waist and sleeves lined with cambric. Shipping wt., 25 oz. **EACH**
No. 31K1820 Navy blue. **$6.45**

GIRLS' DRESS IN NEW EFFECT. Made of good strong quality shepherd check cotton suiting in one-piece open back style with full plaited skirt. Trimmed with red suiting with black embroidered scallops. A pretty serviceable dress. Shipping weight, 18 oz. **EACH**
No. 31K1822 Black and white. **$1.19**

GIRLS' PRETTILY TRIMMED CASHMERE DRESS. Smart little frock for a girl. Made of cashmere with trimmings of plaid and shepherd check suiting, cord pipings and gilt buttons. Dress closes in back. Waist and sleeves lined with cambric. Full plaited skirt. A splendid value. Shipping weight, 18 ounces. **EACH**
No. 31K1824 Navy blue.
No. 31K1825 Red. **$2.48**

GIRLS' DRESS OF NOVELTY SUITING. Pretty new effect. Made of fancy novelty cotton suiting which looks like wool. Dress cut in one-piece open back style with full plaited skirt. Waist lined with cambric. Trimmed with solid color cotton serge, embroidered scallops, silk cord and tassels. Shipping weight, 20 ounces. No. 31K1826 Brown. No. 31K1827 EACH Navy blue. $1.69	GIRLS' DRESS OF PLAID SUITING. Made of good strong quality cotton suiting in plaid effect. Trimmed with solid color cotton serge, novelty braid and gilt buttons. Full plaited skirt. Waist and sleeves lined with cambric. Dress closes in back. Shipping weight, 18 ounces. No. 31K1828 Blue plaid. No. 31K1829 EACH Brown plaid. $1.25	GIRLS' DRESS WITH SMART TRIMMINGS. Made in popular new style of good heavy quality cotton serge, which looks like wool, trimmed with shepherd check suiting, silk cord piping and finished with tie. Cut in one-piece open back style with full plaited skirt. Waist lined with cambric. Shipping wt., 20 oz. No. 31K1830 EACH Navy blue. $1.48	GIRLS' DAINTILY TRIMMED CASHMERE DRESS. Commonly sold as wool cashmere, but contains a small percentage of cotton. In one-piece open back style with full plaited skirt. Waist and sleeves lined with cambric. Dress trimmed with plaid taffeta silk, fancy silk cord and embroidered spray. Large revers on front. Shipping weight, 18 ounces. No. 31K1832 Red. No. 31K1833 EACH Navy blue. $2.79	GIRLS' DRESS OF COTTON SERGE. Made in pretty one-piece style with large sailor collar effect and tie. Material is good heavy quality navy blue cotton serge with trimmings of shepherd check suiting. Made in one-piece open back style with full plaited skirt. Looks like a wool dress. Shipping wt., 18 ounces. No. 31K1834 EACH Navy blue. $1.29	GIRLS' STYLISHLY TRIMMED DRESS. Cut on full roomy pattern, closing in back, with full plaited skirt. Material is a good strong quality shepherd check cotton suiting with trimmings of red French flannel, black silk soutache and gilt buttons. A splendid serviceable dress at a low price. Shipping weight, 17 ounces. No. 31K1836 EACH Shepherd check. $1.25	GIRLS' SPLENDID VALUE BLUE SERGE DRESS. Remember, this dress is furnished in all sizes from 6 years up to 14 years, and is a wonderful value at this price. Made in sailor style, closing in back, with full plaited skirt. Material is fine all wool serge. Trimmed with red silk soutache. Waist and sleeves lined with cambric. Large sailor collar. Shipping weight, 20 ounces. No. 31K1838 EACH Navy blue. $3.45

CLOTH DRESSES

Ages, 2 to 6 years. State Age.

IMPORTANT.

The scale below will help you to decide on the correct size. If your child is large or small for her age, order accordingly. Sizes of children of same age vary a great deal. Measurements may vary somewhat owing to different styles.

Age 2 3 4 5 6
Average length, in.20 22 23 24 26
Average bust, in..22 23 24 25 26
In ordering be sure to state age.

29K7855
88¢

29K7839
49¢

29K7836
$1.18

29K7850
58¢

29K7853
69¢

29K7866
$2.38

29K7859
$1.10

29K7868
$2.48

29K7846
$1.27

29K7863
$1.88

29K7856
$1.95

29K7837
98¢

29K7862
$1.59

29K7865
$3.35

No. 29K7839 Blue plaid.
No. 29K7840 Red plaid.
CHILD'S DRESS in pretty plaid material woven to resemble wool. Yoke of solid color, trimmed with a narrow braid, fancy cord piping and buttons. Comes in pretty small blue or red broken plaid. Waist lined. State age.
Price, each.......... **49c**

No. 29K7850 Blue plaid.
No. 29K7852 Red plaid.
SERVICEABLE COTTON PLAID DRESS in pretty woven pattern resembling wool material. Yoke and panels of plain material neatly trimmed with fancy cord and buttons. Waist lined. State age.
Price, each.......... **58c**

No. 29K7853 Blue plaid.
No. 29K7854 Red plaid.
A PRACTICAL LITTLE DRESS, made of a firmly finished cotton material in neat broken plaid pattern that looks like wool. Trimmed on one side with beautifully colored embroidery banding finished with narrow braid, buttons and fancy cord edge. Waist lined. State age.
Price, each.......... **69c**

No. 29K7837
ATTRACTIVE DRESS of pretty black and white shepherd check woven material that looks like wool. Prettily trimmed with pipings and bands of plain red material. Neatly braided band of plain material extends diagonally across front from shoulder to hem in surplice style. Waist lined. State age.
Price, each.......... **98c**

No. 29K7855 Red plaid.
No. 29K7857 Blue plaid.
PRETTY PLAID DRESS in a firm finished cotton fabric woven to resemble a wool material. Comes in pretty red or blue plaid. Yoke of plain material trimmed with soutache braid. Waist lined. Full plaited skirt. State age. Price, each....... **88c**

No. 29K7859 Red trim.
No. 29K7861 Cadet blue trim.
BEAUTIFUL DRESS of small black and white shepherd check material, woven to resemble wool. Yoke, cuffs and fancy square sailor collar of plain material in contrasting color. Brass button trimmed. Piping on yoke, collar and belt. Tie of mercerized rep cloth. Waist lined. State age.
Price, each....... **$1.10**

No. 29K7836 Blue plaid.
No. 29K7844 Red plaid.
FANCY PLAID CLOTH DRESS, woven in small neat pattern, with a firm finish that looks like wool. Front panel yoke depth, made of plain color material and embroidered in neat design. Piping and buttons to match panel. Waist lined throughout.
State age. Price, each, **$1.18**

No. 29K7846 Navy blue.
No. 29K7848 Red.
SERVICEABLE DRESS, made of a part wool cashmere. Velvet trim around yoke. Collar, yoke, cuffs, belt and front trimmed with piping of bias plaid material and gilt buttons. Waist and sleeves lined. Side plaited skirt. State age. Price, each.... **$1.27**

No. 29K7862
PRETTY DRESS of good quality navy blue wool serge mixed with a little cotton. Revers inlaid with black and white stripe material. Red piping and buttons. Waist lined. State age.
Price, each....... **$1.59**

No. 29K7863 Navy blue with cadet trim.
No. 29K7864 Brown with red trim.
AN ATTRACTIVE DRESS of good quality worsted serge, very firm and durable. Pretty embroidered effect of rope silk on revers. Waist lined. State age.
Price, each....... **$1.88**

No. 29K7856
BLACK AND WHITE SHEPHERD CHECK DRESS, made of a good quality woven cloth, resembling wool. Embroidered red wool cloth collar and cuffs. Red piping and button trimmed. Lined waist. Price, each.. **$1.95**

No. 29K7866 Navy blue with green silk piping.
No. 29K7867 Dark red with black silk piping.
PRETTY DRESS of hard twisted worsted serge. Trimmed with black and white striped bands, piped in contrasting color. Waist lined.
Price, each....... **$2.38**

No. 29K7868
BEAUTIFUL SAILOR COLLAR DRESS of good quality navy blue worsted serge. Embroidered shield and red wool cloth sailor collar. Black mercerized cotton rep cloth tie. Price, each.... **$2.48** age.

No. 29K7865
OUR BEST DRESS, made of hand twisted navy blue serge. Red wool cloth yoke and collar. Black and white satin cord piping. Pretty black lacing over red panel. A charming style. State age.
Price, each **$3.35**

HAPPY HOURS FOR THE CHILDREN

All children like to play Indian, cowboy, policeman and soldier. You can double their pleasure by giving them the dandy play suits offered here. These play suits are specially well adapted for holiday purposes. Inexpensive and sure to please.
Note description for sizes in which each number is furnished. When ordering be sure to state age.

No. 40K636
$1.30 OUR POPULAR INDIAN TEPEE. Made of unbleached white cotton fabric with colored decorations. Very simply constructed, easily put together and taken down. Poles are jointed and collapsible. Include one with your order. Doubles the pleasure of playing Indian. Average shipping wt., 5 lbs.

No. 40K630
95c THE "MEDICINE MAN" INDIAN PLAY SUIT. Popular outfit, consisting of shirt with insert in front and pretty yellow and red fringe trimmings. Splendid war bonnet with colored feathers. Well made garments in good weight tan khaki cloth. SIZES —4 to 10 years. State age. Shipping weight, 22 ounces.

No. 40K628
45c INDIAN PLAY SUIT in "Brownie" style. Made of tan khaki cloth with striking trimmings in red and yellow. War bonnet with seven feathers in assorted colors. Something inexpensive from which the little fellows will derive a great deal of pleasure. SIZES—4 to 10 years. Order by age. Shipping weight, 16 ounces.

No. 40K632
95c INDIAN SQUAW SUIT for little girls. Extremely popular one-piece style in red drill with rich yellow trimmings. Handsome headdress trimmed with feathers in variegated colors, and emblem in front. SIZES—4 to 10 years. Be sure to state age. Shipping weight, 18 ounces.

No. 40K634
$1.50 THE "BIG CHIEF" INDIAN OUTFIT. Made of heavy dark navy blue drill handsomely trimmed with red, white and blue. Long trousers, with red and blue stripe and fringe down sides. Gorgeous war bonnet trimmed with red, white and blue feathers. Tomahawk furnished with this number. SIZES—4 to 10 years. Order by age. Shipping weight, 30 ounces.

No. 40K646
$1.50 POLICEMEN'S UNIFORM of dark blue drill. Blouse with military collar, light blue trimmings, brass buttons, star. Long trousers with white stripe. Leather belt eagle buckle, club and cap. SIZES—6 to 14 years. Shipping wt., 32 ounces.

No. 40K642
$1.25 EXTRAORDINARY VALUE IN COWBOY CHAPS. Genuine leather front, strong khaki drill back. Patch pockets, leather belt, pistol holster, large metal buttons on side seams, and lariat. The most serviceable outfit of the kind. SIZES—6 to 14 years. State age. Shipping wt., 23 oz.

No. 40K644
$1.50 THE REGULAR ARMY PLAY SUIT of olive color khaki drill. Four patch pockets, military collar, shoulder straps, gunmetal eagle buttons. Knickerbocker pants with attached leggings, and hat. SIZES—8 to 16 years. Shipping weight, 24 oz.

No. 40K640
$1.15 OUR GIRL SCOUTS' SUIT. Sure to please the little girls. Consists of blouse, skirt, hat and bandana neckerchief. Made of tan color drill with brown fringe trimmings. SIZES—4 to 10 years. State age. Shipping weight, 29 ounces.

No. 40K650
$2.50 EXTRAORDINARY VALUE IN GENUINE WOOL CHAPS. Sheep's wool pelt leather front, strong khaki drill back. Leather belt and pistol holster, lariat, metal trimmings. Very durable and attractive. SIZES—6 to 14 years. State age. Shipping weight, 36 ounces.

No. 40K648
$1.75 GREAT VALUE IN A COWBOY OUTFIT. Shirt and long trousers made of khaki drill. Imitation leather fringe trimming. Bandana neckerchief, pistol holster and belt, metal pistol, lariat, and hat to match. SIZES—6 to 14 years. Shipping weight, 40 ounces.

No. 40K652
$2.65 THE "WILD WEST" COWBOY OUTFIT. Strong khaki color drill with brown leather trimmings. Double breasted shirt. Long trousers with one hip pocket. Leather belt pistol holster, bandana neckerchief, lariat, and felt hat with leather band. SIZES—6 to 14 years. Shipping weight, 42 ounces.

No. 40K638
95c INEXPENSIVE COWBOY CHAPS. Tan khaki trimmed with imitation leather front. Two large patch pockets, belt, pistol holster and lariat. SIZES—6 to 14 years. Order by age. Shipping wt., 20 oz.

INEXPENSIVE CLOTHING FOR BOYS AND LITTLE FELLOWS

These suits are not our own make and we do not especially recommend them. They are, however, the best that can possibly be produced for the price. We especially recommend our UCANTTEAR Brand of clothing, which is a little higher in price, but will be by far the cheapest in the end. Note sizes in which each number is made and order by age.

$1.50 No. 40N751
BOYS' KNICKERBOCKER SUIT in good weight dark brown soft finished cotton material. Black twill lining, two outside pockets with flap. Knickerbocker pants with side pockets, hip pockets, strap and buckle at knee. Sizes, 8 to 15 years. State boy's age. Shipping weight, 3¼ lbs.

$1.75 No. 40N753
MEDIUM BROWN FANCY STRIPED CASSIMERE SUIT. Strong cotton fabric. Double breasted style, two outside pockets with flap. Knickerbocker pants with side pockets, hip pocket, strap and buckle at knee. Double stitched and taped seams. Sizes, 8 to 15 years. State age. Shipping weight, 3¼ lbs.

$1.85 No. 40N755
DARK BLUE KNICKERBOCKER SUIT in good weight wool and cotton mixed material. Twill lining, two outside pockets with flap. Knickerbocker pants with side pockets, hip pocket, strap and buckle at knee. Sizes, 8 to 15 years. State age. Shipping weight, 3¼ pounds.

$1.95 No. 40N757
BLUISH GRAY STRIPE EFFECT SUIT of extra strong hard finished cotton worsted material. About the most durable inexpensive suit which can be produced. Twill lining, two outside pockets with flap. Knickerbocker pants with side pockets, hip pocket, strap and buckle at knee. Double stitched and taped seams. Sizes, 8 to 15 years. State age. Shpg. wt., 3¼ lbs.

$2.45 No. 40N759
FANCY MEDIUM BROWN MIXED KNICKERBOCKER SUIT with an extra pair of knickerbockers. Serviceable medium weight cotton material. Double breasted style. Two pairs of knickerbocker pants with side pockets, hip pocket, strap and buckle at knee. Sizes, 8 to 15 years. State age. Shipping weight, 3¾ pounds.

$1.75 No. 40N763
LITTLE FELLOWS' DOUBLE BREASTED MANLY SUIT in a dark gray pattern wool and cotton mixed material with a little stripe effect in violet. Twill lining, three outside pockets. Bloomer pants with side pockets, hip pocket, elastic at bottoms. Sizes, 5 to 9 years. State age. Shipping weight, 3 pounds.

$1.48 No. 40N771
LITTLE FELLOWS' OVERCOAT in a dark brown good weight cotton fabric. Double breasted, two outside pockets with flap, cuff effect on sleeves. Collar of same material. Black Italian lining. Sizes, 3 to 8 years. State age. Shipping weight, 3¼ pounds.

$1.25 No. 40N761
LITTLE FELLOWS' BUTTON TO THE NECK SUIT in a strong cotton fabric, medium gray and brown mixed with a neat stripe effect. Fancy imitation plait of brown tape and white and brown soutache braid down front, bow tie, leather belt. Bloomer pants. Sizes, 4 to 9 years. State age. Shipping weight, 3 pounds.

$1.75 No. 40N765
LITTLE FELLOWS' BUSTER BROWN SUIT of a soft finished wool and cotton mixed cassimere. Color, dark brown with a hairline stripe effect in a lighter brown. Silk emblem in center of front, bow tie, leather belt. Bloomer pants. Sizes, 2½ to 6 years. State age. Shipping weight, 3 pounds.

$1.75 No. 40N767
DARK NAVY BLUE BUTTON TO THE NECK STYLE SUIT of soft finished wool and cotton mixed material. Made like illustration, inlaid box plait down front in a little lighter blue, bow tie, leather belt. Bloomer pants. Sizes, 4 to 8 years. State age. Shipping weight, 3 pounds.

$1.85 No. 40N769
LITTLE FELLOWS' MILITARY RUSSIAN SUIT of extra strong hard finished cotton fabric. Color, dark blue with a little stripe effect in olive. Embroidered emblem in center of front, breast pocket. Bloomer pants. Sizes, 2½ to 6 years. State age. Shipping weight, 3 pounds.

$1.60 No. 40N772
LITTLE FELLOWS' OVERCOAT of heavy weight wool and cotton mixed material. Color, dark navy blue. Black twill lining, slit and belt in back, brass buttons. Sizes, 3 to 8 years. State age. Shipping wt., 3¼ lbs.

LATEST NOVELTIES IN HATS AND CAPS FOR CHILDREN

24c No. 40N813
LITTLE FELLOWS' GOLF STYLE CAPS in a great variety of colors and patterns. Near match to our little fellows' suits. Inside fur lined band. Sizes, 6⅛, 6¼, 6⅜, 6½ and 6⅝. State size and color wanted. Shipping weight, 7½ ounces.

39c No. 40N815
LITTLE FELLOWS' DARK NAVY BLUE WOOL SERGE GOLF CAP. Embroidered emblem in front. Inside fur lined band. Sizes, 6⅛, 6¼, 6⅜, 6½ and 6⅝. State size wanted. Shipping wt., 7½ oz.

40c
No. 40N817 Gray with red trimmings.
No. 40N819 Brown with white trimmings.
No. 40N821 Blue with orange trimmings.
CHILDREN'S POPULAR RAH-RAH HATS. Soft finished wool cassimere. Note catalog number and color. Sizes, 6¼, 6⅜, 6½, 6⅝ and 6¾. State size. Shipping weight, 6½ ounces.

35c
No. 40N827 Blue.
No. 40N829 Gray.
LITTLE FELLOWS' BLUE OR GRAY CHINCHILLA POLO CAPS. Wool and cotton mixed. Note catalog number for each color. Sizes, 6¼, 6⅜, 6½, 6⅝ and 6¾. State size wanted. Shipping weight, 7 ounces.

95c
No. 40N831 Gray.
No. 40N833 Brown.
CHILDREN'S BEAUTIFUL TYROLEAN HATS in gray or brown. Silk plush. Silk band to match color and a bunch of feathers on the side. Note catalog number for each color. Sizes, 6¼, 6⅜, 6½, 6⅝ and 6¾. State size wanted. Shipping wt., 8 ounces.

60c
No. 40N823 Blue.
No. 40N825 Gray.
ALL WOOL CHINCHILLA POLO CAPS in blue or gray. Silk lining. Can be pulled down over the ears. Note catalog number of each color. Sizes, 6⅛, 6⅜, 6½, 6⅝ and 6¾. State size. Shipping weight, 7½ ounces.

Boys' Comfortable Hot Weather Suits in Khaki, Linen and Palm Beach Cloth

Note sizes in which each number can be furnished.   Order by age.

$2.25 No. 40R2488
GENUINE LINEN CRASH SUIT. Plain linen color. Norfolk style, plaits front and back. Belt, ivory buttons. Knickerbocker pants. Belt loops, side pockets, hip pocket, strap and buckle at knee. Good quality material and exceptional value at price. SIZES—8 to 16 years. State age. Shipping wt., 2¼ lbs.

$1.95 No. 40R2484
DARK DRAB KHAKI NORFOLK SUIT. Extra strong wearing material. Norfolk style, plaits front and back. Belt all around. Knickerbocker pants, belt loops, side pockets, hip pocket, strap and buckle at knee. SIZES—8 to 16 years. State age. Shipping weight, 2¼ pounds.

$2.25 No. 40R2486
BEST QUALITY KHAKI CLOTH NORFOLK SUIT. Olive tan color. Yoke effect. Plaits front and back. Breast pocket, two lower pockets with flaps, belt all around. Peg top knickerbocker pants, belt loops, side pockets, hip pocket, watch pocket, strap and buckle at knee. SIZES—8 to 16 years. State age. Shipping weight, 2¼ pounds.

$1.50 No. 40R2482
DOUBLE BREASTED SUIT in khaki drill. Tan color. Double breasted coat, three outside patch pockets, belt all around. Knickerbocker pants, belt loops, side pockets, hip pocket, strap and buckle at knee. SIZES—8 to 16 years. State age. Shipping weight, 2¼ pounds.

$3.95 No. 40R2490
FINE QUALITY PALM BEACH CLOTH KNICKERBOCKER SUIT. Linen color. Fancy plaits front and back. Patch pockets made to button. Belt all around. Pearl buttons. Peg top knickerbocker pants. Belt loops, side buckle straps, side pockets, hip pocket, watch pocket, strap and buckle at knee. SIZES—10 to 17 years only. State age. Shipping weight, 2¼ pounds.

═══ BOY SCOUTS' OUTFIT ═══

Furnished in sizes to fit average size boys from 12 to 17 years. Order by age. Not larger than 33 inches breast measure.

No. 40R2570

Made of a splendid quality of khaki cloth in the latest olive tan color. Complete uniform consists of scout coat, scout breeches laced below the knee, strong puttees made of army duck, a campaign hat of khaki cloth, with ventilation eyelets in crown, and the latest style haversack. All made exactly like illustrations. An outfit of practical value, not only as a uniform, but for general wear, at a much more reasonable price than well made goods like these can possibly be obtained elsewhere.

If you want the complete uniform, order No. 40R2570, price, $3.65. Any part of the uniform can be obtained by ordering under the numbers and at prices listed below.

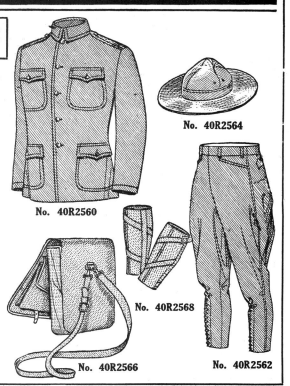

No. 40R2560

No. 40R2564

No. 40R2568

No. 40R2566

No. 40R2562

No. 40R2570
Complete Scout Outfit.. **$3.65**
Shipping weight, 3½ lbs.

No. 40R2560
Scout Coat........... **$1.25**
Shipping weight, 1¾ lbs.

No. 40R2562
Scout Breeches........... **98c**
Shipping weight, 1⅜ lbs.

No. 40R2564
Scout Campaign Hat... **40c**
Sizes, 6½, 6⅝, 6¾, 6⅞, 7 and 7⅛.
Shipping weight, 12 oz.

No. 40R2566
Scout Haversack........ **54c**
Shipping weight, 9 oz.

No. 40R2568
Scout Puttees.......... **48c**
Shipping weight, 9 oz.

GOOD STYLES FOR ALL AGES AT BARGAIN PRICES

$1.25 No. 18R6452 Finest quality genuine patent Milan braid, trimmed with 2⅛-inch satin taffeta ribbon of good quality finished at either side in puffs and trimming loops. A wreath across front of tiny imported muslin June roses with moss. 21 inches around head size. Colors, white with pink, light blue, navy blue, or old rose ribbon; or champagne with light blue ribbon; roses to harmonize. State color. Shipping weight, 1½ lbs.

63c No. 18R6456 Both style and value are embodied in this pretty mushroom hat for girls 7 to 10 years of age. Smooth finished chip braid of good quality with satin braid stripes. Trimmed around crown with 2⅜-inch ribbon of best quality velvetta finished at back in loop and long end. 22½ inches around head size. Colors, white with navy blue, brown, cardinal or light blue ribbon, or in all light blue. State color. Shipping weight, 1¾ lbs.

98c No. 18R6460 Becoming hand made poke bonnet of fancy straw webbing with edging on brim to match, for little girls 3 to 5 years of age. Fine quality satin taffeta ribbon band and loops. Cluster of tiny imported moss rosebuds are nested in ribbon loops at left side. 22 inches around head size. Natural Tuscan color with pink, light blue, white or navy blue ribbon, all with satin stripes in straw cloth to match. State color. Shpg. wt., 1½ lbs.

58c No. 18R6464 Very becoming toque style for children 3 to 6 years of age. Full soft draped crown of good quality white pique with close fitting double brim of fine ratine cloth. Three tiny imported moss rosebuds are held in place with ⅞-inch satin taffeta ribbon. 22 inches around head size. Colors: White crown with light blue brim; also with navy blue, old rose, or white brim, all with trimming to harmonize. State color. Shipping weight, 1 lb.

$1.38 No. 18R6468 Fine quality genuine imported Java hat with pretty fluted mushroom brim for girls 7 to 10 years of age. Full scarf trimming is of fine quality all silk crepe in large polka dot pattern finished at back with full straw cord rosette. 23 inches around head size. Colors, natural cream-white only, with light blue, navy blue, green or old rose dots in trimming. State color. Shipping weight, 1½ lbs.

$1.65 No. 18R6472 Pretty Tam o' Shanter crown hat made of allover straw webbing with brim of all silk pyroxylin braid for girls 6 to 8 years of age. Satin taffeta ribbon, 1¼ inches wide, is artistically draped amongst the folds of crown. Combination wreath of silk centered blossoms and metallic silk rosebuds. 22 inches around head size. Colors, white with pink, light blue, or old rose trimming, or light blue with pink trimming. State color. Shipping weight, 1½ lbs.

$1.75 No. 18R6476 A rich looking hat of high quality for little girls 4 to 6 years of age. Entire top is of good Valenciennes edging sewed row and row. Facing of fine quality satin messaline. Large trimming bows at front, as well as folded drape around crown, are of messaline to match facing. 22 inches around head size. Comes in white with light blue, old rose, navy blue or gold color facing and trimming. State color. Shipping weight, 1½ lbs.

$1.98 No. 18R6480 Beautiful mushroom brim hat of all silk finished hemp braid for girls 6 to 9 years of age. Fine quality satin taffeta ribbon artistically draped around Tam o' Shanter crown and finished with long loop and ends. One of our finest qualities. 23 inches around head size. Comes in white, with pink, light blue, navy blue or gold color ribbon or in solid old rose. State color. Shipping weight, 1½ lbs.

$1.58 No. 18R6484 Full allover lace crown with good quality leghorn brim bound with lace. For girls 9 to 12 years of age. Band and bow of 1½-inch fine quality taffeta silk ribbon. 23½ inches around head size. Two trimming clusters, each with three June roses and pretty wild flowers. Colors, natural leghorn brim with white allover lace crown and pink, light blue, cream-yellow or old rose ribbon; all flowers to match ribbon. State color. Shipping wt., 1¾ lbs.

75c No. 18R6488 Pretty and serviceable poke effect mushroom shape for girls 5 to 7 years of age. Made of satin finished Japanese straw braid with fancy raised edge. Mercerized poplin of good quality is worked in combination with braid in pretty plaited rosette. Band of braid around crown. 21 inches around head size. White and navy blue, as illustrated; white and brown; white and cardinal; all white or all navy blue. State color. Shipping weight, 1¾ lbs.

95c No. 18R6492 Stylish hat with full gathered crown of good quality pique and brim of Swiss embroidery laid over fancy woven cloth. Satin taffeta ribbon, ⅞ inch wide, is laid around crown, finished in loops and ends. Six satin ribbon rosebuds are trimmed across front. 23 inches around head size. For girls 6 to 9 years of age. White with pink, light blue, navy blue old rose, or cardinal trimming. State color. Shipping weight, 1½ lbs.

$1.69 No. 18R6496 Beautiful hat for girls 5 to 7 years of age. Entire top is of excellent imitation baby Irish lace with white Valenciennes lace edging on brim. Combination wreath of velvet forget-me-nots and large satin ribbon rosebuds around crown with extra full ruche of 2½-inch satin taffeta ribbon, also rosette at left side. 21 inches around head size. Colors, white with light blue, white, pink, old rose or navy blue trimming. State color. Shipping weight, 1¾ lbs.

$1.48 No. 18R6501 All silk finished hemp braid poke bonnet for girls 9 to 12 years of age. Drape around crown and large rosette of satin taffeta ribbon, 2½ inches wide. Three tiny muslin June roses and puffs of ribbon at right side. 24 inches around head size. Colors, white with pink, light blue, navy blue or gold color ribbon; champagne with light blue ribbon, or all light blue. State color. Shipping wt., 1¾ lbs.

$1.19 No. 18R6505 Stylish hat for girls 12 to 15 years of age. Genuine closely sewed patent Milan braid hat, effectively trimmed with full ruche of high quality satin taffeta ribbon, 3 inches wide, laid over top of brim. Two large satin covered buttons at side of crown. 24½ inches around head size. Colors, white with pink, old rose, navy blue or white trimming or in burnt straw with light blue trimming. State color. Shipping weight, 2 lbs.

$1.19 No. 18R6509 Stylish deep setting hat for children 12 to 15 years of age. Made of finest quality genuine patent Milan braid closely sewed. All around drape, and long trimming loops, are of good quality satin taffeta ribbon, 3¾ inches wide, set off with cabochon of heavy silk cord. 24 inches around head size. Colors, white with light blue, pink, old rose, navy blue or white trimming. State color. Shipping weight, 2 lbs.

89c No. 18R6513 Stylish and serviceable poke effect mushroom hat of pretty two-tone satin finished Japanese braid for girls 6 to 9 years of age. Trimming band and tailored bows at each side of crown are of 1½-inch mercerized poplin ribbon. 23 inches around head size. We are selling this hat at a very low price, quality considered. Colors, white and navy blue combination, as illustrated; white and cardinal; or white and brown. State color. Shipping wt., 1½ lbs.

17T8512 $3.48

17T8507 $3.98

17T8505 $3.95

17T8501 $4.95

17T8514 $1.98

17T8510 $4.98

17T8500 $6.90

Girls' Winter Coats

Ages, Years	10	12	14
Lengths, Inches	36	39	42

Samples of material of any coat sent on request. Muffs on this page are sold separately.
Average shipping weight of muffs, 1 pound.

Girls' Astralama Cloth Coat. Astralama is woven of bright glossy mohair in a small curl pattern to imitate astrakhan lamb fur. The coat is made in full loose style, fastening with loops and plush buttons. The kimono sleeves are finished with fancy shaped cuffs, trimmed with small plush buttons. Collar is of silk seal plush. Lined throughout with mercerized sateen. **State age and color.** Average shipping weight, 4¼ pounds.
No. 17T8507 Navy blue.
No. 17T8508 Brown.
No. 17T8509 Black.
Price.............................. **$3.98**
Astralama Muff, trimmed with bands of silk seal plush. Colors to match coat. State color.
No. 17T8860 Price.................. **95c**

Girls' Canadian Pony Cloth Coat. A very furlike material of heavy winter weight, woven of brilliant mohair in a circular or whirl pattern to imitate real fur. The coat is made with the new style kimono sleeves. Stitched cuffs and storm collar. Fronts fasten with loops and large plush buttons. Lined with black mercerized sateen. **State age.** Average shipping weight, 4½ pounds.
No. 17T8505 Black.
Price.............................. **$3.95**
No. 17T8851 Canadian Pony Cloth Muff to match coat.
Price.............................. **79c**

Girls' Wool Mixed Cloth Coat. Made of a medium weight wool mixed material in a selection of neat dark patterns. Coat is made full and loose with kimono sleeves and patch pockets. Fronts have deep facings and fasten with large fancy buttons. **State age.** Average shipping weight, 3½ pounds.
No. 17T8514 Dark mixture. **$1.98**
Price..............................

Girls' All Wool Cheviot Coat. Made of a heavy weight all wool cheviot cloth, very warm and durable. Coat is made full and loose with wide Balkan belt and patch pockets. The storm collar and cuffs are of cheviot cloth in contrasting colors. The fronts have deep facings of cheviot and fasten with fancy buttons. **State age and color.** Average shipping weight, 4¼ pounds.
No. 17T8512 Navy blue.
No. 17T8513 Tan.
No. 17T8506 Gray. Price... **$3.48**

Girls' Stylish Winter Coat. Made of a good weight all wool material in very attractive dark plaids. Coat is cut along full loose lines with the new flared flounce. The sleeves are made with the new deep set-in armholes and are finished with fancy cuffs trimmed with buttons. Fronts have deep cloth facings. Patch pockets. **State age and color.** Average shipping weight, 4¼ pounds.
No. 17T8510 Navy blue, green and red plaid.
No. 17T8511 Navy blue and Copenhagen blue plaid.
Price.............................. **$4.98**

Girls' Baby Lamb Cloth Coat. One of the most popular imitation fur cloths. It is of good weight and woven of bright rich mohair in pattern to imitate baby lamb fur. Lined throughout with mercerized sateen, quilted and wadded for additional warmth. The coat is made in the loose box style with the new kimono sleeves. The collar and Balkan belt are of silk seal plush, a rich brown black in color. The cuffs are trimmed with seal plush to match the collar and belt. Fronts fasten with loops and four large plush buttons. **State age.** Average shipping weight, 4¾ pounds.
No. 17T8500 Black. **$6.90**
Price..............................
The Muff shown with this coat is made of black baby lamb cloth trimmed with bands of seal plush.
No. 17T8856 Price............. **$1.25**

Girls' Astralama Cloth Coat. Astralama is a good weight astrakhan cloth, woven of brilliant mohair in small tight curls to imitate astrakhan lamb fur. Coat is made in the Balkan style with kimono sleeves. The pointed belt is trimmed with large plush buttons. The cuffs are trimmed with silk seal plush to match storm collar. Lined with good quality sateen and fastens with loops and large plush buttons. **State age and color.** Ave. shpg. wt., 4¼ lbs.
No. 17T8501 Navy blue. No. 17T8502 Brown.
No. 17T8503 Black. Price........... **$4.95**
Astralama Cloth Muff, trimmed with bands of silk seal plush. Colors to match coat. State color.
No. 17T8860 Price................ **95c**

17R7878
$1.88

17R7893
$3.95

17R7882
$2.25

17R7880
$1.98

17R7883
$2.98

17R7885
$2.88

17R7892
$3.95

17R7888
$2.98

17R7890
$2.98

17R7877
$1.48

SPRING COAT, to fit children from 2 to 6 years. Material is a tan color cotton poplin. Lined throughout with sateen. The circular collar is made of Copenhagen blue cotton ratine to match the cuffs and wide belt. Fronts fasten with pretty colored buttons to harmonize with the trimming of coat. State age. Average shipping wt., 1¼ lbs.
No. 17R7878 Tan. $1.88
Price............

BLACK SATIN COAT, to fit children 2 to 6 years of age. Lined throughout with black mercerized sateen. The garment is cut full and fastens with large fancy buttons. Extra collar and cuffs of white pique, lace trimmed. Shipping weight, 1¼ pounds.
No. 17R7892
Black. Price............ $3.95

SPRING AND FALL COAT, to fit children from 2 to 6 years of age. The material is a good quality all wool smooth finished ladies' cloth. The coat is loose fitting and lined throughout with good quality sateen. The fronts fasten with fancy buttons. Circular collar is inlaid with rich black satin to match the fancy tie and wide plaited Balkan belt. State age. See scale of sizes. Average shipping weight, 1¼ pounds.
No. 17R7893 Red.
No. 17R7894 Navy $3.95
blue. Price............

BEAUTIFUL SPRING AND FALL COAT, to fit children 2 to 6 years of age. Material used is a good quality all wool serge. Made loose fitting and lined throughout with mercerized sateen. The shawl collar of circular design at back is embroidered in scroll and floral design in Persian colors to match the messaline sash. State age. See scale of sizes. Average shipping wt., 1½ lbs.
No. 17R7885 Navy $2.88
blue. Price............

ATTRACTIVE SPRING AND FALL COAT, to fit children from 2 to 6 years of age. Made of a closely woven cotton fabric in small black and white Shepherd check pattern. The coat is lined throughout with good quality gray mercerized sateen. Fronts fasten with attractive fancy buttons. The collar and cuffs are trimmed with Copenhagen blue mercerized cotton poplin. Back has wide belt. State age. See scale of sizes. Average shipping wt., 1¼ lbs.
No. 17R7882 Black and white Shepherd check. $2.25
Price............

DAINTY SPRING AND FALL COAT, to fit children 2 to 6 years of age. Made of all wool serge. Coat is loose fitting and lined throughout with mercerized sateen. Front fastens with good white pearl buttons. The shawl collar is embroidered in tasteful design with silk cord. State age. See scale of sizes. Average shipping wt., 1½ lbs.
No. 17R7888 Navy blue.
No. 17R7889 $2.98
Cream-white. Price............

ALL WOOL SERGE COAT, to fit children from 2 to 6 years of age. It buttons close to the neck with neat turndown collar. Fastens with large fancy pearl buttons. Lined throughout with mercerized sateen. State age. See scale of sizes. Average shipping wt., 1⅜ lbs.
No. 17R7880 Navy blue.
No. 17R7881 $1.98
Cream-white. Price............

ATTRACTIVE COAT, to fit children 2 to 6 years of age. Material used is all wool serge. The garment is lined throughout with good mercerized sateen. The fancy sailor collar is made in pointed design at back and shoulder, with rich tan color silk Bengaline and cardinal and gilt soutache braid. Nobby rosette tie with streamers. State age. See scale of sizes. Average shipping wt., 1½ lbs.
No. 17R7890 Navy $2.98
blue. Price............

NAVY BLUE WOOL MIXED SERGE COAT, to fit children 2 to 6 years of age. The serge is of good quality and the garment is cut loose and full. Lined throughout with sateen. Large collar and turnback cuffs are finished with additional collar and cuffs made of white pique. State age. Average shipping weight, 1⅜ pounds.
No. 17R7883 Navy $2.98
blue. Price............

PONGEE COAT, to fit children 2 to 6 years. Made of a very fine cotton fabric. Collar and turnback cuffs are trimmed with braid embroidery in tan color. Coat lined throughout with sateen and fastens with pearl buttons. State size. Average shpg. wt., 1 lb.
No. 17R7877 Tan. $1.48
Price............

Rompers, Creepers, Dresses, Aprons

No. 29V8925

Girls' Suspender Apron, straps cross in back and button on shoulders. Comes in assorted light patterns of blue, pink, tan or gray pin striped percale with fancy juvenile colored border. **State first and second color choice.** Ages, 2 to 6 years. **State age.** Average shipping wt., 4 oz. Price, each........ **19c**

No. 29V7648 Blue.

Girls' Oliver Twist Dress. Hydegrade percale waist with collar and skirt of pretty plaid Amoskeag gingham. Ages, 2 to 6 years. **State age.** Average shipping wt., 6 oz. Price, each.... **28c**

No. 29V8932 Blue.

Girls' Apron of Manhattan cloth, a splendid wearing material. Plain binding; pocket and belted back. Ages, 2 to 7 years. **State age.** Average shipping weight, 6 oz. Price, each... **19c**

No. 29V2123 Plain blue.
No. 29V2124 Blue and white check.

Babies' Strong Chambray Overalls or Creepers. Neatly trimmed. Well made, with double stitched seams. Ages, 6 months to 2 years. **State age.** Average shipping wt., 4 oz. Price, each.... **22c**

No. 29V8935 Blue stripe.
No. 29V8936 Pink stripe.
No. 29V8937 Solid white.

Neat Seersucker Gingham Rompers; material that needs no ironing. Neatly trimmed in contrasting color. Double stitched seams. Ages, 2 to 7 years. **State age.** Aver. shpg. wt., 7 oz. Price, each... **48c**

No. 29V8978 Cadet blue.
No. 29V8979 Tan.

Children's Serviceable Rompers of fast color Hydegrade Youngster cloth. Good value. Ages, 2 to 6 years. **State age.** Av. shpg. wt., 6 oz. Price, each..... **24c**

No. 29V7805

Practical Dress for the little tots. Made of assorted light and dark pattern percales and ginghams. Ages, 1 to 4 years. **State age.** Average shipping wt., 4 ounces. Price, each.. **19c**

No. 29V8916 Blue and white check gingham.
No. 29V8915 Assorted patterns percale.

Girls' Belted Back Coverall Apron. Pocket. Well made; neatly piped. Ages, 2 to 7 years. **State age.** Average shipping weight, 7 ounces. Price, each..... **24c**

No. 29V8942 Blue and white stripe.
No. 29V8939 Plain blue.

Amoskeag Chambray Rompers. Double stitched flat seams; neatly piped. Sizes to fit ages 2 to 7 years. **State age.** Average shpg. wt., 7 oz. Price, each.... **39c**

No. 29V8966 Blue and white.

Striped Chambray Rompers made for hard wear. Neatly trimmed with dark blue material and white piping. Opens down front to crotch. Double stitched seams throughout. Ages, 2 to 7 years. **State age.** Average shipping weight, 8 ounces. Price, each. **55c**

No. 29V8962 Tan.
No. 29V8963 Blue.

Rompers made of good weight closely woven chambray. Neatly trimmed. Durable, double stitched seams throughout. Ages, 2 to 6 years. **State age.** Average shipping wt., 8 oz. Price, each.. **45c**

No. 29V8933 Blue and white.
No. 29V8934 Pink and white.

Babies' Combination Rompers and Creepers of checked Amoskeag gingham. Buttons down back, also side of leg, so that diaper can be easily removed. Ages, 6 months, 1 and 2 years. **State age.** Average shipping weight, 4 ounces. Price, each.. **48c**

No. 29V8972 Blue and white.
No. 29V8973 Tan and white.

Striped Percale Rompers. Plain banding gives yoke effect. Well made. Ages, 1 to 5 years. **State age.** Shipping weight, 5 oz. Price, each. **19c**

No. 29V8988 White and blue.
No. 29V8989 White and tan.

Popular Oliver Twist Chambray Romper Suit. Detachable blouse of white linene. Ages, 2 to 6 years. **State age.** Average shipping wt., 7 oz. Price, each. **48c**

Comfortable, Sanitary Washable Suits in Pretty Styles and Colors

All full cut, roomy garments, made under our own supervision, at prices from 25 to 50 per cent less than usually offered.

42¢
40V5631

48¢
40V5633

45¢
40V5635

55¢
40V5637

70¢
40V5639

85¢
40V5645

75¢
40V5641

85¢
40V56

All illustrations are actual photographic reproductions of the garments.
Note sizes in which each number can be furnished and order by age. Average shpg. wt., 1 lb.

No. 40V5631 42c
Little Fellows' Russian Blouse Suit with straight pants. Splendid washable cotton material. Natural linen color. Made exactly like illustration. Sailor collar. Laced in front. SIZES—2½ to 6 years. *State age.*

No. 40V5633 48c
Russian Blouse Suit with bloomer pants. Made of Beachwood Union linen, a good weight cotton fabric. Bluish gray color. Belt. Cuffs double thickness. A durable everyday suit. SIZES—2½ to 6 years. *State age.*

No. 40V5635 45c
Military Russian Blouse Suit with bloomer pants, for little fellows. Made of Harvard linen, a good washable cotton fabric in plain white. Breast pocket. Belt. SIZES—2½ to 6 years. *State age.*

No. 40V5637 55c
Russian Collar Blouse Suit with straight pants. Splendid quality of washable madras cloth. Tan sailor collar. Fly front. Four-in-hand tie. Belt effect. Detachable shield. SIZES—2½ to 6 years. *State age.*

No. 40V5639 70c
Russian Sailor Blouse Suit with straight pants. Good washable blue and white striped cotton suiing. Sailor collar. Detachable embroidered shield. Belt effect. SIZES—2½ to 6 years. *State age.*

No. 40V5641 75c
Stylish Pilgrim Blouse Suit with bloomer pants. Holland suiting, a cotton fabric. Linen color with a broken check effect in brown. Breast pocket. Belt. Pearl buttons. SIZES—2½ to 6 years. *State age.*

40V5643 85c
Russian Blouse Suit in fast color Amoskeag blue and white striped cotton suiting. Bloomer pants. SIZES—2½ to 6 years. *State age.*

No. 40V5645 85c
Low Neck Short Sleeve Russian Blouse Suit in plain white batiste cloth with blue and white trimmings. Pearl buttons. Breast pocket. Belt effect. Straight pants. SIZES—2½ to 6 years. *State age.*

No. 40V5647 75c
Russian Sailor Blouse Suit in a fine quality of Amoskeag chambray. Black and white Shepherd plaid pattern. Collar scalloped around edges. Breast pocket. Belt effect. Straight pants. SIZES—2½ to 6 years. *State age.*

No. 40V5649 90c
Eton Collar Double Breasted Effect Russian Suit with bloomer pants. Made of fine domestic rep. Cadet blue color. Breast pocket. Belt effect. Double cuffs made to button. Pearl buttons. SIZES—2½ to 6 years. *State age.*

No. 40V5651 90c
Pretty Plymouth Collar Blouse Suit with bloomer pants. Plain white Hillsboro linen, a cotton fabric. Short sleeves. Broad belt. Breast pocket. Collar and sleeves scalloped in light blue. SIZES—2½ to 6 years. *State age.*

No. 40V5653 $1.15
Long Roll Double Breasted Russian Sailor Blouse Style Suit. Plain white batiste. Belt. Cuffs made to button. Detachable silk embroidered shield. Bloomer pants. SIZES—2½ to 6 years. *State age.*

No. 40V5655 $1.35
A beautiful New Style Suit in imported rep, tan color with red trimmings. Broad box plait. Broad belt with red edges. Pearl buttons. Bloomer pants. SIZES—2½ to 6 years. *State age.*

40V5657 $1.50
Stylish Double Breasted Russian Suit of imported rep in a light blue shade. Illustration shows trimmings. Bloomer pants. SIZES—2½ to 6 years. *State age.*

40V5659 $1.95
Handsome Russian Style Washable Suit. Plain white imported rep with olive tan trimmings. Bloomer pants. SIZES—2½ to 6 years. *State age.*

75¢
40V5647

$1.15
40V5653

90¢
40V5649

90¢
40V5651

$1.35
40V5655

$1.95
40V5659

$1.50
40V5657

Raincoats for Juniors and Children

HAT
17V9861
49¢

HAT
17V9862
59¢

HAT
17V9863
98¢

17V9801
$1.79

17V9806
$1.79

HAT
17V9860
29¢

17V9804
$2.48

17V9810
$5.95

17V9808
$3.98

17V9807
$2.48

17V9800
89¢

Children's Raincoat, to fit ages 6 to 15 years. Material is a good quality highly mercerized sateen, thoroughly rubberized on the inside. Coat is made straight and loose fitting with neat turnover collar, turnback cuffs and patch pockets. State age. See scale of sizes. Average shipping weight, 1⅝ pounds.
No. 17V9804 Navy blue.
No. 17V9805 Tan. Price.. $2.48
Waterproof hat to match. State color. Av. shpg. wt., 10 oz.
No. 17V9860 Price.... 29c

Junior Misses' and Children's Raincoat, made of a fine cotton rainproof fabric in tan color. The coat is thoroughly rubberized on the inside and is made loose and easy fitting, having neat turnover collar, slash pockets and strapped sleeves. Sizes to fit 13 to 19 years and 6 to 12 years. State age. See different scales of sizes.
No. 17V9806 Tan. Junior sizes. Average shpg. wt. 2¼ lbs. Price.. $1.79
No. 17V9814 Tan. Children's sizes. Av. shpg. wt., 1⅝ lbs. Price.... 1.48
Waterproof hat to match. Average shpg. wt., 12 oz.

Junior Misses' Serge Raincoat. The material is a splendid quality all wool French serge thoroughly waterproofed with a good coating of rubber on the inside. The coat is loose fitting with belt across back and has slash pockets and the sleeves are made with deep armholes and wide cuffs. The collar may be worn buttoned up closely about the throat if desired. (See small illustration.) Sizes to fit ages 13 to 19 years. State age. See scale of sizes. Average shipping weight, 3 pounds.
No. 17V9810 Black.
No. 17V9811 Navy blue.
No. 17V9812 Tan.
No. 17V9813 Gray. $5.95
Price.............
Hat to match. State color. Average shpg. wt., 14 oz.
No. 17V9863 Price.... 98c

Junior Misses' Tweed Raincoat. Material is a good serviceable wool mixed tweed in pepper and salt pattern and is thoroughly rubberized on the inside. The coat is made with deep armholes and hangs loose and full with belt across back. The fronts have large fancy pockets and the sleeves are finished with deep cuffs and buttons. The collar may be worn buttoned closely about the throat if desired. Ages, 13 to 19 years. State age. See scale of sizes. Average shipping weight, 3½ pounds.
No. 17V9808 Gray mixed.
No. 17V9809 Tan mixed. Price............. $3.98
Hat of same material to match. State color. Av. shpg. wt., 14 oz.
No. 17V9862 Price.... 59c

Junior Misses' Raincoat of good weight, closely woven fine double texture cotton rainproof fabric in tan color, in sizes to fit girls from 13 to 19 years of age. Inside of the garment shows plaid pattern in colors to harmonize with the outside; and there is a coating of rubber between, making this garment thoroughly waterproof. Neat turnover French band collar. The front is cut straight and loose and has slash pockets. Sleeves trimmed with strap and button. The back hangs loose and full. See scale of sizes below. State size and age wanted when ordering. Average shipping weight, 3¾ pounds.
No. 17V9807 Tan. Price........... $2.48

Girls' Raincape in sizes to fit ages 6 to 15 years. Made of a fine cotton fabric in attractive plaid on the inside. The outside of the cape is thoroughly rubberized showing pattern of two-tone gray stripes. State age or length wanted. See scale of sizes. Average shipping weight, 1⅝ pounds.
No. 17V9800 Gray stripe. 89c
Price.............

Girls' Sateen Raincape, to fit ages 6 to 15 years. Material is a good quality highly mercerized sateen, thoroughly rubberized on the inside. The hood is lined with attractive plaid silk and is made in entirely new Billy Burke style. State age or length. See scale of sizes. Average shipping weight, 1⅝ lbs.
No. 17V9801 Navy blue.
No. 17V9802 Red.
No. 17V9803 Tan. Price............. $1.79

CHILDREN'S SCALE OF SIZES.						
Ages, years................	6	8	10	12	14	15
Length, inches................	33	35	37	39	42	45

JUNIOR SCALE OF SIZES.			
Ages, years.	13	15	17	19
Length, inches................	45	48	50	50
Bust measure, inches................	34	34	36	2

Fur Sets for Girls

For Ages From 8 to 12 Years.

No. 41K6670
Brown Set **$9.25**
Girls' Brown Marmot Fur Set. Generally sold as Russian mink. A short, glossy, blended fur. Cape style scarf and melon style muff with silk ruching. Set silk lined. Average shipping weight, 2 pounds.

No. 41K6650   Brown Set **$3.95**
No. 41K6655   Blue Gray Set .. **3.95**
Girls' Imported China Goat Fur Set. The blue gray imitates wolf and the brown imitates cub bear. A long haired, serviceable fur. Animal style scarf and pillow style muff. Set Skinner's satin lined. Average shipping weight, 2¾ pounds.

41K6650

41K6670

41K6665

41K6680

41K6660

41K6675

41K6635

No. 41K6680   Tan and Black Set **$4.95**
No. 41K6685   Natural Tan and Gray Set **4.95**
No. 41K6690   Brown Set **5.95**
Girls' Imported Coney Fur Set in tan and black to imitate tiger, natural tan and gray or dark brown. Attractive animal style scarf and melon style muff. Set silk lined. Average shipping weight, 2¼ pounds.

No. 41K6665
Dark Brown Set **$7.75**
Girls' Blended Dark Brown Set made of durable muskrat fur. Plain animal style scarf and pillow style muff with satin ruching. Set Skinner's satin lined. Average shipping weight, 2 pounds.

No. 41K6660
White Set **$7.95**
Girls' White Iceland Fox Fur Set. Made from the long haired, soft, combed Thibet fur in imitation of white fox. Animal boa scarf with fur on both sides, and melon style muff with Skinner's satin lining. Average shipping weight, 2 pounds.

No. 41K6675
White Set **$6.50**
Imitation Ermine Fur Set. Made from imported white coney with black imitation ermine tails. New style collarette, which can be worn as in illustration, or with the collar turned up around the neck. Large melon style muff with silk ruching. Set silk lined. Average shipping weight, 2¼ pounds.

No. 41K6635   Natural Tan and Gray Set **$4.75**
No. 41K6640   Brown Set **5.75**
No. 41K6645   Taupe Gray Set **5.75**
Girls' Imported Coney Fur Set in natural tan and gray, brown or taupe gray. New style cape scarf, which can be worn as in the illustration, or tied up close around the neck. Melon style muff. Set Skinner's satin lined. Average shipping weight, 2 pounds.

Low Cuts for Large and Small Girls
Especially Adapted to Growing Feet

No.		Sizes	The Pair
15H3821	Big Misses'	2½ to 7	$2.65
15H7631	Misses'	12 to 2	2.25
15H7632	Children's	8 to 11½	1.95

Patent Leather Lavalliere Sandal—Neat Two-Button Slashed Strap—Nobby Buckle—Sensible Heel—"Banner" Last—Searsmade.
Wide widths.
Shipping wt., 1⅝ lbs.

No.		Sizes	The Pair
15H3815	Big Misses'	2½ to 7	$2.50
15H7629	Misses'	12 to 2	2.15
15H7630	Children's	8 to 11½	1.85

Patent Leather Lavalliere Pump—Dull Kid Quarter and Strap—Button Fastened—Sensible Heel—"Banner" Last—Searsmade.
Wide widths.
Shipping wt., 1 lb. 5 oz.

No.		Sizes	The Pair
15H3814	Big Misses'	2½ to 7	$2.65
15H7627	Misses'	12 to 2	2.25
15H7628	Children's	8 to 11½	1.95

Patent Leather Two-Strap Sandal—Dull Kid Straps and Collar—Neat Bow—Sensible Heel—"Banner" Last—Searsmade.
Wide widths.
Shipping wt., 1 lb. 5 oz.

No.		Sizes	The Pair
15H3812	Big Misses'	2½ to 7	$2.50
15H7623	Misses'	12 to 2	2.15
15H7624	Children's	8 to 11½	1.85

Patent Leather Slashed Strap Sandal—Popular Two-Button Barred Front—Low Heel—"Banner" Last—Searsmade.
Wide widths.
Shipping wt., 1 lb. 5 oz.

No.		Sizes	The Pair
15H3811	Big Misses'	2½ to 6	$2.85
15H7621	Misses'	12 to 2	2.45
15H7622	Children's	8 to 11½	2.15

Stylish Patent Leather Roman Sandal — Broad Toe — Low Heel —"Banner" Last—Searsmade.
Wide widths.
Shipping wt., 1 lb. 5 oz.

No.		Sizes	The Pair
15H3809	Big Misses'	2½ to 7	$2.50
15H7617	Misses'	12 to 2	2.15
15H7618	Children's	8 to 11½	1.85

Gunmetal Two-Strap Sandal—Sensible Heel—Durable Chrome Sole—"Banner" Last—Searsmade.
Wide widths.
Shipping wt., 1 lb. 9 oz.

No.		Sizes	The Pair
15H3810	Big Misses'	2½ to 7	$2.50
15H7619	Misses'	12 to 2	2.15
15H7620	Children's	8 to 11½	1.85

Gunmetal Baby Doll Pump—Neat Pompon—Sensible Heel—"Banner" Last—Searsmade.
Wide widths.
Shipping wt., 1 lb. 5 oz.

No.		Sizes	The Pair
15H3813	Big Misses'	2½ to 7	$2.65
15H7625	Misses'	12 to 2	2.25
15H7626	Children's	8 to 11½	1.95

Patent Leather Ankle Strap Colonial—Sensible Heel—"Banner" Last—Searsmade.
Wide widths.
Shipping wt., 1 lb. 7 oz.

No.		Sizes	The Pair
15H3803	Big Misses'	2½ to 5½	$2.50
15H7609	Misses'	12 to 2	2.15
15H7610	Children's	8 to 11½	1.85
15H8546	Infants' Spring Heel 5 to 8		1.35

Patent Leather Baby Doll Pump—Low Heel—"Banner" Last—Searsmade.
Wide widths.
Shipping wt., 1⅝ lbs.

No.		Sizes	The Pair
15H3804	Big Misses'	2½ to 5½	$2.50
15H7611	Misses'	12 to 2	1.95
15H7612	Children's	8 to 11½	1.75

Gunmetal Button Oxford—Dull Kid Quarter — Chrome Sole — "Banner" Last—Searsmade.
Wide widths.
Shipping wt., 1½ lbs.

No.		Sizes	The Pair
15H3800	Big Misses'	2½ to 5½	$2.50
15H7601	Misses'	12 to 2	2.15
15H7602	Children's	8 to 11½	1.85

Patent Leather Two-Strap Sandal—Sensible Heel—"Ruth" Last—Searsmade.
Wide widths.
Shipping wt., 1⅝ lbs.

No.		Sizes	The Pair
15H3808	Big Misses'	2½ to 7	$2.00
15H7615	Misses'	12 to 2	1.75
15H7616	Children's	8 to 11½	1.55

Dressy Black Velveteen Baby Doll Pump—Sensible Heel—"Banner" Last—Searsmade.
Wide widths.
Shipping wt., 1 lb. 5 oz.

Gunmetal or Patent.

No.	Description	Sizes	The Pair
15H3820	Big Misses' Patent	2½ to 6	$1.65
15H3817	Big Misses' Gun'tal	2½ to 6	1.65
15H7653	Misses' Patent	12 to 2	1.40
15H7654	Children's Patent	8 to 11½	1.20

Nobby Blucher Oxford—Sensible Heel With Rubber Top Lift—"Banner" Last—Searsmade. No. 15H3817 Gunmetal Shoe has no rubber heel.
Wide widths.
Shipping wt., 1½ lbs.

No.		Sizes	The Pair
15H3816	Big Misses'	2½ to 7	$2.50
15H7605	Misses'	12 to 2	2.15
15H7606	Children's	8 to 11½	1.85

Bright Kid Two-Strap Sandal—Sensible Heel—"Ruth" Last—Searsmade.
Wide widths.
Shipping wt., 1 lb. 5 oz.

No.		Sizes	The Pair
15H3563	Big Misses'	3 to 8	$1.09
15H7877	Misses'	12 to 2	.89
15H7878	Children's	9 to 11½	.79
15H8550	Infants'	5 to 8	.69

Tan Grain Barefoot Sandal — New Stitchdown Welt — Nature's Last.
Wide widths.
Shipping wt., 1 lb. 3 oz.

No.		Sizes	The Pair
15H3822	Big Misses'	2½ to 7	$2.25
15H7603	Misses'	12 to 2	1.75
15H7604	Children's	8½ to 11½	1.50
15H8544	Infants' Spring Heel	5 to 8	1.25

Patent Leather Three-Strap Sandal—Low Heel—"Banner" Last—Searsmade.
Wide widths.
Shipping wt., 1 lb. 5 oz.

31H5600 31H5601 31H5602 31H5603 31H5604

31H5605 31H5606 31H5607

GIRLS' ORGANDY DRESS, of neatly embroidered washable organdy. Waist is trimmed in front with pin tucks and lace insertion and in back with pin tucks. The square collar is edged with lace to match edging on sleeves. Plaited skirt made in two-tier effect, trimmed with hemstitching. The tucked belt is finished with two silk ribbon rosettes and small silk buds. Fastens invisibly in back. **State age.** Av. shpg. wt., 1½ lbs.

EACH
No. **31H5600** **$1.73**
White.

GIRLS' EMBROIDERY DRESS. Made of embroidered organdy flouncing in an attractive style. Waist is cut in jacket effect, trimmed with rows of insertion and small buttons. Has neat silk bow tie at neck. Sleeves are of embroidery flouncing to match double skirt. Has soft silk ribbon girdle finished in front with rosette. Buttons invisibly in back. **State age.** Av. shpg. wt., 1¼ lbs.

EACH
No. **31H5602** **$2.68**
White.

GIRLS' EMBROIDERY DRESS. Waist made of embroidery flouncing, with underwaist effect of tucked lawn and insertion in front. Set off with pin tucks in back. Gathered skirt trimmed with embroidery, giving it the tunic effect. Belt finished with silk ribbon rosette at side front. Buttons invisibly in back. **State age.** Average shipping weight, 1¼ pounds.

EACH
No. **31H5604** **$1.43**
White.

GIRLS' VOILE DRESS of good quality washable cotton voile, in an attractive one-piece style. Waist made in drop shoulder effect, and elaborately trimmed with hand embroidery, lace and insertion. Has fancy yoke of Venise lace. Cuffs on sleeves are of insertion and lace edging. Skirt has fancy yoke, also panel of embroidered voile. Trimmed at bottom with clusters of pin tucks and lace edging. Wide sash of soft silk ribbon finished with large bow in back and set off with fancy medallion to match yoke. One of our most attractive styles. Fastens invisibly in back. **State age.** Average shipping weight, 1¾ lbs.

EACH
No. **31H5606** **$6.98**
White.

GIRLS' EMBROIDERY DRESS. Made in a pretty combination of lawn and embroidery, in one-piece button front style. Plaited skirt is neatly trimmed with lace and insertion to match trimming on collar and sleeves, and has panel front of embroidery. Belt of embroidery beading has silk ribbon running through to match bow at neck, and is finished with rosette in front. **State age.** Av. shpg. wt., 1½ lbs

EACH
No. **31H5601** **$1.67**
White.

GIRLS' EMBROIDERY TRIMMED DRESS Made of sheer lawn with revers extending over shoulders and forming tabs in back. V neck and revers edged with lace to match edging on sleeves, which are also trimmed with clusters of pin tucks. The silk ribbon girdle is finished in front with sash tie. The plaited skirt is edged with embroidery and trimmed with row of hemstitching. **State age.** Average shipping weight, 1½ pounds.

EACH
No. **31H5603** **$2.48**
White.

GIRLS' TASTEFUL LAWN DRESS. Made of sheer lawn and trimmed with lace and embroidery both front and back. Embroidered panel extends full length of dress in front. Pretty cape collar extends over shoulders to panel in back of dress. Skirt has flounce on each side of panel. Silk ribbon girdle finished with tie at side front. **State age.** Average shpg. weight, 1¾ pounds.

EACH
No. **31H5605** **$3.48**
White.

GIRLS' EMBROIDERED LAWN DRESS. In one-piece button back style. Front of waist made of dainty embroidery and lace in jacket effect. Back is trimmed with clusters of pin tucks. The gathered skirt of embroidery flouncing in a two-tier effect is neatly hemstitched. Belt is of silk ribbon with rosette in front. Fastens invisibly in back. **State age.** Average shipping weight, 1½ lbs.

EACH
No. **31H5607** **$2.39**
White.

Girls' Dresses offered on this page are furnished in sizes 6 to 14 years. **Be sure to state age when ordering.**

Ages, years	6	8	10	12	14
Average bust measure, inches	28	29	30	32	34
Average length, inches	26	28	32	38	42

New and Snappy Styles in Boys' Long Pants Suits—
Ucanttear Make—Carefully Tailored of Fine Quality Materials

Furnished in sizes to fit average size boys from 14 to 17 years of age only. Not larger than 33 inches breast measure. See bottom of page for scale of measurements and how to order. Average shipping weight, 4 pounds.

$10.00
No. 40H1300
Handsome Gray Mixture Wool Cassimere.
Boys' Long Pants Pinch Back Style Suit of a soft finish pure wool cassimere material in a handsome medium gray mixture with indistinct stripe in darker gray. Single breasted coat with three outside patch pockets. Semi-form fitting. Inverted plait, tucks and stitched-on half belt form the pinch back effect. Serge lining. Five-button vest without collar. Prevailing style pants with usual pockets and cuff bottoms. SIZES—14 to 17 years. **State age and measurements.**

$10.00
No. 40H1302
Dark Navy Blue Pure Wool Worsted.
Boys' Splendid Quality Dark Navy Blue Pure Wool Worsted Suit. Pattern has fancy stripe effect formed by the weave. Three-button single breasted coat has two slanting lower pockets with flap. Seam back, no slit. Latest style five-button single breasted vest with four outside patch pockets. Coat lining and vest back of alpaca. Semi-peg top pants with belt loops, usual pockets, one hip pocket made to button, and narrow cuff bottoms. SIZES—14 to 17 years. **State age and measurements.**

$9.50
No. 40H1304
Fancy Brown Striped Wool Mixed Worsted
Boys' Long Pants School Suit in dark brown herringbone weave effect with indistinct stripe formed by bright blue threads. Threaded tan and maroon color decorations make the pattern a most pleasing one. 90 per cent wool worsted material. Finely tailored. Long roll lapel, two-button single breasted sack coat. Three outside patch pockets. Seam back, with slit. Latest style five-button vest without collar. Coat lining and vest back of alpaca. Semi-peg top pants with usual pockets, one hip pocket made to button, belt loops, side buckle straps and narrow cuff bottoms. SIZES—14 to 17 years. **State age and measurements.**

$5.85
No. 40H1310
Dark Gray Mixture Soft Finish Cassimere.
Boys' Long Pants High School Suit of dark gray wool filled and cotton warp soft finish cassimere. Light gray and tan dotted color decorations and threaded stripe effect in indistinct light gray threads. Made in conservative single breasted style. Coat is semi-form fitting and has two lower pockets with flap. Seam back, without slit. Five-button collarless vest. Coat lining and vest back of twill. Semi-peg top pants with usual pockets, belt loops, side buckle straps, and turnunder at bottoms. SIZES—14 to 17 years. **State age and measurements.**

$10.00
No. 40H1334
Electric Blue Wool Worsted Serge.
Boys' High School Suit in beautiful electric or bright blue shade pure wool worsted serge. Standard dye material. Single breasted coat with patch pockets. Semi-form fitting. Pinch back effect formed by inverted plait, tucks and stitched-on half belt. Wool serge lining. Five-button vest without collar. Prevailing style pants with usual pockets and cuff bottoms. SIZES—14 to 17 years. **State age and measurements.**

HOW TO ORDER

When ordering boys' long pants high school suits state the age of the boy and his height and weight, or give his age and his breast, waist and inseam measurements, taken after the manner explained on the order blanks in the back of this book. Below is a table of measurements according to which our high school suits are cut and made up.

MEASUREMENTS FOR LONG PANTS HIGH SCHOOL SUITS.

Age	Coat	Pants	
	Breast, Inches	Waist, Inches	Inseam, Inches
14	30½	27 or 28	27 or 28
15	31¼	28 or 29	29 or 30
16	32	29 or 30	30 or 31
17	33	30 or 31	31 or 32

ORDER FROM THIS CATALOG.

The illustrations and descriptions of the suits on this page accurately represent the garments, so that you may safely order direct from this catalog. Moreover, our guarantee protects you fully, for if for any reason you are not satisfied with the garments you receive, you are at perfect liberty to return them, and we will make an exchange for a suit you do like, or will return your money. However, if you feel that color illustrations of the materials would enable you to order more satisfactorily, send for our free color Fashion Book of Youths' and Boys' Clothing, No. 88H.

Boys' Winter Overcoats

SIZES—Made in sizes 9 to 15 years, large enough to fit over other clothes. Lengths range from 36 to 40½ inches.

$11.00
Medium Gray.
No. 40N2800

Boys' Overcoat. Made of 20-ounce Cheviot, about half wool and half cotton. Medium dark mottled gray with blue and olive overplaid. Double breasted style, as illustrated. Very broad ulster collar can be buttoned up close about neck. Warmly lined side pockets. Two muff pockets. Inside pocket. Loose half belt with two buttons across back. Seam back, no slit. Lined with dark gray plaid. Sateen yoke and sleeve lining. SIZES — 9 to 15 years. State size. Average shipping weight, 5½ pounds.

EXTRA VALUE

$11.00
Heavy Military Ulster
Dark Brown.
No. 40N2804

Overcoat of heavy, closely woven melton, a 24-ounce fabric, 85 per cent wool and 15 per cent cotton. Just as illustrated. Double breasted style with ulster collar that can be buttoned up close at neck. Warmly lined slash side pockets. Inside pocket. Stitched-on half belt in back. Military seams from shoulders to half belt. Center vent in back. Full lined with heavy black twill. SIZES—9 to 15 years. State size. Average shipping weight, 6 pounds.

$9.50
Heavy Melton.
Oxford Gray.
No. 40N2812

Boys' Heavy Oxford Gray Overcoat. Made of 23-ounce melton cloth, about 80 per cent wool and 20 per cent cotton. Style and color as illustrated at right. Warmly lined muff pockets. Side pockets with flap. Inside pocket. Convertible ulster collar buttons up close about neck. Half belt in back. Seam back with slit. Full twill lined. SIZES —9 to 15 years. State size. Average shipping weight, 6 pounds.

$11.50
Brown.
No. 40N2802

Boys' Overcoat. Made of 20-ounce overcoating, about half wool and half cotton. Brown as illustrated with darker mottling and maroon and olive overplaid. Warmly lined side pockets with flap. Breast pocket. Plain back with center seam and vent. Pretty plaid lining. Twill Venetian yoke and sleeve lining. SIZES — 9 to 15 years. State size. Average shipping weight, 5½ lbs.

Military Ulster.
$11.35
Olive Brown.
No. 40N2810

Boys' Overcoat of 24-ounce olive brown overcoating, about two-thirds wool and one-third cotton. This fabric is very similar to that which is used in army overcoats. Military double breasted style with converging buttons. Extra broad ulster collar can be buttoned up close about neck. Warmly lined slash pockets. Inside pocket. Half belt across back. Seam back; no vent. Full lined with brown twill. SIZES—9 to 15 years. State size. Average shipping weight, 5½ pounds.

$11.00
Dark Gray Melton.
No. 40N2806

Boys' Overcoat. Made of heavy dark gray melton, a 25-ounce fabric, about three-fourths wool and one-fourth cotton. Double breasted style, as illustrated at left. Broad ulster collar can be buttoned up close at neck. Warmly lined side pockets with flap and two muff pockets. Inside pocket. Loose half belt across back with two buttons. Seam back with center vent. Gray plaid lining. Yoke and sleeves lined with black twill. SIZES—9 to 15 years. State size. Average shipping weight, 6 pounds.

$11.50
Navy Blue.
No. 40N2808

Overcoat of navy blue 23-ounce overcoating, about 85 per cent wool and 15 per cent cotton. Style and color as illustrated at left. Warmly lined side pockets. Breast and inside pockets. Ulster collar can be buttoned up close about neck. Half belt stitched on in back. Military seams from shoulder to half belt. Slit in back. Coat lined with strong black twill. SIZES— 9 to 15 years. State size. Average shipping weight, 6 pounds.

$8.50
Medium Gray.
No. 40N2814

Boys' Overcoat. Made of extra heavy weight medium gray overcoating, about three-fourths wool and balance cotton. Double breasted style as illustrated. Broad ulster collar can be buttoned up close about neck. Two side pockets with flap. Two muff pockets are flannel lined. Inside pocket. Loose half belt with two buttons across back. Seam back; no slit. Coat lined with twill. SIZES— 9 to 15 years. State size. Average shpg. wt., 6 lbs.

Girls' Winter Coats, Hats and Muffs

| Ages, years.................. 7 | 8 | 9 |
| Length, inches ....29 | 31 | 33 |

These coats are made very large and cut full in every way.   Hats and muffs are sold separately.   Average shipping weight, 10 ounces.   State age and color when ordering.

17N8914
Velour Plush
$8.48

17N8920
Fancy
Weave Velour
$7.98

17N8925
Corduroy
$7.48

17N8932
Beaver Plush
$7.48

17N8941
Velour Plush
$8.95

17N8940
Seal Plush
$10.98

17N8933
Corduroy
$5.98

17N8949
Velour Plush
$7.48

17N8955
Astrakhan
$5.98

31N2035

31N2040

31N2045

31N2050

31N2055

31N2060

31N2065

31N2070

31N2075

31N2080

Serviceable Three-Piece Sets and Sweaters for the Children

No. 29N9150 Red.
No. 29N9151 Copenhagen blue.
High Grade Three-Piece Set. Knit from select quality all wool zephyr yarn. Consists of full belted, ocean pearl button trimmed sweater with roll top pockets, fancy pompon trimmed toque and full fashioned drawer leggings. Ages, 1 to 6 years. State age. Average shipping wt., 1⅝ lbs.
Price, each set $5.95

No. 29N9056 ☞ Red, white trim.
No. 29N9057 Copenhagen blue, white trim.
Children's Cardigan Knit All Wool Sweater. Made in popular middy style, attractively trimmed in white. Sailor collar. Neck and side lacing. Ages, 2 to 6 years. State age. Av. shpg. wt., 8 oz. Each...... $2.65

No. 29N9146 Navy blue, gold stripes.
No. 29N9147 Maroon, white stripes.
No. 29N9167 Gray, red stripes.
All Wool Two-Piece Jersey Knit Athletic Suit. Double striped sweater. Double fabric close fitting collar, fastening at shoulder with snap fasteners. Full sized bloomers with elastic at waist and knees. Ages, 2 to 6 yrs. State age. Av. shpg. wt., 10 oz. Each suit. $2.98

No. 29N9132 Brown.
No. 29N9133 Red.
Serviceable Four-Piece Angora Finish Set. Knit from all wool yarn with a brushed surface. Fancy toque, full size sweater with roomy pockets, mittens and full fashioned drawer leggings. All seams double stitched and reinforced. Ages, 1 to 6 years. State age. Average shipping weight, 1 pound 13 ounces.
Price, each set............ $6.48

State Age.

No. 29N9159 White.
Little Tots' Norfolk Style Three-Piece Set. Knit from pure wool zephyr yarn in a fancy stitch. Sweater, toque and drawer leggings. Sweater has Byron collar and wide belt, button trimmed both front and back. Well made throughout. A warm and serviceable suit. Ages, 1 to 4 years. State age. Average shpg. wt., 1 lb. 5 oz.
Price, each set... $4.75

No. 29N9114 Khaki, white trim.
No. 29N9115 Copenhagen blue, gray trim.
Stylish Three-Piece Brushed Set. Knit from nearly one-half wool worsted; balance fine quality cotton yarn. Beautiful sweater has close fitting sailor collar, wide, full belt and fancy breast pockets. Hockey cap and drawer leggings. Ages, 1 to 6 years. State age. Average shipping weight, 1⅜ pounds.
Price, each set... $4.12

29N9127 Gray.
29N9143 Red.
29N9144 Copenhagen blue.
Medium Priced Three-Piece Set. Knit from about 15 per cent wool and 85 per cent cotton. Three-quarter belted sweater with double fabric cuffs; double fabric hockey cap; drawer leggings. An exceptional value at this price. Ages, 1 to 6 yrs. State age. Av. shpg. wt., 1¼ lbs.
Each set... $3.18

State Age.

No. 29N9131 White.
No. 29N9130 White, light blue trim.
Special Value All Wool Three-Piece Set. Knit in the popular links and links stitch. Sweater has close fitting collar and full fashioned sleeves with close fitting cuffs. Pompon trimmed toque. Fancy knitted drawer leggings. Ages, 1 to 3 years. State age. Average shpg. wt., 1 pound.
Each set... $4.45

No. 29N6330 Khaki brown.
Popular Military Style Slipover Sweater. Knit from strong yarn, one-half wool; balance cotton. Nobby close fitting collar and breast pocket. Full fashioned sleeves. Ages, 2 to 6 yrs. State age. Av. shpg. wt., 10 oz.
Price, each. $2.75

29N9125 Copenhagen blue.
29N9124 Brown.
29N9123 Red.
Medium Heavy Weight Cardigan Knit Three-Piece Set. Knit in a close stitch from about ½ wool; ⅔ cotton. Double knit cap. Fashioned sleeves, Drawer leggings. Ages, 1 to 6 years. State age. Av. shpg. wt., 1⅜ lbs.
Price, each set... $3.90

No. 29N9168 Navy blue.
No. 29N9169 Cardinal.
Medium Weight Cardigan Knit Three-Piece Set. Knit from all wool worsted yarn. Sweater has two pockets and double fabric cuffs. Heavy double knit sport cap. Full fashioned drawer leggings. A warm and serviceable suit. Ages, 1 to 4 years. State age. Average shipping weight, 1½ pounds.
Price, each set..... $5.35

No. 29N9116 Red, white trim.
No. 29N9117 Copenhagen blue, white trim.
Fancy Three-Piece Set. Knit from about 15 per cent worsted wool and 85 per cent fine quality cotton yarn. Wide all around belt stitched down to form pockets. Double fabric hockey cap. Drawer leggings. Attractive and serviceable. Ages, 1 to 6 years. State age. Av. shpg. wt., 1 lb. 5 oz.
Each set.... $3.45

SWEATER COAT.
29N9072 Cardinal.
29N9073 Copenhagen.
Belted Style All Wool Sweater. Sailor collar, white trim. Two pockets. Ages, 2 to 6 yrs. State age. Av. shpg. wt., 10 oz. Each $2.88
CAP TO MATCH.
29N8126 Cardinal.
29N8127 Copenhagen.
Same material as sweater. Av. shpg. wt., 3 oz. Each.. 65c

29N9170 Rose.
29N9172 Copenhagen.
Attractive Four-Piece Angora Finish Set. Knit from all wool yarn with a brushed surface. Consists of fancy toque, good weight sweater with roomy pockets, full size drawer leggings and mittens. Well made with double seams. Ages, 1 to 6 years. State age. Av. shpg. wt., 1 lb. 13 oz.
Price, each set.... $5.95

No. 29N9112 Red.
No. 29N9113 Navy blue.
Inexpensive Three-Piece Set. Knit from soft cotton yarns. Sweater has double fabric military collar and full belt. Double fabric hockey cap. Fashioned drawer leggings. A set which will stand much hard wear. Ages, 1 to 6 years. State age. Average shipping wt., 1¼ lbs.
Price, each set..... $2.12

Perfect Fitting Shoes for the Baby

No. Pair
15N8182 $1.09
Sizes, 4 to 8. Heel.
15N8183 95c
Sizes, 2 to 5. No heel.
Gunmetal Finish
Side Leather Button
—Dull Leather Top
—Foot Form Shape
—Flexible Turned
Sole.

Average Shipping Weight
of Shoes on This Page,
1 Pound.

All Shoes on This Page
Are Wide Widths.

No. Pair
15N8296 $1.09
Sizes, 4 to 8. Heel.
15N8297 95c
Sizes, 2 to 5. No heel.
Gunmetal Finish
Side Leather Button
—Black Cloth Top—
Foot Form Shape
—Flexible
Turned Sole.

No. Pair
15N8040 $1.09
Sizes, 4 to 8. Heel.
15N8041 95c
Sizes, 2 to 5. No heel.
Patent Leather Button—
Black Cloth Top—Foot
Form Shape—Flexible
Turned Sole.

No. Pair
15N8062 $1.09
Sizes, 4 to 8. Heel.
15N8063 95c
Sizes, 2 to 5. No heel.
Black Kid Blucher—
Patent Leather Tip—
Foot Form Shape—
Flexible Turned Sole.

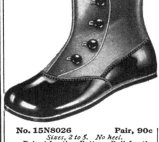

No. Pair
15N8059 $1.09
Sizes, 4 to 8. Heel.
15N8060 95c
Sizes, 2 to 5. No heel.
Black Kid Button—
Patent Leather Tip
and Heel Foxing—Foot
Form Shape—Flexible
Turned Sole.

No. 15N8026   Pair, 90c
Sizes, 2 to 5. No heel.
Patent Leather Button—Dull Leather Top—Foot Form Shape—Flexible Turned Sole.

No. 15N8030   Pair, 90c
Sizes, 2 to 5. No heel.
Black Kid Button—Patent Leather Tip—Foot Form Shape—Flexible Turned Sole.

No. Pair
15N8037 $1.09
Sizes, 4 to 8. Heel.
15N8038 95c
Sizes, 2 to 5. No heel.
Black Kid Lace—
Patent Leather Tip—
Heel Foxing and Lace
Stay—Foot Form
Shape — Flexible
Turned Sole.

INFANTS' WARM LINED SHOES.
No. Pair
15N8135 $1.09
Sizes, 5 to 8. Heel.
15N8136 95c
Sizes, 2 to 5. No heel.
Black Kid Button—
Patent Leather Tip
—Foot Form Shape
—Warm Lining—
Flexible
Turned
Sole.

No. Pair
15N8137 $1.09
Sizes, 5 to 8. Heel.
15N8138 95c
Sizes, 2 to 5. No heel.
Black Kid Lace—
Felt Top—Warm
Lining—Patent
Leather Tip—
Foot Form
Shape—Flex-
ible Turned
Sole.

No. Pair
15N8069 95c
Sizes, 3 to 8. Heel.
15N8070 75c
Sizes, 2 to 5. No heel.
Black Kid Button—
Black Cloth Top—Semi-
Foot Form Shape—
Scout Tip—Flexible
Turned Sole.

Soft Sole Shoes for the Baby

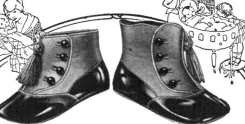

No. Pair
15N8967 59c
Sizes, 0 to 3.
Black Velveteen
Hi-Cut—White Fur
Trimmed—Leather-
ette Soft Sole.

No. Pair
15N8964 59c
Sizes, 0 to 3.
Pato-lite (Not Pat-
ent Leather)—
White Mercerized
Quilted Top—Hi-Cut
—Fur Trimmed—
Leatherette Soft
Sole.

No. 15N8932 Pair, 49c
Sizes, 0 to 3.
Black Velveteen Button
—Leatherette Soft Sole.

No. 15N8904 Pair, 49c
Sizes, 0 to 3.
Pato-lite (Not Patent Leather)
Vamp—Dull Leather Top—Leather-
ette Soft Sole.

No. 15N8915 Pair, 49c
Sizes, 0 to 3.
Pato-lite (Not Patent Leather)
Vamp—Dull Leather Top—Fat An-
kle Pattern—Leatherette Soft Sole.

No. 15N8937 Pair, 49c
Sizes, 0 to 3.
Pato-lite (Not Patent
Leather) Vamp—Black
Velveteen Quarter—Leath-
erette Soft Sole.

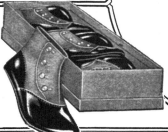

No. 15N8911
Sizes, 0 to 3.
Price, three
pairs of one
size only, 79c
Pato-lite (Not Pat-
ent Leather) Vamp
—Poplin Top—
Leatherette Soft
Sole. Colors: White,
pink and blue.
Packed three colors
to a box.

No. 15N8969
Sizes, 0 to 3.   Price
Three pairs of one size only, 65c
Soft Lambskin — Warm Lined
Moccasin.

No. 15N8919
Sizes, 0 to 3.
Price, three
pairs of one
size only, 89c
Pato-lite (Not
Patent Leather) Vamp
—Leather Top—
Leatherette Soft
Sole. Colors: Blue,
tan and black.
Packed three colors
in one box.

Boys' Furnishing Goods

45c EACH 33T8596 Large Open End Fancy Pattern Four-In-Hand Tie. Made of the better grade neckwear silks in the following colors: Navy blue, light blue, red, brown, purple, gray, lavender or green. State color wanted. Shipping weight, 2 ounces.

25c EACH 33T8574 Boys' and Children's Scotch Plaid Silk Windsor Tie. Large variety patterns. Shipping weight, 2 ounces.
33T8576—Same as above, but in blue with white polka dots only.

29c EACH 33T8590 Silk and Cotton Mixed Reversible Four-In-Hand Tie. Can be worn either side, giving double the wear. The following colors only: Navy blue, red, brown, purple, gray, lavender or green. State color wanted. Shipping weight, 2 ounces.

25c EACH 33T8578 Boys' and Children's Good Quality Silk Windsor Tie. Exceptional value. Plain colors, white, pink, light blue, red, navy blue, black or brown. Be sure to state color. Shipping wt., 2 ounces.

39c EACH 33T8572 Boys' Fancy Pattern Open End Silk and Cotton Mixed Four-In-Hand Tie. Very good value at our price. Colors, navy blue, light blue, red, brown, gray, purple, lavender or green. State color wanted. Shipping weight, 2 ounces.

25c EACH 33T8894—Black. 33T8895—Brown. Sizes, 24, 26, 28 and 30 inches waist measure. State waist measure. Boys' Embossed Cowhide Belt. A neat and attractive pattern. Width, about 1 inch. Nickel plated buckle. Shipping weight, 4 ounces.

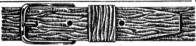

29c EACH 33T8890—Black. 33T8891—Tan. Sizes, 24, 26, 28 and 30 inches waist measure. State waist measure. Boys' Embossed Cowhide Belt. Popular tubular style. Width, about 1 inch. Shipping weight, 4 ounces.

39c EACH 33T8897—Black. Sizes, 24, 26, 28 and 30 inches waist measure. State size. Boys' Genuine Pigskin Belt with self adjusting buckle. About 1 inch wide. A good strong serviceable article. Shipping wt., 6 ounces.

39c EACH 33T8892—Black. 33T8893—Tan. Sizes, 24, 26, 28 and 30 inches waist measure. State size and initial. Boys' Lined Grained Leather Belt, about 1 inch wide. Stamped initial on oxidized steel tongueless buckle. Very pretty. Shpg. wt., 5 oz.

18c EACH 33T8593—Boys' Silk and Cotton Mixed Reversible Bow Tie. Made the same as the men's, only shorter. Plain colors, navy blue, light blue, red, brown, purple, gray, lavender, green or black. Good quality. State color. Shipping wt., 2 oz.

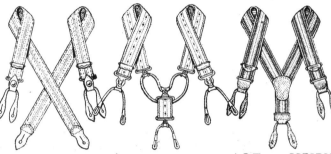

35c EACH 33T8765 Our Boys' Best Quality Dress Suspenders. Made of fancy weave fine lisle webbing. Non-rusting brass plated steel buckles and white leather ends. Workmanship guaranteed. Full length. Shipping weight, 4 ounces.

31c EACH 33T8768 Boys' Self Adjusting Cord Back Suspenders. Made of good quality web. Instantly conform to movements of wearer and will not pull out buttons. Made full length, 30 inches. Shipping weight, 4 ounces.

25c EACH 33T8762 Boys' Police Web Suspenders. Good quality elastic web, strong buckles and trimmings, leather ends. Regular police style construction. Full length. Shipping weight, 4 ounces.

18c EACH 33T8594 Boys' Silk and Cotton Mixed Band Bow. Can furnish in almost any color or pattern. State color and pattern. Shpg. wt., 2 oz.

12c EACH 33T8598 Boys' Silk and Cotton Mixed Shield Bow. Comes in a large variety of colors and patterns. State color wanted. Shipping weight, 2 ounces.

50c For Six 33T9300 Boys' Plain White Cotton Handkerchief with hemstitched border. Size, about 15½x16 inches. Shpg. wt., 5 oz.

$1.15 EACH 33T1091—Boys' Medium Weight Flannelette Nightshirt. Neat striped patterns. Garment is made large and roomy and is well finished. Ages, 8, 10, 12, 14 and 16 years. State age. Shipping weight, 9 ounces.

$1.50 EACH 33T1093—Genuine Amoskeag "Teazeldown" Flannelette Nightshirt. The same as our men's nightshirt, only in boys' size. Excellent value for the money. Ages, 10, 12, 14 and 16 years. State age. Shipping weight, 15 ounces.

$1.65 SUIT 33T1094 Boys' Flannelette Pajamas. Made of good weight material in neat striped patterns. Warm and comfortable garments. Ages, 8, 10, 12, 14 and 16 years. State age. Shipping weight, 13 oz.

$1.35 EACH Boys' Heavy Weight Flannelette Nightshirt. Striped patterns. A good warm garment well made. Ages, 8, 10, 12, 14 and 16 years. State age. Shipping weight, 13 oz.

33T1092

89c EACH 33T1082—Boys' Good Quality Muslin Nightshirt. Made collarless style. A well made full length garment. Sizes, 6, 8, 10, 12, 14 and 16 years. State age. Shipping weight, 12 ounces.

CHILDREN'S FLANNELETTE WEAR

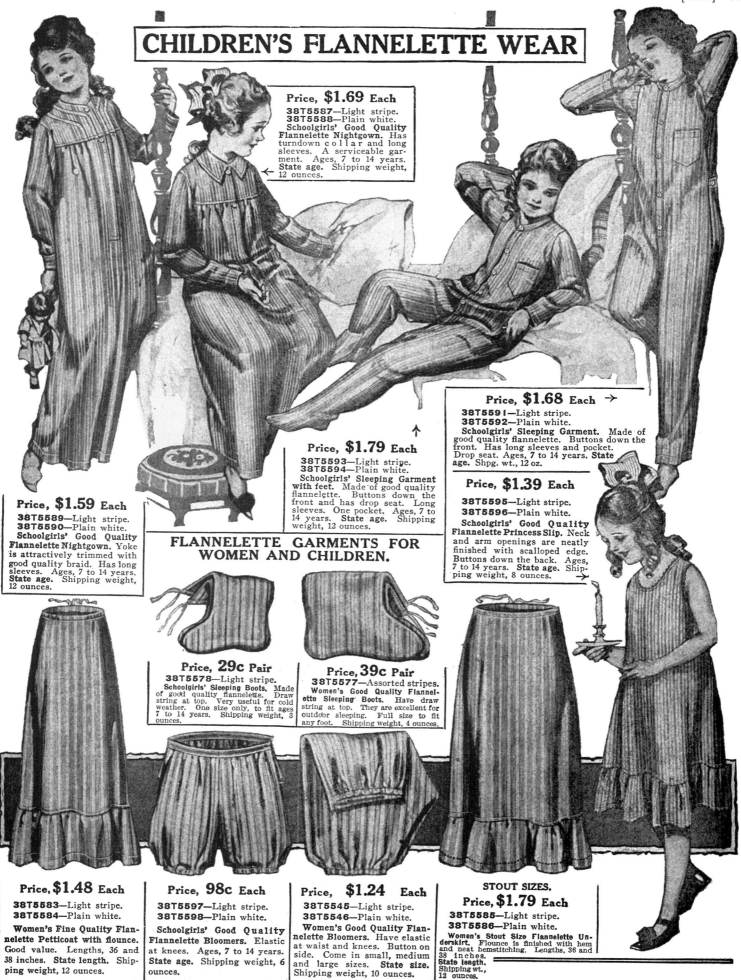

Price, $1.69 Each

38T5587—Light stripe.
38T5588—Plain white.
Schoolgirls' Good Quality Flannelette Nightgown. Has turndown collar and long sleeves. A serviceable garment. Ages, 7 to 14 years. State age. Shipping weight, 12 ounces.

Price, $1.68 Each →

38T5591—Light stripe.
38T5592—Plain white.
Schoolgirls' Sleeping Garment. Made of good quality flannelette. Buttons down the front. Has long sleeves and pocket. Drop seat. Ages, 7 to 14 years. State age. Shpg. wt., 12 oz.

Price, $1.79 Each

38T5593—Light stripe.
38T5594—Plain white.
Schoolgirls' Sleeping Garment with feet. Made of good quality flannelette. Buttons down the front and has drop seat. Long sleeves. One pocket. Ages, 7 to 14 years. State age. Shipping weight, 12 ounces.

Price, $1.39 Each

38T5595—Light stripe.
38T5596—Plain white.
Schoolgirls' Good Quality Flannelette Princess Slip. Neck and arm openings are neatly finished with scalloped edge. Buttons down the back. Ages, 7 to 14 years. State age. Shipping weight, 8 ounces.
→

Price, $1.59 Each

38T5589—Light stripe.
38T5590—Plain white.
Schoolgirls' Good Quality Flannelette Nightgown. Yoke is attractively trimmed with good quality braid. Has long sleeves. Ages, 7 to 14 years. State age. Shipping weight, 12 ounces.

FLANNELETTE GARMENTS FOR WOMEN AND CHILDREN.

Price, 29c Pair

38T5578—Light stripe.
Schoolgirls' Sleeping Boots. Made of good quality flannelette. Draw string at top. Very useful for cold weather. One size only, to fit ages 7 to 14 years. Shipping weight, 3 ounces.

Price, 39c Pair

38T5577—Assorted stripes.
Women's Good Quality Flannelette Sleeping Boots. Have draw string at top. They are excellent for outdoor sleeping. Full size to fit any foot. Shipping weight, 4 ounces.

Price, $1.48 Each

38T5583—Light stripe.
38T5584—Plain white.
Women's Fine Quality Flannelette Petticoat with flounce. Good value. Lengths, 36 and 38 inches. State length. Shipping weight, 12 ounces.

Price, 98c Each

38T5597—Light stripe.
38T5598—Plain white.
Schoolgirls' Good Quality Flannelette Bloomers. Elastic at knees. Ages, 7 to 14 years. State age. Shipping weight, 6 ounces.

Price, $1.24 Each

38T5545—Light stripe.
38T5546—Plain white.
Women's Good Quality Flannelette Bloomers. Have elastic at waist and knees. Button on side. Come in small, medium and large sizes. State size. Shipping weight, 10 ounces.

STOUT SIZES.
Price, $1.79 Each

38T5585—Light stripe.
38T5586—Plain white.
Women's Stout Size Flannelette Underskirt. Flounce is finished with hem and neat hemstitching. Lengths, 36 and 38 inches. State length. Shipping wt., 12 ounces.

Double Stretch Elastic.

A flat elastic, specially desirable for waists, petticoats and underwear. Colors: Black or white. **State color.** Width, about ¼ inch.
25T2905—Price, per yard. **4c**

Cable Elastic Web. Good heavy quality mercerized cotton cable elastic web woven on heavy rubber strands. Colors: Black, white, pink or light blue. **State color.** Width, about ⅞ inch.
25T2911—Per yard. . . . **12c**

Frilled Elastic. Used for making garters and for other trimming purposes. Comes in a neat pattern on a durable elastic. Colors: Black, white, pink or light blue. **State color.** Width, about 1½ inches.
25T2907
Price, per yard. **12c**

Buster Brown Hose Supporters

STRENGTH WHERE STRENGTH IS NEEDED AND IT GIVES WHERE IT OUGHT TO GIVE

Children's Size 19c A Pair
Misses Size 21c A Pair
Young Women's Size 23c A Pair
Women's Size 25c A Pair

Buster Brown Hose Supporters are correctly made from the best material, and leading authorities recommend Buster Brown as the best supporter on the market. Made along practical lines. Has wide non-elastic top which gives strength where it is needed, and you can make the adjustment to sizes without the metal cutting the fabric or lessening the elasticity. The bottom is made of extra wide elastic which has no great strain to stand, but which gives freely to every movement of the body. Has rubber snap buttons. All metal parts are heavily nickel plated. Comes in white or black. **State color.** Shipping weight, per pair, 3 ounces.

25T5023—Children's size. Length, about 8½ inches. Price, per pair. **19c**
25T5025—Misses' size. Length, about 10½ inches. Price, per pair. **21c**
25T5027—Young Women's size. Length, about 12 inches. Price, per pair. . . **23c**
25T5029—Women's size. Length, about 14 inches. Price, per pair. **25c**

Elastics and Hose Supporters

White Coutil Hip Supporter. Bound with tape top and bottom. Laces in back. Fastens in front with corset clasps. Rubber button hose supporters attached. Sizes, 24 to 34 inches waist measure. **State waist measure.** Shipping weight, 12 ounces.
25T4961
Price. . . . **89c**
each. . . . . .

Arm Bands, made of flat shirred elastic trimmed with ribbon bow. Colors: White, pink or light blue. **State color.** Width, about ½ inch. Shipping weight, 2 ounces.
25T5266
Per pair. **10c**

TUBULAR ELASTIC

Tubular Hat Elastic. Narrow Tubular Elastic, used for children's hats, boudoir caps and dressmaking purposes. Black or white. **State color.**
25T2901
Price, per yard. **5c**

FLAT HAT ELASTIC

Mercerized Hat Elastic. A mercerized Flat Hat Elastic, used for children's hats and boudoir caps. Width, about ¼ inch. Colors: Black or white. **State color.**
25T2903—Per yard. **5c**

Good quality non-elastic webbing with elastic hose supporters attached. Black or white. **State color.** Shpg. wt., 3 oz.
25T5048 Children's size. Each, **23c**
25T5050 Misses' size. Each, **25c**
25T5052 Women's size. Each, **28c**

Girdle Hose Supporters are used extensively when a corset is not worn, also for bathing and athletics. Made of a good quality cotton cloth. Can be adjusted to fit from 23 to 34-inch waist measure. Garters are made of a good quality webbing and have rubber cushion clasps. Colors: Black, white, pink or light blue. **State color.** Shipping weight, 6 ounces.
25T5060—Price, each. **55c**

So-On Hose Supporters. To be sewed on to your corset. Made of good heavy elastic webbing with rubber button fastener clasps. Shpg. wt., 3 oz.
25T5016—Per pair. **19c**

Hickory Waist and Garters for Girls and Boys.

The Hickory Waist will appeal to mother as a sensible and comfortable child's waist. Made of mercerized sateen that will wear and launder well. It has a front breast strap that will always hold the waist in place. The garters are made of white rubber, with cushion clasps that will not tear the stockings. Easily adjusted buckle. Comes in sizes from 2 to 14 years. **State age.** Shipping wt., 8 ounces.
25T5033
Price, each. **65c**

Kazoo Waist for the small boy. Scientifically made. Can be easily adjusted to fit the figure. Acts as a body brace, hose and trouser support. Strongly made throughout of heavy lisle elastic webbing with nickel plated adjustment buckles. Sizes, 2 to 12 years. **State age.** Shipping weight, 6 ounces.
25T5056
Price, each. **59c**

Kazoo Waist for girls. Serves as a perfect brace as well as a hose support. Growing girls should wear a waist that will prevent the shoulders from drooping. Made of strong white elastic with durable trimmings. Ages, 4 to 14 years. **State age.** Shipping wt., 6 oz.
25T5058 Price, each. . . **59c**

Kazoo Waist for boys. Properly constructed in every way. Hose supporters are attached to hose directly in front, thereby preventing the shoulder straps from slipping from shoulders, also keep child from becoming round shouldered. Made of strong elastic webbing with durable suspender buckle and non-elastic buttonhole ends. Sizes, 6 to 16 years. **State age.** Shipping weight, 6 ounces.
25T5057
Price, each. **59c**

Exceptionally good medium priced Hose Supporters. Made of an extra wide heavy elastic webbing, with rubber fasteners. In black or white. **State color.** Shpg. wt., 3 oz.
25T5017—Children's size. Lgth., abt. 7 in. Per pair. **14c**
25T5018—Misses' size. Length, about 9½ in. Per pair. **14c**
25T5019—Young Women's size. Lgth., abt. 11¾ in. Pair. . . . **14c**

HEAVY PLAIN LISLE ELASTIC

¼ INCH · ½ INCH · ¾ INCH · ⅞ INCH · 1 INCH

25T2909—Heavy plain lisle elastic of a good quality. Comes in black or white. **State width and color.**
Width, about ¼ inch. Per yard. **6c**
Width, about ½ inch. Per yard. **8c**
Width, about ¾ inch. Per yard. . . . **10c**
Width, about ⅞ inch. Per yard. . . . **13c**
Width, about 1 inch. Per yard. . . . **15c**

This is an extra heavy elastic webbing.

Men's, Boys' and Youths' Vulcanized Rubber Sole Footwear

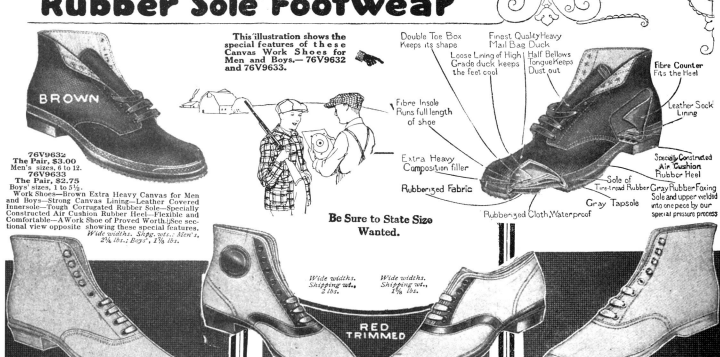

This illustration shows the special features of these Canvas Work Shoes for Men and Boys.— 76V9632 and 76V9633.

Double Toe Box Keeps its shape
Finest Quality Heavy Mail Bag Duck
Loose Lining of High Grade duck keeps the feet cool
Half Bellows Tongue Keeps Dust out
Fibre Counter Fits the Heel
Fibre Insole Runs full length of shoe
Leather Sock Lining
Extra Heavy Composition filler
Rubberized Fabric
Specially Constructed Air Cushion Rubber Heel
Sole of Tire-tread Rubber
Gray Tapsole
Gray Rubber Foxing Sole and upper welded into one piece by our special pressure process
Rubberized Cloth, Waterproof

Be Sure to State Size Wanted.

76V9632
The Pair, $3.00
Men's sizes, 6 to 12.
76V9633
The Pair, $2.75
Boys' sizes, 1 to 5½.
Work Shoes—Brown Extra Heavy Canvas for Men and Boys—Strong Canvas Lining—Leather Covered Innersole—Tough Corrugated Rubber Sole—Specially Constructed Air Cushion Rubber Heel—Flexible and Comfortable—A Work Shoe of Proved Worth. See sectional view opposite showing these special features. *Wide widths. Shpg. wts.: Men's, 2¼ lbs.; Boys', 1⅛ lbs.*

76V9658   **The Pair, $3.00**
Our Best Men's Shoe in This Style—Extra Quality White Canvas Shoe—Canvas Lining—Leatherette Covered Innersole—White Hooks and Eyelets—Smooth White Rubber Sole and Specially Constructed Air Cushion Rubber Heel—Flexible and Comfortable—A Splendid Shoe for Summer Wear. Popular Custom Last—Style, Durability and Comfort Combine to Make This a Splendid Shoe for Summer Wear.
Sizes, 6 to 12.
Wide widths. Shipping wt., 2¼ lbs.

76V9662   **The Pair, $2.75**
Our Best Men's Oxford in This Style—Extra Quality White Canvas Oxford—Canvas Lining—Leatherette Covered Innersole—White Eyelets—Smooth White Rubber Sole and Specially Constructed Air Cushion Rubber Heel—Popular Custom Last—Cool, Comfortable and Neat.
Sizes, 6 to 12. Wide widths.
Shipping wt., 1⅞ lbs.

	Sizes		
76V9582—Men's Oxfords.	6 to 12	The Pair,	$1.40
76V9583—Boys' Oxfords.	1 to 5½	The Pair,	1.30
76V9585—Men's Shoes.	6 to 12	The Pair,	1.50
76V9586—Boys' Shoes.	1 to 5½	The Pair,	1.40

Men's and Boys' Standard Quality Brown Canvas Lace Shoes and Oxfords — Unlined — Corrugated Brown Rubber Sole—Composition Innersole.
Wide widths. Shipping wts.: Men's, 2 lbs.; Boys', 1½ lbs.

RED TRIMMED

Wide widths. Shipping wt., 2 lbs.

Wide widths. Shipping wt., 1⅞ lbs.

76V9607   **The Pair, $2.50**
Men's sizes, 6 to 12.
76V9608   **The Pair, $2.25**
Boys' sizes, 1 to 5½.
76V9609   **The Pair, $2.00**
Youths' sizes, 11 to 13½.
Men's, Boys' and Youths' Standard Quality White Canvas Lace Shoe—Red Trimming—Ankle Patch—Corrugated Red Rubber Sole and Specially Constructed Air Cushion Rubber Heel—Unlined—Composition Innersole.

76V9604   **The Pair, $2.25**
Men's sizes, 6 to 12.
76V9605   **The Pair, $2.00**
Boys' sizes, 1 to 5½.
76V9606   **The Pair, $1.75**
Youths' sizes, 11 to 13½.
Men's, Boys' and Youths' Standard Quality White Canvas Oxfords—Red Trimming—Corrugated Red Rubber Sole and Specially Constructed Air Cushion Rubber Heel—Unlined—Composition Innersole.

WHITE OR BROWN

Wide widths. Shipping wts.: Men's, 2 lbs.; Boys', 1⅞ lbs.

Wide widths. Shipping wts.: Men's, 2 lbs.; Boys', 1⅞ lbs.

Oxford.
76V9640   **The Pair, $2.00**
White—Men's sizes, 6 to 12.
76V9641   **The Pair, $1.75**
White—Boys' sizes, 1 to 5½.
76V9646   **The Pair, $2.00**
Brown—Men's sizes, 6 to 12.
76V9647   **The Pair, $1.75**
Brown—Boys' sizes, 1 to 5½.
Men's and Boys' Standard Quality White and Brown Canvas Oxfords — Unlined — Corrugated Rubber Sole — Specially Constructed Air Cushion Rubber Heel — Composition Innersole.

Shoe.
76V9643   **The Pair, $2.25**
White—Men's sizes, 6 to 12.
76V9644   **The Pair, $2.00**
White—Boys' sizes, 1 to 5½.
76V9649   **The Pair, $2.25**
Brown—Men's sizes, 6 to 12.
76V9650   **The Pair, $2.00**
Brown—Boys' sizes, 1 to 5½.
Men's and Boys' Standard Quality White and Brown Canvas Lace Shoes — Corrugated Rubber Sole — Specially Constructed Air Cushion Rubber Heel — Unlined — Composition Innersole.

76V9601—Men's Shoes.   Sizes, 6 to 12   **The Pair, $1.40**
76V9602—Boys' Shoes.   Sizes, 1 to 5½   **The Pair, 1.30**
76V9598—Men's Oxfords.   Sizes, 6 to 12   **The Pair, 1.30**
76V9599—Boys' Oxfords.   Sizes, 1 to 5½   **The Pair, 1.20**
76V9581—Youths' Oxfords.   Sizes, 11 to 13½   **The Pair, 1.10**
Men's, Boys' and Youths' Standard Quality White Canvas Shoes and Oxfords—Light Gray Corrugated Rubber Sole—Unlined—Composition Innersole.

76V9620—Men's sizes, 6 to 12.   **The Pair, $2.25**
76V9621—Boys' sizes, 1 to 5½.   **The Pair, 2.00**
Our Best Shoe in the No Heel Style—Men's and Boys' Extra Quality White Canvas Shoe—Canvas Lining—Leather Covered Innersole—Smooth White Extra Thick Rubber Sole and ¼-Inch Heel Lift—The Superior Qualities of This Shoe Make It Particularly Desirable for Tennis and Other Sports.
Wide widths. Shipping wts.: Men's, 2⅛ lbs.; Boys', 1⅝ lbs.

76V9616—Men's sizes, 6 to 12.   **The Pair, $2.00**
76V9617—Boys' sizes, 1 to 5½.   **The Pair, 1.75**
Our Best Oxford in the No Heel Style—Men's and Boys' White Canvas Oxford—Canvas Lining—Leather Covered Innersole—Smooth White Thick Rubber Sole and ¼-Inch Heel Lift.
Wide widths. Shipping wts.: Men's, 2⅛ lbs.; Boys', 1⅝ lbs.

BLACK

76V9592—Men's Oxfords.	6 to 12	Pair,	$1.30
76V9593—Boys' Oxfords.	1 to 5½	Pair,	1.20
76V9580—Youths' Oxfords.	11 to 13½	Pair,	1.10
76V9595—Men's Shoes.	6 to 12	Pair,	1.40
76V9596—Boys' Shoes.	1 to 5½	Pair,	1.30

Men's, Boys' and Youths' Standard Quality Black Canvas Shoes and Oxfords—Unlined—Corrugated Brown Rubber Sole—Composition Innersole.
Wide widths. Shipping wts.: Men's, 2 lbs.; Boys', 1½ lbs.

PRETTY WHITE DRESSES FOR GIRLS
SIZES 7 TO 14

31E2640—White.   EACH $4.29
SOMETHING UNUSUALLY SMART and dainty is this frock of COTTON NET. The waist in front and softly gathered skirt are embroidered in pleasing pattern. Frilled collar and sleeves with lace edging. Silk ribbon belt. No underslip included. Closes invisibly in back. Sizes, 7 to 14. State size. Average shipping weight, 1¼ pounds.

31E2645—White.   EACH $2.48
GIRLISH STYLE of washable white ORGANDIE. Pretty lace and embroidery trim the waist with silk ribbon bow. Pin tucks and hemstitching adorn the softly gathered skirt. Lace edged elbow length sleeves. Buttons invisibly in center of pin tucked back. Silk ribbon belt. Sizes, 7 to 14. State size. Av. shpg. wt., 8 oz.

31E2650—White.   EACH
31E2651—Flesh color. $11.98
A SILK GEORGETTE DRESS is always a well chosen selection for best wear. The waist is very pretty with its ruffle trimming and becoming neckline with lace in front and back. Foundation of Jap silk increases the rich appearance. Elbow length sleeves and soft belt. Closes invisibly in back. Sizes, 7 to 14. State size. Average shipping weight, 1¼ pounds.

31E2640

31E2645

31E2650

Keep quality in mind as well as price when you are trying to make your money do its full duty. We work to keep prices as low as quality will permit.

SIZE SCALE
Size	7	8	10	12	14
Average bust measure, in	28	29	30	31½	33
Average length, inches	27	28	32	38	42

31E2655

31E2660

31E2665

31E2670

31E2655—White.   EACH $1.98
THIS YOUTHFUL STYLE is made of ORGANDIE, a washable and good wearing material. The deep embroidered yoke effect hangs free from shoulders over waist and the neckline is finished with lace. The gathered skirt has clusters of pin tucks and the lace trimming at bottom gives such a dainty appearance. Tucked belt. Elbow length sleeves with tucks and lace edging. Invisible back closing. Sizes, 7 to 14. State size. Average shipping weight, 8 ounces.

31E2660—White.   EACH $3.98
THIS GIRLS' CHARMING DRESS is made of good quality COTTON VOILE, a soft durable material easy to launder. The hand embroidery of dainty coloring on waist and belt is artistic and increases the smartness of this style. An unusual and becoming touch of trimming is the neat band at neckline and on elbow length sleeves. Clusters of pin tucks breaks the plainness of the softly gathered skirt. Closes invisibly in back. Sizes, 7 to 14. State size. Average shipping weight, 1 pound.

31E2665—White.   EACH $2.39
A GENERAL SERVICE WHITE WASH DRESS of good quality COTTON VOILE and a reasonable price is quoted. The waist is trimmed with embroidery and lace insertion in vestee effect, and clusters of pin tucks are featured in front and back. Neatness predominates in the gathered skirt with pin tucks and hemstitching. Dainty lace finishes the neckline, sleeves and bottom of skirt. A silk ribbon belt adds a dainty touch. Closes in back. Sizes, 7 to 14. State size. Average shipping weight, 8 ounces.

31E2670—White.   EACH $3.48
THAT "DRESSY APPEARANCE" is presented by this smart style made of embroidered ORGANDIE, attractive and dainty. The waist in bolero effect is trimmed with tucks and lace. Dainty tucks and hemstitching adorn the gathered skirt with pressed in plaits. An added style feature is the silk ribbon belt running through lace loops in front. Little ribbon rosettes and covered buttons add further trimming. Closes invisibly in back. Sizes, 7 to 14. State size. Average shipping weight, 1 pound.

SCHOOLGIRLS' NIGHTGOWNS and PRINCESS SLIPS
Ages, 7 to 16 Years.

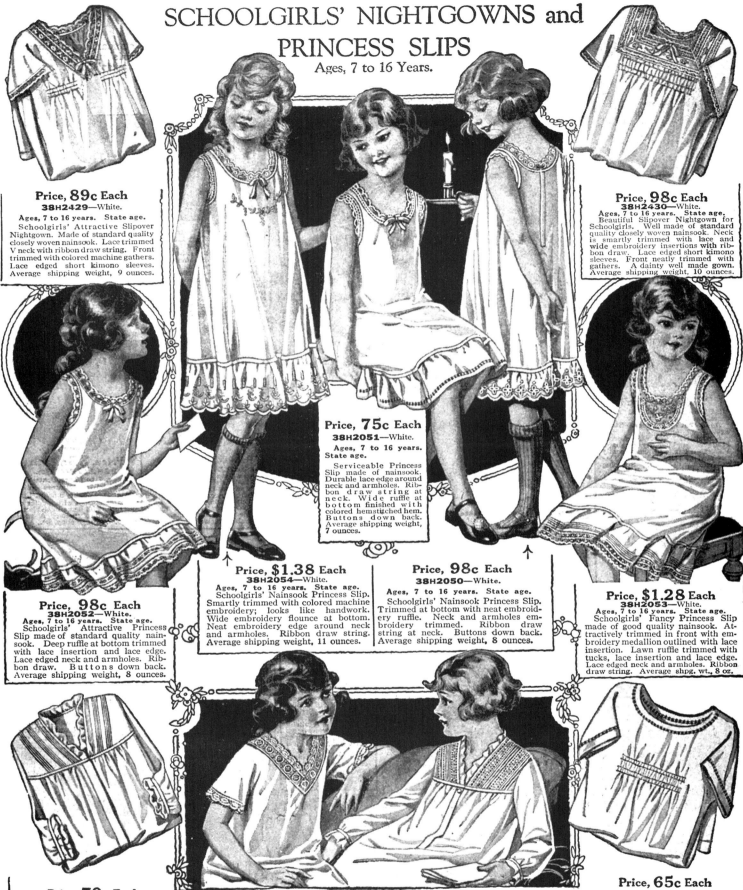

Price, 89c Each
38H2429—White.
Ages, 7 to 16 years. State age.
Schoolgirls' Attractive Slipover Nightgown. Made of standard quality closely woven nainsook. Lace trimmed V neck with ribbon draw string. Front trimmed with colored machine gathers. Lace edged short kimono sleeves. Average shipping weight, 9 ounces.

Price, 98c Each
38H2430—White.
Ages, 7 to 16 years. State age.
Beautiful Slipover Nightgown for Schoolgirls. Well made of standard quality closely woven nainsook. Neck is smartly trimmed with lace and wide embroidery insertions with ribbon draw. Lace edged short kimono sleeves. Front neatly trimmed with gathers. A dainty well made gown. Average shipping weight, 10 ounces.

Price, 75c Each
38H2051—White.
Ages, 7 to 16 years. State age.
Serviceable Princess Slip made of nainsook. Durable lace edge around neck and armholes. Ribbon draw string at neck. Wide ruffle at bottom finished with colored hemstitched hem. Buttons down back. Average shipping weight, 7 ounces.

Price, 98c Each
38H2052—White.
Ages, 7 to 16 years. State age.
Schoolgirls' Attractive Princess Slip made of standard quality nainsook. Deep ruffle at bottom trimmed with lace insertion and lace edge. Lace edged neck and armholes. Ribbon draw. Buttons down back. Average shipping weight, 8 ounces.

Price, $1.38 Each
38H2054—White.
Ages, 7 to 16 years. State age.
Schoolgirls' Nainsook Princess Slip. Smartly trimmed with colored machine embroidery; looks like handwork. Wide embroidery flounce at bottom. Neat embroidery edge around neck and armholes. Ribbon draw string. Average shipping weight, 11 ounces.

Price, 98c Each
38H2050—White.
Ages, 7 to 16 years. State age.
Schoolgirls' Nainsook Princess Slip. Trimmed at bottom with neat embroidery ruffle. Neck and armholes embroidery trimmed. Ribbon draw string at neck. Buttons down back. Average shipping weight, 8 ounces.

Price, $1.28 Each
38H2053—White.
Ages, 7 to 16 years. State age.
Schoolgirls' Fancy Princess Slip made of good quality nainsook. Attractively trimmed in front with embroidery medallion outlined with lace insertion. Lawn ruffle trimmed with tucks, lace insertion and lace edge. Lace edged neck and armholes. Ribbon draw string. Average shpg. wt., 8 oz.

Price, 79c Each
38H2426—White.
Ages, 7 to 16 years. State age.
Schoolgirls' Long Sleeve Nightgown made of standard quality cambric finish muslin. Yoke trimmed with clusters of pin tucks. Plain frill in neck and sleeves. Average shipping weight, 8 ounces.

Price, 79c Each
38H2428—White.
Ages, 7 to 16 years. State age.
Slipover Style Nainsook Nightgown for Schoolgirls. Neck trimmed with embroidery insertion and lace edge. Lace edged kimono sleeves. A practical, inexpensive garment, well made and will give excellent service. Average shipping wt., 9 ounces.

Price, 89c Each
38H2425—White.
Ages, 7 to 16 years. State age.
Girls' Practical Long Sleeve Cambric Nightgown. Front yoke trimmed with pin tucks and embroidery insertions. Narrow frill finishes neck and sleeves. Double back yoke. A very serviceable garment. Average shpg. wt., 8 ounces.

Price, 65c Each
38H2427—White.
Ages, 7 to 16 years. State age.
Exceptional value in a Slipover Gown for Schoolgirls. Made of standard quality nainsook. Trimmed with colored machine gathers. Colored hemstitched hem finishes neck and kimono sleeves. Average shipping weight, 9 ounces.

Prices That Save Many Dollars for Mother

WE HAVE had the suits on these pages made up according to our own specifications, of HIGH GRADE STANDARD FABRICS, tested in our own laboratories for COLOR FASTNESS, STRENGTH and WEARING QUALITIES.

The styles—look for yourself!—you wouldn't want a finer assortment to choose from. They cover all details demanded by the most "hard to please" mothers. In addition to this, these garments are made over FULL SIZE PATTERNS; nothing but HIGH GRADE WORKMANSHIP clear through. All important seams are DOUBLE STITCHED and covered, so there are no raw edges.

Practical Flannel Rompers.

$1.19

40K3618—Medium gray.
40K3620—Dark blue.
40K3623—Brown. Durable Winter Weight Flannel Rompers, about 30 per cent wool. Made in neat, plain style that is easy to launder. Drop seat. SIZES—2 to 7 years. State size. Av. shipping weight, 1¼ lbs.

Golden Brown Corduroy.
Warm, Winter Romper.

$1.19

40K3625—Corduroy wears so well and is so warm and comfortable in chilly weather that it makes an ideal romper for indoor winter wear. Simple one-piece style makes it easy for the little fellow to dress himself. Drop seat. Good quality pearl buttons. SIZES—2 to 7 years. State size. Average shipping weight, 1¾ pounds.

Better Quality Corduroy Romper.
Golden Brown.

$1.49

40K3627—Style as above, except better quality throughout. SIZES—2 to 7 years. State size. Average shipping weight, 1¾ pounds.

Handsome Brown Corduroy.
Oliver Twist Style Suit.

40K3321

$1.79

A very fine Oliver Twist Suit of good quality brown corduroy. Buttons down front with plait effect. Long sleeves button at cuff. Fancy breast pocket with flap. Silk cord and tassel tie. Straight style pants with button trim at knee. SIZES—2 to 7 years. State size. Average shipping weight, 1¾ pounds.

Dark Brown Corduroy, Braid Trimming.

40K3319

$2.85

Good quality Oliver Twist Suit in dark brown corduroy. Collar and cuffs are trimmed with two rows of white braid. Waist buttons down front with plait effect. Breast pocket. Straight style pants are button trimmed. A dressy, comfortable suit for cold weather. SIZES—3 to 8 years. State size. Average shipping wt., 1¾ lbs.

Dark Brown Corduroy Pants.
Tan Peggy Cloth Waist.

$1.48

40K3315
Oliver Twist Style Suit. The square collar is trimmed with three rows of braid. Cuff effect on sleeve, finished with braid. Good quality smoked pearl buttons. Pretty black tie. SIZES—2 to 7 years. State size. Av. shpg. wt., 1½ lbs.

Dark Blue.
40K3317 **$1.48**
Same style, with dark blue corduroy pants and blue Peggy cloth waist. SIZES—2 to 7 years. State size. Av. shpg. wt., 1½ lbs.

They're Practical

Very Attractive

Genuine Black Sateen Rompers.
Fast Color Trimmings.
40K3628

89c

Heavy weight Genuine Black Sateen Rompers with fast color red trimming on collar, belt, pocket and cuffs. Drop seat. A neat looking, practical romper that will save washing. SIZES—2 to 7 years. State size. Average shipping weight, 8 oz.

Gray Stripe Flannelette.
Standard Quality, Inexpensive Rompers.
40K3617

69c

Warm, Bloomer Style Rompers of gray stripe flannelette. Fast color red piping at collar, pocket and belt. Double stitched seams for strength. Drop seat. SIZES—2 to 7 years. State size. Average shipping weight, 10 oz.

Heavy Weight Galatea.
Wears Exceptionally Well
40K3654

$1.45

Washable Galatea Oliver Twist Style Suit. Straight style pants of plain dark blue. Waist of narrow blue and white stripe with braid trimmed collar and cuffs of plain blue. Plain white dickey and pretty black tie. SIZES—2 to 7 years. State size. Av. shpg. wt., 13 oz.

Heavy Weight Crash Suiting.
Washes Beautifully.
40K3651 **$1.39**

Strong, heavy weight Wash Suit of linen color cotton crash suiting. Plain blue Peggy cloth collar and piping on pockets and cuffs. Waist has plaited panel effect in front, as shown. Black cord and tassel tie. SIZES—2 to 7 yrs. State size. Av. shpg. wt., 14 oz.

Playtime Overalls.
Durable and Priced Low.
MEDIUM WEIGHT BLUE DENIM.

40K3100 Sizes, 3 to 8 years. **50c**

40K3102 Sizes, 9 to 14 years. **65c**

Low priced overalls that will give good service. Made of double and twist medium weight blue denim. Attached suspenders and patented buttons. Three pockets with corners bar tacked to prevent ripping. State size. Average shipping weight, 14 ounces.

Economical Play Garment.
Fast Color Trimmings.
Genuine Stifel INDIGO BLUE Shadow Stripe DRILL.

40K3608 Sizes, 2 to 7 years. **45c**
Good Weight Washable KHAKI DRILL.

40K3610 Sizes, 2 to 7 years. **45c**
Slip it on over the dressy clothes when on visits, at picnics, etc., or it can be worn with blouse only. Strongly made of durable materials. **Double stitched seams.** State size. Average shipping weight, 8 ounces.

BIG PAL SUITS
Every Boy Wants One of These.
Easy to Slip Into—Easy to Take Off.
Button Front—Drop Seat.
Made Extra Strong of Durable
FAST COLOR KHAKI.

40K3611 — Sizes, 3 to 8 years. **89c**
40K3613 — Sizes, 9 to 12 years. **98c**

Nothing pleases the boy more than to dress and act like his daddy. He'd be just tickled to do those little chores around the house if he had one of these suits to wear. Made big and roomy so they can be worn with ease and comfort over his other clothes. They make practical play garments, too. Material is firmly woven. Seams are strongly reinforced. Riveted buttons. State size. Average shipping weight, 1¼ pounds.

Rufplay Overalls
Will Stand Hard Wear.
Double Seat and Double Knees.
MEDIUM WEIGHT INDIGO BLUE DENIM.

40K3122 Sizes, 3 to 8 years. **79c**

40K3124 Sizes, 9 to 14 years. **95c**
Double stitched seams; all points of strain securely bar tacked to prevent ripping. Riveted brass buttons that will pass through wringer easily. Attached suspenders. Made of double and twist indigo blue denim that will give excellent wear. State size. Average shipping weight, 1⅛ pounds.

Have You Tried Our Famous
Rufplay Rompers **?**
for the Little Fellows

Lowest Prices
—and Better Quality too!

For Dad's Helper.
Medium Heavy Weight BLUE DENIM OVERALLS.
40K3108 Sizes, 3 to 8 yrs. **79c** **40K3110** Sizes, 9 to 17 yrs. **89c**
Strongly made of medium heavy weight double and twist blue denim. **Triple stitched legs;** pockets are reinforced. Attached suspenders. **State size.** Average shipping weight, 1¼ pounds.

Double and Twist BLUE DENIM JACKET.
To Match Overalls 40K3110 Listed Above.
40K3112 Sizes, 9 to 17 years. **89c**
Very convenient to slip on when working around the yard or the garage. Strongly made, sleeve and shoulder seams **triple stitched;** pockets reinforced to prevent ripping. State size. Average shipping weight, 1 pound.

Every Garment Made Over Full and Roomy Patterns.

Genuine Stifel INDIGO BLUE DRILL With Dotted White Stripe.
Illustrated at the LEFT.
Sure to Satisfy.

40K3104 Sizes, 3 to 8 years. **55c**

40K3106 Sizes, 9 to 17 years. **69c**
This garment is a big value at our price. Made of the well known genuine Stifel INDIGO BLUE DRILL of medium weight with dotted white stripes. Double stitched throughout. Corners of all three pockets are securely bar tacked. Patent buttons will not tear out. **State size.** Average shipping weight, 14 ounces.

Age	Waist of Boy, Inches	Waist of Ov'all, Inches	Overall Inseam, Inches
3	22	24	14
4	23	24	15
5	24	26	16
6	25	26	17
7	25½	27	18
8	26	27	19
9	26½	28½	20
10	27	29	21
11	27½	30	22
12	28	30	23
13	28½	31	24
14	29	31	25
15	29½	32	26
16	30	32	27½
17	30½	33	28½

SCALE OF SIZES FOR BOYS' OVERALLS.

40K3126, 40K3128, 40K3130, 40K3134 and 40K3138 have longer inseams, allowing for turn up bottoms.

Dresses and Knicker Suits for Girls
Ages 7 to 14 Years

31L2800 *Gingham* **$1⁵⁹**

31L2815 *Organdie* **$1⁹⁸**

31L2830 *Hills Jean* **$1⁹⁸**

31L2820 *Gingham Bloomer Dress* **$1⁰⁰**

31L2805 *Crepe and Gingham* **$2³⁹**

31L2810 *Hills Khaki Jean Knickers* **98¢**

31L2811 *Middy* **98¢**
31L2812 *Shirt* **98¢**

31L2825 *Separate Skirts for Girls. Sizes 7 to 14*

Crisp, cool **gingham** is combined with sheer **organdie** to make this little washable frock. Piping edges the short sleeves, organdie collar and loose hanging organdie panels on skirt.
SIZES—7 to 14. State size. Shipping weight, 1 pound.
31L2800—Lavender and white check.
31L2801—Blue and white check.
31L2802—Tan and brown check. **$1.59**

A Two-Piece Dress, made of reliable material. Separate blouse is of plain **Tokio crepe**. Collar and cuffs of white repp; attached belt; pearl buttons. The plaited skirt is of contrasting checked **gingham**, attached to a sleeveless body lining.
SIZES—7 to 14. State size. Shipping weight, 1 pound.
31L2805—Maize with black and white check.
31L2806—Blue with blue and white check. **$2.39**

Here are comfort garments, army style shirt, well made knickers and middy blouse. All are made of durable genuine Hill's Jean in Khaki tan. Don't confuse this splendid guaranteed fabric with ordinary cheap khaki—Hill's Jean wears like iron. Buy all three of these garments—they make a practical, easily laundered summer outfit.
SIZES—7 to 14. State size. Shipping weight, each, 1½ pounds.
31L2810—Khaki Knickers.
31L2811—Khaki Middy.
31L2812—Khaki Shirt. **98c**

Dainty Frock of sheer **organdie**, with panels of Swiss embroidered organdie bordered by insertions of fine Valenciennes lace. Trimming of Valenciennes lace edging. Back tucked in clusters and lace trimmed. Skirt is of embroidered organdie flouncing. Silk satin ribbon sash.
SIZES—7 to 14. State size. Shpg. wt., 1 lb.
31L2815—White. **$1.98**

Big values in girls' nicely made plaited Skirts for wear with separate waists or blouses. Skirts are designed with button trimmed pockets and attached to sleeveless body lining. Your choice of five materials.
SIZES—7 to 14. State size. Shipping weight, 1¼ pounds.
31L2825—Cotton plaid...**89c**
31L2826—Navy blue Peggy cloth.....................**89c**
31L2827—White jean.....**98c**
31L2828—Khaki.........**98c**
31L2829—Navy blue all wool serge..................**$1.98**

Girls' solid comfort Bloomer Dress. Easily laundered and well made of fast color fancy **checked gingham**. Dress is trimmed with colored piping on the neck, sleeves, pockets, down front and around the bottom. Separate bloomers to match, with elastic at knees and waistband.
SIZES—7 to 14. State size. Shipping weight, 1¼ pounds.
31L2820—Red plaid.
31L2821—Blue plaid. **$1.00**

In this smart white Jean Two-Piece Middy Dress you'll find style and serviceability combined. The separate middy blouse has sailor collar and cuffs, trimmed with contrasting braid. Embroidered tie loop. Wide attached belt, fastening at sides with buttons. The plaited skirt is attached to a sleeveless body lining.
SIZES—7 to 14. State size. Shipping weight, 1 pound.
31L2830 White. **$1.98**

A Three-Piece Outfit to delight the active, healthy girl. Outfit includes comfortable knickerbockers; stylish sleeveless "meadowbrook" sports jacket, both made of finest quality iron wearing **Hill's tan khaki jean**; also a cool waist of washable white **cotton crepe**. Jacket has tuxedo revers, and belt of imitation leather. Knickers are in regulation style. These are well made "quality" garments.
SIZES—7 to 14. State size. Shipping weight, 2 pounds.
31L2835 Khaki tan. **$2.79**

STATE SIZE WHEN ORDERING.
The Girls' Dresses on this page are furnished in sizes as follows:

Sizes, years	7	8	10	12	14
Average bust measure, inches	30	31	32	33	34
Average length, inches	27	28	32	36	40

Girls' Coats for Spring and Fall

Ages 10-12-14 Years
Lengths 34-37-40 Inches

17L4930
All Wool Polo Coat
$5.49

17L4935
All Wool Polo Coat
$7.59

17L4940
All Wool Knitted
$3.98

17L4955
All Wool Polo Cape
$6.98

17L4950
All Wool Polo Coat
$8.48

17L4945
All Wool Polo Coat
$9.98

A **finely tailored, stylish practical coat for spring and fall.** Made of high grade light weight **all wool coating** with a soft fleecy nap. Coat has inverted plait in back, stitched to yoke depth, and trimmed with buttons. Two large button trimmed patch pockets, finished with tailored stitching. All around belt of self material. Unlined. About 36 inches long. **An excellent coat for general wear, carefully made and moderately priced. State age.** Shipping weight, 2½ pounds.

17L4930—Tan.
17L4931—Blue.
$5.49

A stylish Polo Cape of fine material and workmanship, made of superior quality light weight **all wool** fleecy material. Heavy worsted and artificial silk embroidery in tasteful color contrast are used with charming effect to elaborate the collar and the tailor stitched bands which cover the arm vents. Cape is cut on circular lines, with shaped shoulders, and fastens with buttons and has string tie of self material. Length, 38 inches. Unlined. **A fine spring and fall garment very moderately priced. State age.** Shipping weight, 3 pounds.

17L4955—Blue.
17L4956—Tan.
17L4957—Light brown.
$6.98

Girls' Polo Coat of exceptionally smart style, just the thing for spring and fall wear. Made of light weight **all wool fleecy coating.** It is cut on full flare lines and tastefully embellished on sides, back and sleeves with stitching in harmonizing color. Has raglan sleeves, button trimmed pockets and belt crossed in front. Unlined. **A splendid value. State age.** Shipping wt., 3 lbs.

17L4935—Tan.
17L4936—Blue.
17L4937 Light brown.
$7.59

Here is a stylish spring and fall novelty. A graceful cape knitted of fine **all wool worsted** in fancy stitch. Deep cape collar and borders down front are of contrasting color fleecy brushed wool in Angora finish. There are contrasting stripes around the bottom. Fastens with worsted tie ending in pompons. Length, about 38 inches. **Our special economy price makes this cape a bargain. State age.** Shipping weight, 3 pounds.

17L4940—Brown-buff.
17L4941 Navy-tan.
$3.98

Smart style, high grade workmanship and splendid material are all in this up to date girls' Polo Coat. It is made of high grade spring weight **all wool material**, which will give splendid wear. Back is designed with a graduated tailored stitched panel, ending in points tastefully trimmed with large tassels. Stitched box plait down center of back. Crossed belt at front. Unlined. **An exceptional value. State age.** Shpg. wt., 3 lbs.

17L4950—Blue.
17L4951—Tan.
$8.48

We present a stunning Polo Coat for spring and fall wear, made of a beautiful quality **all wool** soft, fleecy material in spring weight. In the back the coat is richly hand embroidered in wool and artificial silk in contrasting shades. Pockets in front are hand embroidered. Deep inverted plaits in back. Coat unlined. **A coat of high class** priced very low considering fine quality. State age. Shipping weight 3 lbs.

17L4945—Blue.
17L4946—Tan.
$9.98

Fine Corsets for Growing Girls

These garments have been carefully styled to properly guide the figure of the young miss and prevent misshaping. This line has helped us to be known as "The Place to Buy Corsets."

WITH WOVEN BONING

ELASTIC GIRDLE NO LACERS

Popular With Misses.
18N236 Pink. **$1.85**

A very popular back lacing corset, made of fancy pink brocaded material which combines fine appearance with good wear. Woven wire boning makes an ideal support for girls. All stays correctly placed. Neat embroidered binding at top. Low bust, 2¾ inches. Skirt, 11 inches. Clasp, 8½ inches. Four good supporters. Sizes, 20 to 28. **Order corset size 2 inches smaller than waist measure taken tight over corset. State size.** Shipping weight, 1 pound.

Misses' Back Lacer.
18N122 Pink. **95c**

Back lacing corset, made of strong pink corset material. Only a few bone wires on each side to correctly guide and support the figure. Neat trimming. Four hose supporters. Medium bust, 2¾ inches. Skirt, 11 in. Clasp, 8½ in. Sizes, 20 to 28. **State corset size.** Shipping weight, 14 oz.

Misses' Corset Waist.
18N107 Pink. **95c**

For growing girls. Made of durable pink corset material, reinforced with a few well placed stays and rows of cording on each side. Clasp front. Adjustable shoulder straps. Sizes, 20 to 28. Measure waist and subtract 1 inch for spread of lacers. Thus, if waist measure is 24 in., order size 23. **State size, not age.** Shpg. wt., 14 oz.

Misses' Front Lacer.
18N115 Pink. **$1.48**

Special bargain price on well made corset of fancy figured pink material. Elastic section on each side at bust. Flexible boning and front clasp. Four hose supporters. Low bust, 1¾ inches. Skirt, 12 inches. Front clasp, 8 inches. Sizes, 20 to 28. **State size.** Shpg. wt., 12 oz.

Elastic for Comfort.
18N142—8 inches. **$1.29**
18N144—10 inches. **1.48**

Elastic Girdle Corsets are very comfortable and give good support. No lacers—only a few well placed stays and light weight flexible front clasp. Made of strong surgical elastic in two widths; strong coutil front section. Color, pink only. (**Do not order like usual corsets.**) **Order your natural waist measure taken without your corset on.** Sizes, 22 to 30; also size 32. **State size.** Shpg. wt., 12 oz.

THESE ARE VERY POPULAR

95c 18N231 Pink.

$1.19 18N226 Pink.

New Model for Misses.
No Lacers. **18N117 95c**

Wonderful value. Jacquard figured pink, cotton material. Lightly boned at sides and back and with four short strips of boning placed diagonally at each side at front. Deep bust gores of surgical elastic and wide elastic section all the way down back. Clasp, 6½ inches. Length from top to bottom, 11½ inches at hips, 8¼ inches back and 11½ inches front. Four supporters. Sizes, 22 to 30. (**Do not order like usual corsets.**) **Order your natural waist measure taken without your corset on.** State size. Shipping weight, 8 oz.

For the young miss, also for very slender women. Well made of fancy figured pink cotton material with surgical elastic. Tape shoulder straps. Fastens in back. Four good hose supporters. Even sizes, 30 to 38 inches bust measure. **State measure taken tight around bust.** Shipping wt., 8 ounces.

Corset Bandeau of dainty mercerized brocaded cotton cloth. Elastic all the way down back, fastening with hooks and eyes. Strip of two-inch surgical elastic at sides at waistline adds to comfort. Tape shoulder straps. Drawstring at top of bust. Four supporters. Even sizes, 30 to 38 inches bust measure. **State bust measure taken tight around bust.** Shpg. wt., 6 ounces.

For Misses and Growing Girls.
18N275 $1.00

Made of strong white corset jean, well reinforced and closely corded. Soft plaited bust. Good strong buttons, strongly attached. One pair of two-button hose supporters. Sizes, 20 to 28. **Do not order by age. Measure your girl's waist and subtract 1 inch for spread of lacers.** Thus, if girl's waist measure is 24 inches, order size 23. **Be sure to state size.** Shipping weight, 12 ounces.

For Misses and Slender Women.
Back Lacing. **18N121 $1.39**

A well known favorite. Medium bust, 3½ in. Skirt length, 11½ in. Clasp, 10½ in. Sizes, 19 to 30. A splendid corset for growing girls. Well made of good quality white batiste. Moderately boned, to give good support. **Order your corset size 2 inches smaller than your waist measure taken over your corset.** State corset size. Shpg. wt., 14 oz.

Merchandise up to your expectations and even better is assured in buying from these pages. We do not have the opportunity to meet you personally so must depend on our merchandise to speak for itself. If ever we disappoint you, let us make good on our guarantee.

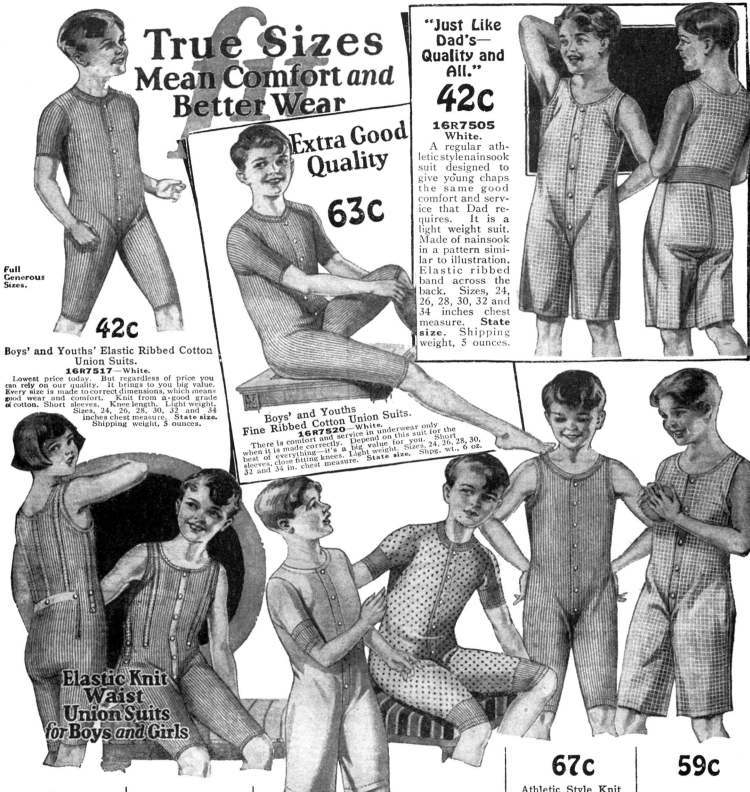

True Sizes
Mean Comfort and Better Wear

Full Generous Sizes.

42c

Boys' and Youths' Elastic Ribbed Cotton Union Suits.
16R7517—White.
Lowest price today. But regardless of price you can rely on our quality. It brings to you big value. Every size is made to correct dimensions, which means good wear and comfort. Knit from a good grade of cotton. Short sleeves. Knee length. Light weight. Sizes, 24, 26, 28, 30, 32 and 34 inches chest measure. **State size.** Shipping weight, 5 ounces.

Extra Good Quality

63c

Boys' and Youths Fine Ribbed Cotton Union Suits.
16R7520—White.
There is comfort and service in underwear only when it is made correctly. Depend on this suit for the best of everything—it's a big value for you. Short sleeves, close fitting knees. Light weight. Sizes, 24, 26, 28, 30, 32 and 34 in. chest measure. **State size.** Shpg. wt., 6 oz.

"Just Like Dad's—Quality and All."
42c

16R7505 White.
A regular athletic style nainsook suit designed to give young chaps the same good comfort and service that Dad requires. It is a light weight suit. Made of nainsook in a pattern similar to illustration. Elastic ribbed band across the back. Sizes, 24, 26, 28, 30, 32 and 34 inches chest measure. **State size.** Shipping weight, 5 ounces.

Elastic Knit Waist Union Suits for Boys and Girls

69c

Combed Cotton Brings to You Suits of Real Quality and Value.
16R7095—White.
Mothers who seek the best in Waist Suits for their young daughters or sons come to an abrupt stop here. It's real value we offer in fine suits made of high grade combed cotton yarn. Medium low neck, sleeveless. Knee length. Drop seat. Reinforced with tubular straps. Pin tubes for garters. Medium light weight. Sizes, 2-3, 4-5, 6-7, 8-9, 10-11 and 12-13 years. **State age.** Shipping weight, 7 ounces.

47c

Quality and Price That's Hard to Beat Any Place.
16R7090—White.
Made of good quality cotton. Medium low neck, sleeveless. Knee length. Reinforced with tubular straps. Pin tubes for garters. Drop seat. Medium light weight. Ages, 2-3, 4-5, 6-7, 8-9, 10-11 and 12-13 years. **State age.** Shipping weight, 5 ounces.

48c

There Is Quality Here in Flat Knit Cotton Union Suits.
16R7524—White.
Strongly made and exceptionally well finished in every detail. Short sleeves with elastic knit cuffs. Loose fitting knee length. Light weight. Sizes, 24, 26, 28, 30, 32 and 34 inches chest measure. **State size.** Shipping wt., 6 oz.

59c

Mesh Knit.
Cool and Comfortable for Boys.
16R7521—Cream color.
When Old Sol seems to smile and does his best to make things pop under scorching rays—what a comfort it will be for the young fellow who wears a fine mesh weave union suit. They're light weight and cool. Made with one big thing in mind, and that's comfort, when the days are good and warm. Elastic knit close fitting cuffs at knees and short sleeves. Sizes, 24, 26, 28, 30, 32 and 34 inches chest measure. **State size.** Shipping weight, 6 oz.

67c

Athletic Style Knit Combed Cotton Union Suit.
A Regular Suit for any Young Chap.
16R7528—Cream color.
It is only natural that every thrifty person looks about before making a purchase of any kind, but we honestly believe that it would be useless in this instance. This suit offers quality that is the making of such a remarkable value. Knit of fine combed cotton yarn. Sleeveless, knee length. Elastic ribbed. Sizes, 24, 26, 28, 30, 32 and 34 inches chest measure. **State size.** Shipping weight, 6 oz.

59c

Our Best Nainsook Athletic Suit.
16R7523—White.
We preach quality—yes—and this suit is proof that we sell it as well. A good comfortable suit made of a light weight, fine checked nainsook patterned similar to illustration. Sleeveless. Knee length. Elastic ribbed band across back. Sizes, 24, 26, 28, 30, 32 and 34 inches chest measure. **State size.** Shipping weight, 6 ounces.

31L2910
Voile
$1¹⁹

Crepe
Bloomer
Dress

**Dainty
Dresses**
for
Warm Weather
*Ages 7-14
Years*

31L2925
Tissue
Gingham
$2⁴⁸

31L2930
Crepe
$2²⁹

31L2915
Crepe
$2⁹⁵

31L2920
Crepe
$1⁹⁵

31L2935
Voile
$1⁷⁹

31L2950
Peggy
Cloth
98c

31L2940
Gingham
$2¹⁹

31L2945
Voile
$1⁹⁵

31L2955
Organdie
$1⁹⁵

Warm Pretty Coats for Your Girl

Ages   2 - 3 - 4 - 5 - 6   Years
Lengths   22 -23 -24 -25 -26   Inches

17T5000
All Wool
Velour
$5.98

Beaverette
Fur
Collar

Viatka
Coney Fur
Collar

Beaverette
Fur Collar →

7T5015
All Wool
Blocked
POLAIRE
$7.89

17T5005
All Wool Plaid
POLAIRE
$7.48

17T5010
All Wool
Chamo
Suede
Velour
$7.95

17T5020
All Wool
Chamo Suede
Velour
Beaverette
Fur Collar
and Cuffs
$8.98

17T5025
Wool Faced
Chinchilla
$7.59

Viatka
Coney Fur
Collar
and Cuffs

Beaverette
Fur Collar

17T5030
All Wool
Velvo-
Sheen
Broadcloth
$9.98

PRETTY TOGS *for* LITTLE TOTS

← 59c
38T5230
Assorted stripes.
38T5231
Assorted light checks.
Ages, 1, 2 and 3 years. State age size.
Warm dress for the little tots. Made of good quality medium striped flannelette or assorted check patterns. Skirt gathered on yoke both front and back. Will keep the little one comfortably warm. Shipping weight, 7 ounces.

FLANNELETTE

Average Length Short Dresses.	
Size, 6 months.....20 inches	Size, 2 years.......20 inches
Size, 1 year........19 inches	Size, 3 years.......22 inches

$1.00 →
38T5210—White.
Ages, 6 months, 1 and 2 years. State age size.
Unusual in value and in wearing qualities is this little tots' walking length dress. Made of the well known "Fruit of the Loom" nainsook. Famous for its soft finish and long wearing qualities. Neat collar and cuffs finished with serviceable edging. A well made garment that will surprise you with its ability to stand up after many washings. Shipping weight, 4 oz.

FRUIT OF THE LOOM

79c
38T5207—White.
Ages, 6 months, 1 and 2 years. State age size.
Serviceable and dainty. This dress is made of nice quality nainsook effectively trimmed at bottom with rows of lace, embroidery insertion and pin tucks. Round yoke made up of alternate panels of lace and embroidery insertion. Lace edged neck and sleeves. Gathered in back. Shipping weight, 4 ounces.

$1.48
38T5251—White.
Ages, 6 months, 1 and 2 years. State age size.
Beautiful lace trimmed dress of fine quality nainsook. Fancy embroidered yoke tastefully trimmed with silk ribbon rosette. Bottom of skirt smartly trimmed with embroidery and rows of lace insertion. Finished with lace trimmed scalloped ruffle. Neck and sleeves lace edged. Shpg. wt., 4 oz.

98c
38T5243—White.
Ages, 6 months, 1 and 2 years. State age size.
A dress of this style is much in demand. Made of an attractive pattern lawn embroidery flouncing and neat embroidered yoke, trimmed with silk ribbon rosette. Lace edged neck and sleeves. Well made throughout and will give satisfactory service. An exceptional value at this price. Shipping weight, 4 ounces.

58c

39c ↑
38T5301—White.
Ages, 6 months, 1 and 2 years. State age size.
Easy to dress the little tots with this underskirt. No buttons or buttonholes to try the mother's patience. Simply slip garment over the head. Well made of good quality nainsook. Trimmed with pin tucks and embroidery ruffle. Shipping weight, 4 ounces.

39c ↑
38T5200—White.
Ages, 6 months, 1 and 2 years. State age size.
A remarkable value in a well made, full size plain bishop style dress for babies. Made of standard quality nainsook. Lace edged neck and sleeves. Gathered front and back. Pearl buttons. Easy to launder. Shpg. wt., 4 oz.

For Babies' Shoes, see page 270-271.

38T5254
Black "Luster" cloth.
38T5255
Tan pongette.
Ages, 1, 2 and 3 years. State age size.
This winning style was designed by a clever mother to save on the little tots' washing. Made of good quality black "Luster" cloth or tan pongette (cotton pongee). Colored piping across front and around neck. Gathered front and back. Shipping weight, 5 oz.

↑ 49c
38T5205—White.
Ages, 6 months, 1 and 2 years. State age size.
Unusual value in this little tots' walking length dress. Made of standard quality nainsook. Round front yoke made of assorted patterns embroidery. Neat embroidery edge at bottom of skirt. Lace edged neck and sleeves. Gathered back. Shpg. wt., 4 oz.

↑49c
38T6010 — Black Luster cloth, red trim.
Ages, 6 months, 1 and 2 years. State age size.
This garment will be a big relief to mothers who have a creeping baby. Saves on laundry, wear and tear of clothing. Made of a durable "Luster" cloth; will not show the soil readily and launders well. Red trim. Buttons at shoulders, also across bottom, making it easy to change diaper. Shpg. wt., 4 oz.

$1.00
38T6047—Blue.
38T6048—Pink.
Ages, 6 months, 1 and 2 years. State age size.
Smart Little Creeper of durable Peggy cloth. Checked gingham collar, front panel, belt and top of pockets. Juvenile applique design on front. Buttons down back and across bottom. Elastic at knees. Shipping weight, 7 ounces.

89c
38T6045—Yellow.
38T6046—Blue.
Ages, 6 months, 1 and 2 years. State age size.
Very good quality Peggy cloth creeper. Trimmed with contrasting piping on collar and cuffs and with embroidery designs on pockets. Buttons down back and across bottom, making it easy to change diaper. Elastic at knees. Shipping weight, 7 ounces.

38T6055
White, blue trim.
38T6056—White, gold trim.
Ages, 6 months, 1 and 2 years. State age size.
$1.45
Exceptionally dressy creeper for the little tot. Made of fine quality mercerized cotton poplin. Trimmed with hand embroidery designs on front yoke and collar. Collar, cuffs and pocket trimmed with hand running stitch. Creeper buttons in back and across bottom, making it easy to change diaper. Elastic at knees. Our best creeper and a great value at this price. Shipping weight, 7 ounces.

FLANNELETTE

38T6016—Blue.
Ages, 6 months, 1 and 2 years. State age size.
65c
A sensible Creeper, made of good quality chambray. Attractively trimmed with hand smocking and white pipings. Buttons in back and across the bottom, making it easy to change diaper. Elastic knees. Shipping weight, 6 ounces.

59c ↑
38T6022—Gray stripes.
38T6023—Light stripes.
Ages, 6 months, 1 and 2 years. State age size.
This nice, warm flannelette creeper offers protection for your baby's health on cool days. Made of good quality flannelette. Body attached to square front yoke. Trimmed with piping. Buttons in back and across bottom, making it easy to change diaper. Shipping weight, 6 ounces.

Values in Quality and Workmanship as Well as Price.

STYLISH COATS *for* LITTLE TOTS
Attractive Styles ~ Reasonably Priced

$3.98
38T6660—Cream-white.
38T6661—Red.
38T6662—Brown.
Ages, 1, 2 and 3 yrs. State age.
There is a lot of style in this attractive Coat, which is made from a serviceable quality one-fourth wool medium weight chinchilla finish eiderdown cloth. Close fitting double fabric collar. Full belt and two pockets. Well made throughout. Lined with good quality sateen. Shipping weight, 1½ lbs.
For Cap to match see opposite page.

$3.98
38T6659—Cream-white.
Ages, 6 months, 1 and 2 years. State age.
Babies' high grade Walking Length Cape Coat. Made of a fine quality two-thirds wool closely woven cashmere. Deep circular cape has beautiful patterns of embroidery, resembling handwork and is finished with scalloped embroidered edge. Lined with a good quality sateen and interlined with flannelette. Cuffs trimmed with scalloped embroidered edge. Shipping weight, 1¼ pounds.

$1.98
38T6671—Light blue, white trim.
38T6672—Pink, white trim.
One size only, for babies up to 2 years of age.
Babies' knitted Capes are very popular just now and this attractive model is knit from a good quality all wool yarn in a block pattern. Convenient side openings for the arms. The revers are daintily hand embroidered with artificial silk buds. Draw string at neck permits snug fit. Shipping weight, 7 ounces.

$1.98
38T6657—Cream-white.
Ages, 6 months, 1 and 2 years. State age.
This attractive walking length Coat is made of cotton cashmere and is exceptionally low priced. Circular cape on round yoke is richly embroidered and finished with scalloped embroidered edge. Beautiful embroidered design on skirt matches cape. Lined with cambric and substantially interlined. Shpg. wt., 12 oz.

$2.75
38T6658—Cream-white.
Ages, 6 months, 1 and 2 years. State age.
A very popular style Walking Length Cape Coat of a fine quality closely woven mercerised cotton cashmere. Circular cape has rich pattern of embroidery resembling handwork and is finished with scalloped embroidered edge. Sateen lining. Flannelette interlining. Shipping weight, 10 ounces.

$1.69
38T6656—Cream-white.
Ages, 6 months, 1 and 2 years. State age.
Babies' inexpensive walking length Coat made of cotton cashmere. The cape is gathered on round braid trimmed yoke and is nicely embroidered and finished with scalloped embroidered edge. Lined with flannelette. Braid trim on cuffs. Shipping weight, 8 ounces.

$2.39
38T6525
Cream-white.
Infants' size only.
Infants' attractive cotton cashmere long coat. Cape is trimmed with braid and is elaborately embroidered and finished with scalloped edge. Deep pattern of rich embroidery on skirt matches cape. Lined with cambric and substantially interlined. Shipping wt., 13 oz.

$1.98
38T6524—Cream-white.
Infants' size only.
Infants' inexpensive yet attractive cotton cashmere long Coat. Neatly embroidered and scalloped circular cape is trimmed at yoke with fancy braid. Flannelette lining. Excellently made throughout. Shpg. wt., 10 oz.

$3.98
38T6527—Cream-white.
Infants' size only.
Our best quality long Coat, made of a finely woven two-thirds wool cashmere. Shoulder cape is beautifully embroidered resembling handwork; scalloped embroidered edge. Lined with sateen of good wearing quality and interlined with flannelette. Shipping weight, 1¼ pounds.

$2.38
38T6514—Cream-white.
No baby's wardrobe is complete without a Bag Style Wrap With Hood. This garment is made of serviceable quality ripple eiderdown cloth with an all wool face and cotton back. Adjustable hood is lined with mercerized sateen and fitted with elastic. Trimmed with mercerized sateen. Warmly lined throughout with flannelette, making it a cozy little wrap for baby's outing. Made according to our own specifications, insuring proper workmanship and fit. Shpg. wt., 1⅜ lbs.

$5.98
38T6665—Navy blue.
38T6666—Brown.
Ages, 1, 2 and 3 years. State age.
Little misses' stylish flared model winter weight Coat, made from a heavy weight excellent quality all wool cheviot. Cut on the very latest lines with raglan shoulders and full bell shape skirt. Attractive coney fur collar. Slash pockets. Neatly stitched and button trimmed back. Good quality sateen lining. Shipping weight, 2¾ pounds.

$5.65
38T6667—Gray.
38T6668—Brown.
Ages, 1, 2 and 3 years. State age.
Little tots' extra heavy weight Overcoat of nearly all wool chinchilla cloth. Durable sateen lining. Quality and workmanship usually found only in much higher priced garments. Shipping weight 2¼ pounds.

HATS TO MATCH.
38T6727—Gray.
38T6728—Brown.
98c
Sizes, 6¼ to 6¾. State size.
Sailor hat to match above coat. Shipping weight, 9 ounces.

$2.89
38T6526
Cream-white.
Infants' size only.
Exceptionally pretty and becoming style long Coat, made of a better quality closely woven mercerized cotton cashmere. Shoulder cape is neatly embroidered, resembling handwork and finished with scalloped embroidered edge. Lined with sateen and warmly interlined with flannelette. Shipping weight, 13 ounces.

$5.48
38T6663—Navy blue.
38T6664—Brown.
Ages, 1, 2 and 3 years. State size.
Little fellows' sailor style winter weight Overcoat. Made from a good quality all wool cheviot. Gilt navy buttons. Close fitting double fabric collar, patch pockets with flaps and full belt. Embroidered emblem on sleeve. Sateen lining. Shipping wt., 2¼ lbs.

Hats to Match.
$1.15
38T6747—Navy Blue.
38T6740—Brown.
Sizes, 6¼ to 6¾. State size.
Sailor Hat to match above coat. Shipping weight, 12 oz.

Youthfully Correct
for the Younger Generation

Ages
7 to 14
Years

31D 4770
*All Wool
Serge*
$4.95

31 D 4780
*Ensemble Style
All Wool
Cashmere Serge*
$4.98

31D 4765
*Excellent
Quality
Cotton
Flannel*
$1.98

31D 4785
*Suede
Duvetyn*
$2.59

31D 4775
*Wool Mixed
Check Suiting*
$3.98

31D 4790
*Wool
Mixed
Homespun*
$3.98

31D 4795
*Ensemble
Style
All Wool
Homespun
Velour*
$4.98

31D 4800
*Gabardine
Serge*
$2.49

31D 4805
*All Wool
Plaid
Homespun*
$4.95

Youth Is Typified By These Swagger Styles

Ages 10 - 12 - 14 Years Lengths 36 - 39 - 42 Inches

Beaverette Fur Trimmed

17 D 3485 All Wool Velva Bloom $18 98

Belgian Lynx Coney Fur

Mandel Fur Collar

Opossum Fur Collar

17 D 3495 All Wool Polaire $13 48

17 D 3490 All Wool Blocked Velour $10 98

Sizes 10 to 16 Years

17 D 3480 All Wool Cheviot $12 95

Sizes 10 to 16 Years

Mandel Fur Trimmed

Mandel Fur Collar and Border

17 D 3510 All Wool Velo Sheen Broadcloth $24 95 Guaranteed Satin de Chine Lined

Belgian Lynx Coney Collar and Border

Sizes 10 to 16 Years

17 D 3500 All Wool Velour $9 95

17 D 3515 Romandi Bolivia $14 95

Sizes 10 to 16 Years

17 D 3505 All Wool Buxkin Velour $18 98 Guaranteed Satin de Chine Lined

A $1 35

B $1 69

C $1 98

D $1 35

E $1 19

F $1 48

G $1 25

H $1 75

J $1 50

K $1 65

L $1 59

M $1 25

N $2 35

O $2 69

P $1 69

R $1 45

S $1 98

T $1 19

U $1 35

V 98¢

Season's Smartest Frocks for Little Girls Ages 2 to 6 Years

A — All Wool Jersey $2.98

B — All Wool Crepe $2.98

C — French Serge $3.00

D — Velveteen $3.98

E — Cotton Serge $1.48 | All Wool Serge $2.98

F — All Wool Homespun $2.98

G — All Wool Jersey $3.65

H — All Wool Cashmere $3.89

Cotton Print — **Peggy Cloth** — **Cotton Print**

$1.48
38D5614—Tangerine and white.
38D5615—Blue and white. Ages, 2, 3, 4, 5 and 6 years. State age size.
Shipping weight, 7 ounces.
Becoming and charming dress of fancy cotton print. White collar, binding on turn-back cuffs and banding with pearl button trim in front. Hand embroidered design on collar. Neck vent closing with ribbon streamers. Has ¾ length sleeves.

$1.59
38D5611—Blue. Ages, 2, 3, 4, 5 and 6 years. State age size. Shpg. wt., 7 oz.
Wash Frock of closely woven **Peggy cloth** trimmed with shirring and hand embroidery in pretty colors. Hand running stitch on contrasting color collar and cuffs. Slashed pockets. Neck vent closing. Long sleeves.

$1.98
38D5616—Coral red check.
38D5617—Blue check. Ages, 2, 3, 4, 5 and 6 years. State age size. Shipping weight, 8 ounces.
This smart bloomer dress of nice quality **checked cotton print** is trimmed with poplin collar, pocket, panel down front and fancy cuffs, cleverly hand embroidered. Bloomers on waistband with elastic at knees. Has ¾ length sleeves.

J — Cotton Serge $1.75

K — Silk Taffeta $4.95

L — Striped Broadcloth $2.35

M — Cotton Print and Broadcloth $1.98

P — All Wool Flannel and Velveteen $3.75

Every Girl's Favorite *Class-mate* Styles Every Mother's Choice

TRADE MARK REG.

(A) $1.29

(B) $2.45

(C) 2.35

(D) $1.75

(E) $1.63
Felt

(F) $1.48
Ajour

(G) $1.85

(H) $1.35

(J) $1.65

(K) $1.29

(L) $1.00

(M) $1.95

Our Finest *Class-mate* **Exquisite Swiss Hair**

Velvet Ribbon Trim
For Misses
$2.98
13 to 16 Years
Fits 21 to 21¾
inches, headsize.
78H6622
Colors: Copenhagen
blue with colors, as illustrated;
Tiger lily (salmon color) with
Wild honey (light brown) ribbon, Meadow pink (rose shade)
with Black ribbon, or Black hat
with Bright Yellow forget-me-
nots. Measure and state color.
Shpg. wt., 2½ lbs.
Darling summer model we are
indeed proud to offer. Shape is
also the latest wide brim droop
with new deep back. Made of
very sheer, genuine Swiss Hair
braid. Carefully reinforced with
concealed wire at edge. Exquisite
streamer trimming of high grade
satin back velvet ribbon. Dainty
bunches of imported forget-me-
nots. Unusually pretty design
and fine quality.

Many Choices—Charming Colors

Class-mate Hats
Wonders for Style and Value

A $2³⁹
Crochet Visca

B $1⁹⁸
Transparent Ajour

C $1⁴⁸

D $2⁷⁵
Ajour Crown
Crepe de Chine
Brim

E $1⁶⁵

$2⁴⁸

For 8 to 10 years
78H6570— (This fits 20¼ to 20¾ inches, headsize.)
Colors: **Tiger lily** with touch of Green, as illustrated; **Copenhagen blue** with touch of Rose color, **Bright Red** with touch of sand, or **Sand** with touch of Oakwood brown. **Measure and state color.** Shipping weight, 1¾ lbs.
One of the most adorable little hats we have ever shown. Attractive crown of fancy two-tone **visca straw braid.** Soft shirrings of **silk Georgette crepe** cover the becoming oval shaped brim which is cut away to a snug fitting back. Dainty ribbon loops and crown band. Handmade ribbon ornament adds dainty trimming touch. Hats to equal this in quality would cost two to three times this price elsewhere.

F $2⁴⁵
Fine Taffeta

G $1⁵⁸ Fine Hemp

H $1⁷⁹

J $1⁸⁵
Ajour Brim
Taffeta Crown

K $1⁹⁸

L $1⁸⁹

Distinctive Features of These Three Sweaters

HAND FINISHED THROUGHOUT

ALL WOOL

REINFORCED SHOULDER SEAMS

Useful Sweaters Astounding Values

Ages 8 to 14 Years

Knitted OUTERwear *deserves the preference*

Double Body Jersey Lined

D $2⁷⁵~

A $4⁹⁸~

B *Two-Piece Set* $4⁹⁸~ PER SET

C $4⁹⁸~

E $2⁹⁸~

L $2⁹⁸~

J $3⁹⁸~

G $1⁷⁹~

H $2⁹⁸~

F $3⁹⁸~

K *Double Body Jersey Lined* $3⁹⁵~

M $3⁶⁵~

Popular Styles
in Boys' Sports Wear

A $2.75 EACH

C Cap 89¢

B Jacket $3.48

E Cap 89¢ EACH

D Sweater $4.59 EACH

F $3.50 EACH

G $4.98

H $1.48

J $2.19 EACH

K $2.19 EACH

L 89¢ EACH

M $1.89

N $2.98 EACH

P 50¢ EACH

Snappy Styles *for* Little Men

$3.98

Dress Up Suits That Wear

40H3333—Dark Blue Serge Weave Cassimere, About One-Half Wool.. **$3.98**

40H3307—Dark Navy Blue Medium Twill, All Wool Worsted Serge... **$5.98**

Sizes, 5 to 9. State age size. Shipping weight, 2½ pounds.

A popular suit that active, sturdy boys get real service out of—and appearance, too. Coat has good quality lining, knickerbocker pants are full lined. A good buy at our low price, and there is nothing more dressy than a beautiful dark blue.

Suit With Extra Pants $5.95

For That Boy of Yours!
Style and Value

40H3314—Brown Plaid Cassimere. Sizes, 4 to 9 years........ **$5.95** State age size. Shipping weight, 3½ pounds.

A four-piece suit at the price of an ordinary suit! That's a real value! And style—the latest thing! Made of nearly all wool cassimere, very firmly woven, in a neat medium brown shade in plaid effect pattern. The single breasted two button coat, unlined, is a snappy, peppy style. Vest, single breasted also, has two pockets. Long pants are collegiate, cut full with wide cuff bottoms. Extra straight style knee pants are full lined. One of our biggest suit bargains.

All Wool $4.98

All Wool $5.45

A Dressy Suit That Wears Well!

40H3341—All Wool Medium Brown Cassimere........ **$4.98**

40H3342—Same as above, with extra knickers.... **$6.65**

Sizes, 5 to 9 years. State age size. Shipping weight, 2½ and 3½ pounds.

Snappy all wool diamond weave cassimere in a medium brown shade. Two button coat has good quality lining. Pants are full lined.

Fellows! This is a Real Suit!

40H3309—Sizes, 4 to 9 years........... **$5.45** State age size. Shipping weight, 3 pounds.

Made of all wool cassimere in a popular blue gray shade in a Glenurquhard plaid pattern. Coat is popular two-button. Five button vest. Straight style pants, full lined. Will give excellent service. At a price that's a real saving.

Washable $1.98

All Wool $3.98

All Wool $5.48

Collegiate! More Popular Than Ever

40H3315—Sizes, 4 to 9 years........... **$3.98** State age size. Shpg. wt., 2¼ lbs.

The blazer suit has earned its popularity by its snappy style and the good, hard, practical service it gives. A new pattern, this all wool blazer coat is in large lumberjacket plaid of green, gray and blue. Two flap pockets. The long pants, collar, cuffs, and waist band are of all wool cassimere in a medium brown shade in the popular diamond weave. The trimmings on the blazer match the pants.

The Warm Weather Suit For Young Vacationists

40H3327—Knickerbocker Suit........................ **$1.98**

Sizes, 5 to 10 years. State age size. Shipping weight, 1¾ pounds.

40H3328—Long Pants Suit.......................... **$2.98**

Sizes, 7 to 16 years. State age size. Shipping weight, 2 pounds.

Ideal for all around summer wear, this suit has lots of style, yet it is most practical, for it launders beautifully. Made of bluish gray smooth Daytona crash after the manner of the English lounge suit — single breasted, with patch pockets. Pants have the usual pockets, and the long pants have cuffs. Every fashionable lad wants a suit like this. The price is low.

The Very Newest Smart Wide Lapels

40H3324—Long Pants Suit........................ **$5.48**

40H3325—Long Pants Suit with extra knickerbockers.......... **6.98**

Sizes, 4 to 9 years. State age size. Shipping weight, 2½ and 3½ pounds.

When such fashionable suits for the small lads are offered at such low prices, every boy should have a suit like this! Blue gray all wool in the effective diamond weave. Double breasted coat has striped alpaca lining. The long pants have regular pockets and wide cuff bottoms. Extra knickerbocker pants are full lined and well made. A dependable quality.

Swagger Top Coat For Chilly Weather

40H3838—Blue Gray All Wool Cassimere........ **$4.98**

Sizes, 2 to 9 years. State age size. Shipping weight, 2 pounds.

Tailored after the fashion of the most stylish men's coats. The material has a smooth finish, in a very popular shade of blue gray firmly woven ll wool cassimere, with very neat Rayon (artificial silk) decorations in a large plaid effect pattern. Wool alpaca lining. Large patch pockets. A very serviceable coat. A good value at this low price.

Clever Top Coat Smartly Tailored

40H3837—Medium Light Gray. All Wool............ **$3.98**

Sizes, 2 to 9 years. State age size. Shipping weight, 2 pounds.

An up-to-the-minute style, this top coat is very practical and dressy as well. Made of all wool material in a neat diamond weave, medium light gray shade. Lined with good quality twill lining. Has two pockets with flaps. Very neatly finished throughout. At this low price, it's a good buy.

Wooly Coats

A $6⁷⁵

B $2⁷⁵

C $4⁷⁵

D $4⁵⁰

E $3⁵⁰

F $5⁹⁵

G $3⁴⁵

H $7⁷⁵

J $4⁷⁵

K $4⁵⁰

RA-KUNA REGISTERED-
L $9⁵⁰

M $2⁹⁸

N $3⁹⁸

P $4⁹⁸

R $4⁹⁸

We've Never Offered *Such Bargains* *IN* Quality Dresses

$2.98 Two Piece Middy Dress
For School and Everyday

31N9225—Navy Blue Skirt and All White Blouse

Practical two-piece middy dress. The blouse is made of strong Lonsdale Jean Cloth. Has non-rip placket cuffs, braid trimming, deep sailor collar and swagger black Sateen tie. Skirt of fine All Wool Serge is gracefully pleated and attached to a cambric bodice.
Ages 7, 8, 10, 12 and 14 years. State age size. See size scale below. Shpg. wt., 1½ lbs.

31N9250 All Wool Flannel With All Silk Scarf Collar

Ages 7 to 14 Years

Genuine Kalburnie
Rayon Plaid Crepe $1.98
Serviceable Frock

31N9235—Green
31N9236—Medium Blue

A charming frock in a smart and youthful two-piece effect style. The collar, yoke, cuffs and hip band are of matching color, solid tone Cotton Crepe.
Frock is prettily trimmed with hand embroidery stitching and fancy buttons.
It has a tie drawn through openings on the yoke. The skirt is made with two wide box pleats at the front.
Ages 7, 8, 10, 12 and 14 years. State size. See size scale. Shpg. wt., 1½ lbs.

Bargain Offer
Girls Coverall Aprons
2 for $1.00

31N9230—B—Green
A—Blue

Style B is fashioned of solid tone, standard grade green Chambray—fast color and durable. Has trimming of Printed Cotton Pongette and novelty buttons.
Style A is made of fast color blue Figured Mercerized Cotton Pongette. The trimming is of solid blue Chambray.
Both frocks are pretty, well made, washable and practical. Ideal for play and everyday service.
Ages 7, 8, 10, 12 and 14 years. State age size See size scale below. Shpg. wt., 3 lbs.

Chambray

A **B**

Pongette

Your Choice
$4.98 Serviceable All Wool Flannel School Frock

31N9250—Rust
31N9251—Medium Blue $4.98

Fashioned in a youthful manner of good quality All Wool Flannel, and attractively trimmed with Figured All Silk Radium which was used for piping the neck and cuffs, as well as for a jaunty tie.
The skirt shows a group of pleats at one side, and an inverted pleat on the other side.
Ages 8, 10, 12, 14 years. State age size. See size scale. Shpg. wt., 1½ lbs.

Two-Piece Effect Style

31N9245—Red and Black $4.98
31N9246—Tan and Brown

The blouse is of good quality All Wool Flasha; the skirt of good quality twill back Velveteen. The blouse is trimmed with Velveteen bandings, a pretty hand embroidered motif and fancy buttons. Pleats lend desirable fulness to the skirt.
Ages 8, 10, 12 and 14 years. State age size. See size scale. Shpg. wt., 2 lbs.

31N9245 All Wool Flasha and Twill Bach Velveteen

Just Think of It !
$4.98 For This All Silk Crepe de Chine Dress
Charming All Silk Frock

31N9240—Light Green and Tan
31N9241—Rose and Tan

The style is youthful and smart; the material is fine quality All Silk Crepe de Chine. Gathers below the yoke and shirring on the skirt, lend a graceful effect. Prettily trimmed with Tan Silk Crepe and silk satin ribbon.
At the special price quoted this dress is truly a marvel of value—priced far below what you would pay elsewhere for such quality.
Ages 7, 8, 10, 12 and 14 years. State age size See size scale. Shpg. wt., 1½ lbs.

SIZE SCALE	7	8	10	12	14 yrs.
Dresses for ages					
Fit chest measures	26	27	29	31	33 in.
Come in lengths	26	28	31	34	38 in.
See Index Pages for measuring instructions.					

Middies and Sportswear
Famous for Sturdy Quality

Admiral BRAND S.R. AND Co.

FOR AGES 7 TO 16 YEARS

Regulation Style "Gym" Middy

HALF WOOL FLANNEL

LONSDALE DRILL CLOTH

Lonsdale Jean Cloth Middy Blouses for Women

98¢

A Bargain

31N9675—
White and Blue
31N9676—**All White**

Well made, good looking middy—popular for sport and general wear. Fashioned of a strong, sturdy fabric with a sailor collar, jaunty black tie and non-rip placket cuffs.

Women's and Misses' Sizes—34 to 44 inches bust measure. State size. Shpg. wt., ¾ pound.

$1 39

Braid Trimmed

31N9670—
White and Blue
31N9671—**All White**

Strong, serviceable middy at a very low price. Made in regulation style with a sailor collar, breast pocket and non-rip placket cuffs. Has braid trimming and a long black tie.

Women's and Misses' Sizes—34 to 44 inches bust measure. State size. Shpg. wt., ¾ pound.

Special Value for Girls

98¢

Good Quality Mercerized Broadcloth

31N9690—White 31N9691—Tan

Girl's Tailored style blouse with snug fitting buttoned waistband and buttoned cuffs. The front is smartly pin tucked and the collar is finished with a jaunty tie drawn through a buckle ornament.

Ages 7, 8, 10, 12, 14 and 16 years. Chest measure 25, 26, 28, 30, 32 and 34 inches. State age size and chest measure. Shpg. wt. ¾ pound.

for Girls and Misses Ages 7 to 20 Years

$1 98

Of Warm Flannel

31N9680—**Navy Blue**

Smart Admiral Brand middy, prettily trimmed with red braid and a long black Sateen tie. Has deep sailor collar and non-rip placket cuffs. A real bargain at **$1.98**.

Misses' and Girl's Sizes—7, 8, 10, 12, 14, 16, 18 and 20 years. State age size and chest measure. Shpg. wt., ¾ pound.

$1 29

"Gym" Middy

31N9665—**White**

Made according to strict specifications with a deep sailor collar, breast pocket and lace tie. It is strong and sturdy wearing. Extra service is assured by double stitched seams.

Misses' and Girl's Sizes—7, 8, 10, 12, 14, 16, 18 and 20 years. Bust measure 25 to 38 inches. State age size and bust measure. Shpg. wt., ¾ pound.

The Ideal Play Outfit for Active Girls

Genuine HONG KONG Jean Cloth Sport Shirt

$1 19

Tailored Sport Shirt

31N9685—**Tan**
31N9686—**Blue**
31N9687—**White**

Made of a sturdy wearing fast color, washable fabric. Has convertible collar and buttoned cuffs.

Ages 7 to 14 years. State age size. Shpg. wt., ¾ pound.

Well Tailored Knickers in Your Choice of Three Sturdy Wearing Fabrics

31N9720—Gray
All Wool Tweed   **$2.48**
31N9721—Tan
All Wool Tweed

31N9722—Tan **Khaki Cloth**
31N9723—Gray   **98c**
Cotton Tweed
31N9724—Tan
Cotton Tweed

Ages 7 to 14 years. State age and exact waist measure. Shpg. wt., 2 pounds.

All Wool Tweed Knickers

$2 48

Khaki Cloth or Cotton Tweed

98¢

Lonsdale Jean Cloth Middy Blouses for Girls

$1 29

31N9695—
White and Blue
31N9696—
All White

Prettily braid trimmed middy. Has long black tie and non-rip placket cuffs.

Girl's Sizes—7, 8, 10, 12, and 14 years. Chest measure 25, 26, 28, 30 and 32 inches. State age size and chest measure. Shpg. wt., ¾ lb.

98¢

31N9697—
White and Blue
31N9698—
All White

Good looking, serviceable middy. Has deep sailor collar, long tie, breast pocket and non-rip placket cuffs.

Girl's Sizes—7, 8, 10, 12 and 14 years. Chest measure 25, 26, 28, 30 and 32 inches. State age size. Shpg. wt., ¾ lb.

Bodice Top Skirts for School Girls

(1) (2) (3)

All Wool Serge or All Wool Crepe Detachable Bodice Top

$2 98

Half Wool Scotch Plaid Detachable Bodice Top

$2 98

Cotton Serge

98¢

Smartly Pleated Skirts In Your Choice of Four Serviceable Fabrics

(1) 31N9717—Navy Blue All Wool Serge
(1) 31N9718—Navy Blue All Wool Crepe   **$2.98**
(2) 31N9716—Half Wool Scotch Plaid

(3) 31N9715—Navy Blue Cotton Serge   **98c**

Skirts one and two are made with detachable cambric bodices that fasten with buttons beneath the Skirt number three has attached bodice.

Ages 7 to 14 years. State age size and exact waist measure. Shpg. wt., 1½ pounds.

17 T 2820
VELOUR
CLOTH
WITH....
MANDEL
FUR

$4.98
POSTPAID

17 T 2825
ALL
WOOL
"DEERHEAD"
CHINCHILLA

$9.95
POSTPAID

17 T 2830
ALL
WOOL
VELOUR
WITH....
MANDEL
FUR

$8.98
POSTPAID

17 T 2835
ALL
VELOUR
CLOTH
WITH....
BEAVERETTE
CONEY

$7.98
POSTPAID

FOR AGES 7•8•9 YEARS

17T2835—Reindeer Tan
17T2836—Light Navy Blue
$7.98 POSTPAID

AN ADORABLE coat with fur trimmed flowing scarf ties; the fur matching the collar, cuffs and perky bow at back of rich Beaverette (Coney). Of warm Velour Cloth (more than half wool) with strong Rayon Twill lining. State age size. See size scale.

17T2830—Reindeer Tan
17T2831—Wine
$8.98 POSTPAID

ITS fabric is a good quality winter weight All Wool Velour enriched with a collar and cuffs of handsome Mink shade Mandel fur. Rayon stitchings and pocket strap-tabs add to its smartness. Lined with strong Twillsheen. State age size. See size scale.

17T2825—Navy Blue
17T2826—Red
17T2827—Powder Blue
$9.95 POSTPAID

THIS little coat of tailored smartness is made of the well known "Deerhead" All Wool Chinchilla—famed for its luxurious warmth. Lined with attractive Plaid Flannel. State age size. See size scale.

17T2820—Reindeer Brown
17T2821—Grackle Blue
17T2822—Wine
$4.98 POSTPAID

WHEN you see it—you will marvel at its low price. Of winter weight Velour Cloth (more than half wool) with strong Venesheen lining. Collared with Mandel fur. State age size. See size scale

SO SMART FOR SCHOOL
$7.98 POSTPAID FOR SET

3-PIECE CHINCHILLA OUTFIT

[NINE TENTHS WOOL]

A COAT—BERET—AND BAG OUTFIT—
THAT SPELLS SMARTNESS FOR THE SCHOOLGIRL

← 17T2833—Navy Blue

AN OUTFIT that will be the envy of all the girls at school—so jaunty—so new—so completely practical—and altogether in the spirit of the day—stressing that grown-up popular ensemble theme, which is all the rage just now. Made of sturdy wearing, cozily warm high grade Chinchilla Cloth (nine-tenths wool). The swagger cut coat is lined with red suede flannel; the bag is strongly made and leatherette trimmed; the beret is sateen lined.
Ages 7, 8, and 9 years. State age size. See size scale.

TWO WONDERFUL VALUES
$10.98 EACH POSTPAID

17T2840—Reindeer Tan
17T2841—Copenhagen Blue

A COAT of straight swagger lines topped with a graceful shoulder cape and with a dressy collar of plucked Imported French Coney fur: (gray fur on the blue coat—tan on the tan). Made of a soft napped supple weave All Wool fabric; warmly interlined; lined with strong Rayon Twill.
Ages 7, 8 and 9 years. State age size.

17T2845—Light Brown
17T2846—Gray

A LUXURIOUSLY warm handsome coat of Rollinson's genuine Silverpelt fur-like fabric. Introduced in New York—sold at Sears for a special low price. A coat—soft to the touch—smart to the eye—luxuriously warm —and unbelievably sturdy wearing. It has a deep, close clipped nap in the effect of genuine fur. Trimmed with leatherette; lined with gay Plaid Flannel.
Ages 7, 8 and 9 years. State age size.

17 T 2840
ALL WOOL
FLANNEL
BROADCLOTH
WITH....
FRENCH
CONEY
FUR

17 T 2845
ROLLINSONS'
GENUINE
SILVERPELT
WITH....
PLAID
FLANNEL
LINING

SIZE SCALE

Coats For Ages:	7—8—9 Years
Come In Lengths:	28—30—32 Inches
To Fit Chest Measures:	26—27—28 Inches

THE YOUNGER MISS HAS HER OWN SMART FASHIONS
AGES 7 TO 14 YEARS

31 T 3887
WASHABLE
PRINTED
PONGETTE
$**1**00
POSTPAID

31 T 3884
ALL
WOOL
JERSEY
$**3**98 POSTPAID

31 T 3881
GUARANTEED
WASHABLE
"FRUIT OF THE
LOOM"
$**1**98 POSTPAID

$**4**98
POSTPAID

Bloomer Dresses For Ages—7-8-9 Years

31T3881—*White Ground Blue Print*
31T3882—*White Ground Rose Print*
$1.98 POSTPAID

AN ADORABLE two-piece bloomer frock. Its attractive print fabric is guaranteed tubfast and famed for wear. Youthfully smart in style details. Trimmed with good quality solid tone cotton broadcloth, touches of dainty hand embroidery and a ribbon tie. Has matching bloomers.
State age size. See size scale.

31T3884—*Medium Green*
31T3885—*Light Blue*
$3.98 POSTPAID

A TWO-piece model of fine All Wool Jersey with matching color lustrous Sateen bloomers. The hand embroidered collar is of imported Linen; the bow tie of silk Crepe de Chine.
State age size. See size scale.

31T3887—*White Ground Fancy Print*
$1.00 POSTPAID

TWO-piece bloomer dress. Tubfast—durable—pretty in style—neat in workmanship. Made of printed Cotton Pongette of a dainty pattern; trimmed with shirrings and solid tone pongette. Has bloomers to match.
State age size. See size scale.

Two-Piece Ensemble of Novelty Homespun with Rayon Crepe Dress

31T3878—*Medium Tan*

THIS swagger two-piece ensemble will please the exacting young "miss"—who wants what is new and smart; the thrifty mother—who looks for practical qualities and value! The neatly tailored, full length coat and the bandings on the frock are of good looking, serviceable Homespun; the long sleeved, charming frock of lustrous Rayon Crepe. The coat can be worn with other frocks.
Ages 8, 10, 12 and 14 years. State age size. See size scale.

COTTON
SERGE
$**1**98 POSTPAID
ALL WOOL SERGE
$**3**98 POSTPAID

98¢ POSTPAID

$**4**98 POSTPAID

$**1**98 POSTPAID

Size Scale

Dresses for Ages, Years . . 7, 8, 10, 12, 14
Fit chest measures, Inches 26, 27, 29, 31, 33
Come in lengths, Inches 26, 28, 31, 34, 37

31T3870 — *Cotton Serge* **$1.98** POSTPAID
31T3869 — *All Wool Serge* **$3.98** POSTPAID

THE regulation style Navy Blue sailor dress. In your choice of fine quality All Wool Serge or serviceable Cotton Serge. Trimmed with soutache braid and an embroidered sleeve emblem.
Ages 7, 8, 10, 12 and 14 years. State age size.

Washable Woven Check Gingham

31T3872 — *Red and White Check*

SO TRIM and youthful—a pleasing choice from every standpoint. A sensible, practical, washable school frock! The collar and cuffs are of cotton broadcloth.
Ages 7, 8, 10, 12 and 14 years. State age size.

All Silk Crepe de Chine

31T3875 — *Red*
31T3876 — *Garland Green*

A LOVELY silk frock for "best wear." It is shirred at the shoulders and on top of the skirt—the shirrings trimmed with Rayon stitchings. Has ribbon tie. *Ages 7, 8, 10, 12 and 14 years. State age size.*

Washable Print and Broadcloth

31T3866 — *Tan and Fancy Print*

A SENSIBLE school and play frock. It is prettily styled in two-piece effect—combining an attractive cotton print with solid tone broadcloth.
Ages 8, 10, 12 and 14 years. State age size. See size scale.

True Values at GREAT SAVINGS in Rough Wear Play Suits

Washable Crash

Khaki Jean

Baseball Outfit
There's twice the fun in the game if you wear one of these cracker jack baseball suits. Dress like the big league players. They'll stand the gaff when you slide into "home," because they're strongly made of good wearing washable gray crash with colored stripes and trimmings. Pants have back pocket. Outfit includes cap, shirt, pants and leather belt. Glove not included. SIZES—4 to 16 years. State age size. We pay the postage.
40R3382 Baseball Outfit....**$1.49**

For the Outdoor Boy
Popular flapper style play suit of strong fast color washable khaki jean. Two chest pockets with buttons. Colored collegiate belt. Pants button to waist. All seams are triple stitched and bar tacked at strain points to assure long service. SIZES—3 to 8 years. State age size. We pay the postage.
40R3386 — Khaki Flapper Suit............. **85c**

Indian Chief Outfit
Made of strong khaki drill. Large headdress of many bright feathers. Bright color stencil design on the front of coat. Blue and gold fringe trimming on coat and pants. State age size. We pay the postage.
40R3373—Chief's Outfit. Sizes, 4 to 14 years........**$1.89**
40R3372—Brave's Outfit. Similar to above, but with less trimmings and fewer feathers. Sizes, 2 to 10 years...**95c**

Serviceable
Standard quality—fast color materials.
Seams strongly stitched and bar tacked. Button back drop seat. Fast color trimmings. Buttons riveted on. SIZES—2 to 6 years. State age size. We pay postage.
40R3620—Blue and White Pincheck..........**57c**
40R3618—Blue and White Stifel Stripe...............**57c**

Boys' Sweaters, Caps and Gloves Refer to Index for Page Listings

Camping Suit

Genuine TOM MIX Cowboy Outfit

New **AVIATORS SUIT**
Be a Real Aviator!
Quite the thing for backyard transatlantic flights. Natty looking aviator style suit, consisting of good strong khaki twill coat with four pockets with flaps to button and lace bottom style riding breeches. Sam Brown style belt, which goes over the shoulders and around the waist. Leatherette puttees and overseas style cap. Mercerized aviation emblem on the sleeve and metal emblem on the coat and hat. They're a brand new idea and bound to make a big hit with any real boy. Cane and field glasses are not included. SIZES—6 to 16 years. State age size. We pay the postage.
40R3380—Complete Aviation Outfit.....**$3.69**

PLAYBOY SUITS

For the Young Camper
Especially designed for outdoor rough wear. Shirt, pants and hat are made of good weight khaki drill. Shirt has two pockets with flap to button, and military collar. Regular style breeches with laced bottoms. Campaign style hat, stockings and belt included in this outfit. SIZES—6 to 16 years. State age size. We pay the postage.
40R3378 Boys' Camp Outfit..**$2.98**

This regular Tom Mix Cowboy Suit brings the Wild West home to every boy. Tom Mix signature on emblem on the shirt. The outfit includes a check cotton twill flannel shirt with two patch pockets with flap; pants of khaki drill with corduroy front and nickel spangles; large toy cork pistol, holster, belt, bandana handkerchief, lasso and large tan beaver felt hat. SIZES—4 to 14 years. State age size. We pay the postage.
40R3384—Tom Mix Cowboy Outfit....**$3.75**

WE *Pay the Postage*
Our low prices are all you pay! Send no money for parcel post charges as *We Pay the Postage* on all play suits on this page. Consider this additional saving when comparing prices.

Enduring Quality Priced Low

This suit will give your boy many hours of pleasure, save money for you and save wear on his other clothes. Has all the trimmings including bandana, lasso, toy pistol and holster. Good quality khaki drill shirt, pants and cowboy style hat. Fringe trimming down side of pants. Sturdily made to stand up under hard wear. Small sizes have elastic waistband. SIZES—4 to 14 years. State age size. We pay the postage.
40R3383—Complete Cowboy Outfit..**$1.39**

A New Cowboy Suit
Khaki shirt has leatherette vest style front with fancy colored designs and letterings. Khaki pants have leatherette trimmings down the side; pockets with fancy designs. Large toy cork pistol with belt, holster, lasso, bandana and cowboy style khaki hat. Small sizes have elastic waistband. SIZES—4 to 14 years. State age size. We pay the postage.
40R3376 Cowboy Outfit....**$2.48**

It's Fun to SAVE BETTER CLOTHES in These Play Suits

Double Seat Knees

They'll Stand the Gaff
Made double at places of greatest wear, seat and knees. All points of strain securely bar tacked. Button back and drop seat. Fast color red trimmings. Riveted brass buttons. SIZES—2 to 8 years. State age size. We pay postage.

4OR3600—Fast Color Indigo Blue Stifel Drill........ **79c**

4OR3605—Fast Color Indigo Blue Denim (Plain Color)........ **79c**

Sturdy Play Suits
These play suits will stand a lot of hard wear and launder well. Strongly stitched throughout and bar tacked at strain points. Patent buttons. Drop seat. Fast color trimmings. SIZES—2 to 8 years. State age size. We pay the postage.

4OR3604 — Genuine Stripe Stifel Drill........ **69c**

4OR3607—Blue and White Hickory Stripe........ **69c**

All Wool and Silk Cassimere
For cooler days of spring and summer this suit will prove just the thing. Double breasted. Has neat sport style collar and cuffs that button. Pants button to the waist, full lined. All wool and silk cassimere with Rayon decorations in an attractive medium brown stripe effect. SIZES — 3 to 8 years. State age size. We pay the postage.

4OR3349 — All Wool and Silk Cassimere Suit........ **$2.25**

A Dandy Outfit
Pants are of fancy brown all wool and silk cassimere with Rayon decorations. Waist is fast color woven Rayon striped broadcloth. Regular shirt style collar and open cuffs that button. A belt of the same material as the pants, and regular belt loops together with the bright color four-in-hand tie. Waist is detachable and can easily be washed. SIZES—3 to 8 years. State age size. We pay the postage.

4OR3302 Complete Suit. **$1.79**

WE PAY the POSTAGE

Khaki Aviation Suit

Rodeo Playsuit

Double Seat Knees

Hickory Stripe

Heavy Weight White Back Blue Denim

ROUGH WEAR
Fast color yarn dyed blue and white striped Hickory cloth, a favorite for long, hard service. Open front style with drop seat. Sport style collar. Triple stitched seams and bar tacked at all points of strain. Riveted buttons will not come off or rust. A demon for wear! SIZES—3 to 8 years. State age size. We pay the postage.

4OR3608—Hickory Cloth Play Suit........ **88c**

It's practically wearproof! Made of fast color indigo blue heavy weight white back denim. Has triple stitched seams, bar tacking at all points of strain, and riveted brass buttons that won't rust and can't come off. Note the large chest pockets with flap and button. SIZES—3 to 8 years have drop seat, and 9 to 12 years have closed back and front openings. State age size. We pay the postage.

4OR3622 Sizes, 3 to 8 years. **$0.95**

4OR3624 Sizes, 9 to 12 years. **1.15**

NEW! Aviation Style Play Suit
Ensure your boy's happiness by getting him one of these dandy play suits. Just like the pilot wears. The bottoms of the pants and the sleeves have adjustable tabs which can be tightened or loosened as desired. Note the chest pockets set on a slant so that the contents cannot easily fall out. Has belt in front closing with a buckle. Embroidered aviation emblem. A very practical and sturdy garment, as it is made of good quality fast color khaki jean and all seams are triple stitched. Has open front and concealed drop seat, all buttons being covered. State age size. We pay the postage.

4OR3626 Sizes, 3 to 8 years...... **$1.00**

4OR3628 Sizes, 9 to 12 years..... **1.19**

Built to Stand Rough Treatment
He'll have many hours of fun in this practical "Rodeo" style play suit and, at the same time, he'll save his regular clothes. It's a dandy with its bell bottoms with extra piece of fast color red Galatea cloth sewed in the side and red Galatea cloth cuffs and trimmings on the pockets. Large chest pockets have flap and buttons. All seams are triple stitched and bar tacked. Open front style with drop seat. Riveted brass buttons that will not come off or rust. Material is fast color blue cotton fabric with woven white pin stripes. SIZES—3 to 8 years. State age size. We pay the postage.

4OR3632—Blue and White Pin Stripe Play Suit.. **98c**

Here is our famous "Hercules" play suit, one of the strongest play suits made. They're double where the greatest strain comes—the seat and the knees. Seams are triple stitched and strongly bar tacked at strain points. Open front style with drop seat. Riveted brass buttons. Your choice of two sturdy fast color materials. SIZES—3 to 8 years. State age size. We pay the postage.

4OR3631 Indigo Blue Denim.. **87c**

4OR3633 Khaki Twill........ **87c**

HERE They Are BOYS!

ALL THE BOYS WANT'EM

With Full Vision Goggles

98c

93F4912—Black.
93F4913—Brown. Be sure to state size. Sizes, 6⅞ to 7⅛. Shpg. wt., ¾ pound.
Top notch aeronauts have detachable goggles with their helmets! Made of selected sheepskin leather. Cotton lining. Goggles are fastened on by snap fasteners. Sliding buckle fastens under chin.

Just Like Real Aviators

79c

93F4900—Black.
93F4901—Brown. Be sure to state size. Sizes, 6⅜ to 7⅛. Shpg. weight, 5 ounces.
Don't confuse this flashy professional style with cheaper helmets at this price elsewhere. Fine quality horsehide. Cotton lining. Adjustable sliding buckle that fastens under the chin. A Top-Notcher.

For Future Aviators!

$1.49

93F4918—Black.
93F4919—Brown.
Sizes, 6⅜ to 7⅛. State size. Shipping weight, ¾ pound.
Boys' Aviation Helmet of selected sheepskin leather. The goggles are fitted with rubber eye rests making them very comfortable. Fastens around cap with an elastic band. Tabs on sides hold goggles in place. Cotton suede cloth lining. Adjustable sliding buckle.

How's This for Value?

42c

93F4923—Black.
93F4924—Brown.
Sizes, 6⅜ to 7⅛. State size. Shipping weight, 8 oz.
Boys' Aviation Helmet of good quality artificial leather. Goggles are fastened to cap with snap fasteners and when reversed goggles fit over the eyes, giving protection in bad weather. Durable cotton lining. Adjustable sliding buckle fastens under chin.

89c

93F4780 Gray Mixture
93F4781 Tan Mixture
93F4782 Brown Mixture.
Sizes, 6⅜ to 7⅛. State size. Shpg. wt., ¾ lb.
Boys' Eight-Quarter Top Golf Style Cap without inband. This season's newest cap fabrics have been selected for these caps. Made of assorted shades, patterns, materials. Many are all wool, others are about three-fourths wool. Lustrous rayon lining. Leather front piece. Cap can be adjusted one size smaller or larger.

59c

93F4700 Gray Mixture.
93F4701 Tan Mixture.
93F4702 Brown Mixture.
Sizes, 6⅜ to 7⅛. State size. Shpg. wt., ¾ lb.
Boys' One-Piece Top Golf Style Cap without inband. Made of assorted shades, patterns, materials. Many are all wool; others about one-half wool. Cotton twill lining. Leather front piece. Cap can be adjusted one size smaller or larger.

89c

93F4795 Gray mixture.
93F4796 Tan mixture.
93F4797 Brown Mixture.
Sizes, 6⅜ to 7⅛. State size. Shpg. wt., ¾ lb.
Boys' One-Piece Top Golf Style Cap without inband in assorted shades, patterns and materials. Many are all wool; others about three-fourths wool. Lustrous rayon lining. Leather front piece. Can be adjusted one size smaller or larger.

$1.29

93F6030 Sand Tan
93F6031 Gray
93F6032 Medium Brown
Sizes, 6⅜ to 7⅛. State size. Shpg. wt., 2 lbs.
Boys' hat of good quality wool felt in popular snap brim style. Crown, about 5¼ in. high. Welt edge brim, about 2¼ in. wide. Neat ribbon band. Leather sweatband.

Selected Styles for the Little Fellows

39c

93F4730—Gray Mixture.
93F4731—Tan Mixture.
93F4732—Brown Mixture.
Sizes, 6⅛ to 6⅞. State size. Shpg. wt., ¾ lb.
Little Fellows' Eight-Quarter Top Prince of Wales Cap without inband. Made of assorted shades, patterns and materials. Many are all wool; others about one-half wool. Trimmed with ribbon band. Cotton twill lining. Indestructible canvas visor.

49c

93F4735—Gray Mixture.
93F4736—Tan Mixture.
93F4737—Brown Mixture.
Sizes, 6⅛ to 6⅞. State size. Shpg. wt., ¾ lb.
Little Fellows' One-Piece Top Golf Cap. Made of assorted shades, patterns, materials. Many are all wool; others about one-half wool. Made without inband. Cotton lining. Leather front piece. Cap can be adjusted one size smaller or larger.

79c

93F4925 Gray
93F4926 Tan Mixture.
93F4927 Brown Mixture.
Sizes, 6¼ to 6⅞. State size. Shpg. wt., ¾ lb.
Little Fellows' Eight-Quarter Top Golf Style Cap. Made of materials more than four-fifths wool, in this season's newest designs. Cotton twill lining. Inside turn-down lined band. These caps are very popular. Cap can be adjusted one size smaller or larger.

Boys' and Children's HATS AND CAPS

See table for size corresponding to your measurements.

HOW TO MEASURE

Place tape measure around head as illustrated. **Free tape measure on request.**

If Head Measures, in.	Order Size
19	6⅛
19¾	6¼
19¾	6⅜
20⅛	6½
20½	6⅝
20⅞	6¾
21¼	6⅞
21⅝	7
22	7⅛

FOR WINTER WEAR

59c

93F4930 Brown.
93F4931 Navy Blue.
93F4932 Maroon.
93F4933—Oxford Gray.
One size only. Shpg. wt., 4 oz.
Boys' Double Thickness Knitted Muffler Cap of good quality yarns of about two-thirds wool, balance cotton. Double thick to protect head and ears in cold weather. Can be buttoned under chin.

All Wool

79c

93F4962 Gray Mixture.
93F4963 Tan Mixture.
93F4964 Brown Mixture
Sizes, 6⅜ to 7⅛. State size. Shpg. wt., 1 lb.
Boys' Golf Style Cap in the season's newest fabric. Made of All Wool Cloth in the favorite eight-quarter top-style. Cotton twill lining. Indestructible canvas visor. Inside turn-down lined band. Cap can be adjusted one size smaller or larger.

FRONT QUARTER
GENUINE HORSEHIDE
LOWEST PRICE
SEARS
EVER NAMED

WE GUARANTEE A SAVING!

OUR BARGAIN KING!

OUR FAMOUS
Arctic Giant

A $7⁵⁰ Post Paid

B $7⁴⁵ Post Paid

C $2⁹⁸ Post Paid

D $3⁴⁸ Post Paid

E $4⁹⁸ Post Paid

F $3⁹⁸ Post Paid

G $2⁷⁹ Post Paid

H $2⁹⁸ Post Paid

Lovely Things
· FOR LITTLE CHILDREN ·

A B
Our Finest Quality
ALL WOOL JERSEY
DRESS OR SUIT
$1⁶⁹ EACH

C
DOLL INCLUDED

D
APRON INCLUDED

98¢ EACH
"FRUIT-of-the-LOOM"
Tub-fast Guaranteed Fabrics

E
POCKET BOOK INCLUDED

F
Hand Embroidered
AGES 1-2-3 YEARS
TWO FOR $1⁰⁰

G
LUSTROUS COTTON BROADCLOTH 89¢

H
PART WOOL FLANNEL $1⁵⁹

J
SOFT ALL WOOL JERSEY $1⁶⁹

K
All SILK TAFFETA $1⁹⁵

L
COAT AND BERET SET $4⁹⁸ POST PAID

M
LEGGINGS $1⁵⁹
COAT AND BERET SET $3⁹⁸ POST PAID

N
Dubfast 79¢ EACH
COTTON BROADCLOTH

ONE-PIECE ALL WOOL JERSEY $1²⁹

TWO-PIECE ALL WOOL JERSEY $1⁶⁹

FINE QUALITY ALL WOOL CREPE $1⁹⁵

A
3-PIECE SET
$5.79
COAT AND HELMET **$3.45**

B
HAND SMOCKED SILK RADIUM
$2.29 SET

Let it Blow!
BEACON CHINCHILLA CLOTH (10% Wool)
...will keep us warm

C
3-PIECE SET
$2.98

TALON HOOKLESS FASTENERS

D
SNOW SUIT AND HELMET
$2.48

COAT AND BERET
$1.98
F

E
HAT, COAT AND LEGGINGS COMPLETE SET
$3.69

Conquer Old King Cold!
In this Fine ALL WOOL 3-Piece Outfit

G
Outfit
$4.98
COMPLETE

H
¾ WOOL SNOW SUIT
$3.45

J
HAT, COAT AND LEGGINGS COMPLETE SET
$5.98

K
Lustrous FINE QUALITY COTTON SUEDE CLOTH 3-PIECE SET
$3.79

L
ALL WOOL CHINCHILLA HELMET
59c

JIFFY BUTTONLESS LEGGINGS *Save Mother's Time*
GENUINE HOOKLESS FASTENERS

M
98c
AGES 1-2-3 YEARS

N
$1.00
AGES 2 TO 6 YEARS

P
90% WOOL CHINCHILLA COAT
$1.98
BERET **39c**

"I'm a Little Rebel!"

I haven't any more mercy for a pair of shoes than a paper doll. But since Mother began buying my shoes from Sears I just can't seem to wear them out, try as I do. My Mother is clever, she's buying more than ever now before prices scoot up.

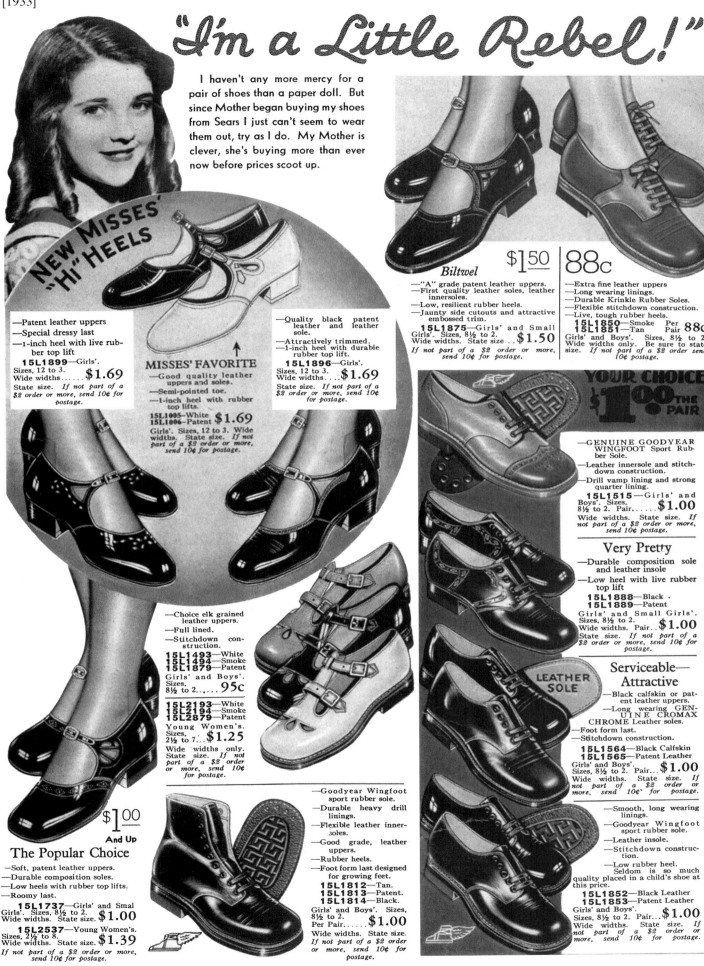

NEW MISSES' "Hi" HEELS

—Patent leather uppers
—Special dressy last
—1-inch heel with live rubber top lift.
15L1899—Girls'. Sizes, 12 to 3. Wide widths...... **$1.69**
State size. *If not part of a $2 order or more, send 10¢ for postage.*

MISSES' FAVORITE
—Good quality leather uppers and soles.
—Semi-pointed toe.
—1-inch heel with rubber top lifts.
15L1005—White
15L1006—Patent **$1.69**
Girls'. Sizes, 12 to 3. Wide widths. State size. *If not part of a $2 order or more, send 10¢ for postage.*

—Quality black patent leather and leather sole.
—Attractively trimmed.
—1-inch heel with durable rubber top lift.
15L1896—Girls'. Sizes, 12 to 3. Wide widths.... **$1.69**
State size. *If not part of a $2 order or more, send 10¢ for postage.*

—Choice elk grained leather uppers.
—Full lined.
—Stitchdown construction.
15L1493—White
15L1494—Smoke
15L1879—Patent
Girls' and Boys'. Sizes, 8½ to 2..... **95c**
15L2193—White
15L2194—Smoke
15L2879—Patent
Young Women's. Sizes, 2½ to 7... **$1.25**
Wide widths only. State size. *If not part of a $2 order or more, send 10¢ for postage.*

$1.00 And Up
The Popular Choice
—Soft, patent leather uppers.
—Durable composition soles.
—Low heels with rubber top lifts.
—Roomy last.
15L1737—Girls' and Small Girls'. Sizes, 8½ to 2. Wide widths. State size. **$1.00**
15L2537—Young Women's. Sizes, 2½ to 8. Wide widths. State size. **$1.39**
If not part of a $2 order or more, send 10¢ for postage.

—Goodyear Wingfoot sport rubber sole.
—Durable heavy drill linings.
—Flexible leather innersoles.
—Good grade, leather uppers.
—Rubber heels.
—Foot form last designed for growing feet.
15L1812—Tan.
15L1813—Patent.
15L1814—Black.
Girls' and Boys'. Sizes, 8½ to 2. Per Pair..... **$1.00**
Wide widths. State size. *If not part of a $2 order or more, send 10¢ for postage.*

Biltwel $1.50
—"A" grade patent leather uppers.
—First quality leather soles, leather innersoles.
—Low, resilient rubber heels.
—Jaunty side cutouts and attractive embossed trim.
15L1875—Girls' and Small Girls'. Sizes, 8½ to 2. Wide widths. State size .. **$1.50**
If not part of a $2 order or more, send 10¢ for postage.

88c
—Extra fine leather uppers.
—Long wearing linings.
—Durable Krinkle Rubber Soles.
—Flexible stitchdown construction.
—Live, tough rubber heels.
15L1850—Smoke Per **88c**
15L1851—Tan Pair
Girls' and Boys'. Sizes, 8½ to 2. Wide widths only. Be sure to state size. *If not part of a $2 order send 10¢ postage.*

YOUR CHOICE $1.00 THE PAIR
—GENUINE GOODYEAR WINGFOOT Sport Rubber Sole.
—Leather innersole and stitchdown construction.
—Drill vamp lining and strong quarter lining.
15L1515—Girls' and Boys'. Sizes, 8½ to 2. Pair...... **$1.00**
Wide widths. State size. *If not part of a $2 order or more, send 10¢ postage.*

Very Pretty
—Durable composition sole and leather insole
—Low heel with live rubber top lift
15L1888—Black
15L1889—Patent
Girls' and Small Girls'. Sizes, 8½ to 2. Wide widths. Pair.. **$1.00**
State size. *If not part of a $2 order or more, send 10¢ for postage.*

Serviceable—Attractive
—Black calfskin or patent leather uppers.
—Long wearing GENUINE CROMAX CHROME Leather soles.
—Foot form last.
—Stitchdown construction.
15L1564—Black Calfskin
15L1565—Patent Leather
Girls' and Boys'. Sizes, 8½ to 2. Pair... **$1.00**
Wide widths. State size. *If not part of a $2 order or more, send 10¢ for postage.*

LEATHER SOLE

—Smooth, long wearing linings.
—Goodyear Wingfoot sport rubber sole.
—Leather insole.
—Stitchdown construction.
—Low rubber heel. Seldom is so much quality placed in a child's shoe at this price.
15L1852—Black Leather
15L1853—Patent Leather
Girls' and Boys'. Sizes, 8½ to 2. Wide widths. State size. *If not part of a $2 order or more, send 10¢ for postage.* **$1.00**

Smart SLEEPING OR BEACH PAJAMAS

Glad Sleepy Hours
38L2428—Blue
38L2429—Green **79c**
Ages—7-8, 9-10, 11-12, 13-14, 15-16 years. State age. Postage, 6c each.
—One-piece style.
—Better quality Cotton Prints.
Everything dear to the junior heart. NEW, wide shouldered "pinafore" style; ties in back! Style, quality, workmanship not excelled in $1 garments elsewhere.

more dash and charm in—
"7 to 16 year" Fashions

Bargain in Health and Style
45c
38L2425—Assorted Bright Floral Prints. Ages—7-8, 9-10, 11-12, 13-14 yrs. State age.

Nothing Half So Joyously Smart As This SMOCK-JAMA **$1.00**
38L2438—Fancy Floral Print.

SUBSTANTIAL **SMARTNESS IN RUN-RESISTANT KNIT RAYONS**

(A) Panty **29c**
38L2121 Flesh Each
38L2122—Peach
Ages—7-8, 9-10, 11-12, 13-14, 15-16 yrs.

(C) One-Piece Sleeveless Pajama with "Topper" Jacket
38L2426 Lido Blue **$1 59**

(D) Underslip
38L2080 Flesh **55c**
38L2081 Peach EACH

(E) One-Piece Pajama
38L2439 Scarlet Red **89c**

SEARS GYM CLOTHING
Made to Stand Hard Wear

Makes an Ideal Play Suit

Girls' One-Piece Gym Suit
—Standard size specification.
—Best quality cotton suiting material.
—Button on one shoulder and down side.
—Guaranteed fast colors—Vat Dyed.
—½-inch elastic at knee.
—Colors: light blue or light green.
Sizes, 8 to 22 years.
This garment has been adopted as the official gym suit by many schools and colleges throughout the country; also used for camp and play. State color and size. Postpaid if part of $2 order.
6K1983
Shpg. wt., 1 lb. 8 oz..... **$1.00**

Combination Gym Suit
Same specification and material as in 6K1983.
Detachable Pleated Skirt Suit Constructed With Drop Seat
Especially adapted for children in Grade Schools. This garment is constructed so as to serve two purposes. One: a gym suit, the other an every day school or play garment. Colors: Blue or Green. State color and age. Ages: 8 to 16.
6K1984—Shpg. wt., 2 lbs. Postpaid if part of $2 order..... **$1.75**

Cotton Gym and Play Bloomers
—Henrietta Cotton twill.
—Black color only.
—Full pleated extra full size.
—Strongly sewed.
—Adjustable fastening at waist.
—Elastic at knee.
Tailored to allow freedom and fit comfortably. Even sizes, 26 to 36 in. waist measure. Shpg. wt., 12 oz. Postpaid if part of $2 order.
6K2083 State size.... **$1.00**
6K2096 Same as 6K2083 except in children's sizes 10-12, 14, 16 years. State size.
Shpg. wt., 6 oz..... **89c**
Sateen Bloomer—Black Color
Tailored or narrow pattern. This garment and our 6K2067 middie make an ideal gym combination. Even sizes, 26 to 36 inch waist. State size.
6K2068—Shpg. wt., 1 lb..... **95c**

Ballet or Gym Slippers
Black Kid Leather Upper

—Canvas lined. —Draw strings.
Used not only for dancing but also very popular as a gym shoe because of their perfect fit and light weight. Shpg. wt., 1 lb. Postpaid if part of $2 order. State size.
6K1389—Sizes and half sizes, 2½ to 7 inclusive..... **$1.75**
6K1388—Sizes 12, 12½, 13, 13½, 1, 1½, and 2..... **$1.65**

Middy Blouse
—Form fitting.
—White bleached cotton Jean Cloth.
—Guaranteed against shrinking.
—Regulation sailor collar.
—Double stitching.
—Full length sleeves.
—Patch pocket.
—Black Middie Tie.
Used for gym, camp and every day wear. Even bust sizes, 26 to 44-inch. Postpaid if part of $2 order. Shpg. wt., 12 oz.
6K2067—State size....**95c**
Cotton Gym Knicker.
—Well tailored.
—Henrietta cotton twill.
—Black color.
—Adjustable waist band.
—Button on both sides.
—Elastic at knee.
This knicker and our 6K2067 middie make an ideal gym or basket ball suit. Even waist sizes 26 to 36 in. State size.
6K2078—Shpg. wt., 1 lb..... **$1.00**

Girls' White Canvas Shoe

—Specially designed for girls and women.
—Lace to toe style.
—White canvas upper.
—Loose lined.
—White foxing and trim.
—Built-in arch support.
—Cushion heel.
—White toe cap.
—White toe guard.
—Compounded Gum Rubber Soles
Constructed so as to give all necessary protection the feet should have. Sizes, 2½ to 8. State size. Postpaid if part of $2 order. **$1.79**
6K1304—Shpg. wt., 1 lb. 12 oz.
Women's Canvas Shoe
The same sizes and style as 6K1304 except single lined, and crepe rubber sole. State size. Postpaid if part of $2 order.
6K1308—Shpg. wt., 1 lb. 12 oz..... **$1.49**

Girls' Athletic Socks
—Good Grade Soft Cotton 12-Inch Length.
White with green or blue trim. An ideal sock to use with 6K1983 gym suit. Sizes 7, 8, 9 and 10. State size and color trim. Postpaid if part of $2 order.
6K2053—Shpg. wt., 3 oz.....**17c**

WE PAY THE POSTAGE ON ORDERS OF $2.00 OR MORE

Warm Winter Wear

SIZE SCALE
Ages: 6- 7- 8- 9-10 Years
Chest: 25-26-27-28-29 Inches
Lengths: 27-28-30-32-34 Inches
Be Sure to State Age Size

All Wool MARABEAUX COATING — $6.98

Our finest coat for little girls. Made of beautiful, sturdy-napped All Wool Marabeaux Sport Coating. Rayon and cotton lining. Interlined. A marvelous coat at twice the price.
Sizes: 6, 7, 8, 9 and 10 years. *State age size.*
17 D 3635—Cocoa Brown
17 D 3636—Medium Red
17 D 3637—Skipper Blue
Sent direct from New York to you ... but you pay the postage only from our nearest Mail Order Store. Shpg. Wt. 3 lbs., 8 oz.

Attractive KEMP COATING — $5.98

High quality and a style "just like big sister's"! Material is about three-fourths Wool, balance Rayon and Cotton, that has a frosty, lovely nap. Fine quality, soft genuine imported Coney fur collar and cuffs. Rayon and Cotton lining. Interlining. *State age size.*
Sizes: 6 to 10 years.
17 D 3640—Medium Blue
17 D 3641—Medium Red
17 D 3642—Reindeer Tan
Sent direct from New York to you ... but you pay the postage only from our nearest Mail Order Store. Shipping Weight, 3 lbs., 10 oz.

WARM, HEAVY CHINCHILLA 70% Wool $3.98

Isn't this Adorable! $4.98

BOTH HAVE Berets to Match

Popular "Regulation" Chinchilla Coat—Beret to Match

(A) Real coat "Classic"! Regulation brass-buttoned, bright emblemed style. Warm, long wearing Chinchilla cloth—70% Wool, balance Rayon and Cotton. Snug, soft cotton suede cloth lining. An outfit of the same fine quality would cost much more elsewhere. *See scale size.*
Sizes: 6, 7, 8, 9 and 10 years. *State age size.*
17 D 3645—Navy Blue ... $3.98
Sent direct from New York to you ... but you pay the postage only from our nearest Mail Order Store. Shipping Weight, 3 lbs., 14 oz.

(B) And quite the newest style, too! Good quality Warm Wool coating, more than three-quarters Wool, balance Rayon and Cotton, with lustrous Sateen lining and warm interlining. Jaunty scalloped oversleeves. Tucked elbow fullness fits into neat cuffs. Genuine Coney fur collar in harmonizing colors sets off the attractive shoulder yoke. A matching beret is included. *State age size.*
Sizes: 6, 7, 8, 9 and 10 years.
17 D 3650—Winetone
17 D 3651—Med. Brown
17 D 3652—Med. Blue $4.98
Sent direct from New York to you ... but you pay the postage only from our nearest Mail Order Store. Shipping Weight, 3 lbs., 2 oz.

Sheepskin Lined ARTIFICIAL LEATHER — $3.98

LET it snow—she'll be as warm as can be in this winter warm jacket of sturdy embossed artificial leather. Wide overlapping double breasted style with wooly warm, sheepskin lining from neckline to waist. Warm wristlets in sleeves. Deep piled genuine Wombat Fur collar.
Sizes: 8, 10, 12 and 14 years. *State age size.* Length, about 23 inches.
17 D 3880—Med. Red
17 D 3881—Med. Blue
17 D 3882—Black........ $3.98
Sent direct from New York to you ... but you pay the postage only from our nearest Mail Order Store. Shipping Weight, 4 lbs., 12 oz.

Chinchilla 70% Wool or ALL WOOL MELTON — $3.98

YOUR choice of two famous fabrics in a warm Jacket. Both are lined with soft, warm Cotton Suede cloth. Both have fluffy Wool and Rayon fur fabric collar that extends inside the coat to form an extra warm yoke across back, shoulders and chest. Hip length.
Sizes: 8, 10, 12, 14 and 16 years. *State age size.*
70% Wool Chinchilla Cloth
17 D 3885—Navy Blue $3.98
All Wool Smooth Melton
17 D 3888—Navy Blue $3.98
Each sent direct from New York ... but you pay the postage only from our nearest Mail Order Store. Shipping Weight, 4 lbs., 12 oz. each.

Du Pont ARTIFICIAL LEATHER BERET TO MATCH $1.89

ARTIFICIAL LEATHER BERET TO MATCH $1.19

STURDY JACKETS

FINE artificial leather jackets. Windproof. Rainproof. Looks like real leather. Beret to match coat, included.
Sizes: 6, 8, 10, 12, and 14 years. Hip length. *State age size.*
Double-Breasted Artificial Leather
17 D 3890—Medium Red
17 D 3891—Medium Blue
17 D 3892—Medium Green ... $1.89
Single-Breasted Artificial Leather
27 D 3895—Medium Red
27 D 3896—Medium Blue
27 D 3897—Medium Green ... $1.19
Not Prepaid, Shpg. Wts. 3 lbs., 6 oz.

Gay *Sport* Togs
FOR 8 TO 16 YEAR OLDS

"Romp-about"
2 PIECE
PLAY SUIT
95¢

I know the place to get Riding Togs! Sears are honeys— and are the prices low!

You can't do without "TWIN" SWEATER SUITS

This four piece Twin Sweater set in Honeycomb weave, all Cotton Boucle Knit, looks like expensive wool knit. Slip-over sweater, Cardigan and skirt. Adorable beret. Sizes: 8 to 14 years. *State size.*
31 E 5107—Red.
31 E 5108—Med. Blue... **$2.98**

Sent direct from New York to you ... but you pay postage only from our nearest Mail Order Store. Shpg. Wt., 1 lb. 4 oz.

Ⓐ Everybody's wearing "shorts" for play this year! Gives you the freedom and comfort you want for active wear. You'll adore this cute tailored outfit of Cotton Linene. Blouse and Shorts have sport trim and belt of striped Percale. Washable. Smart, practical, sensible. Bargain priced. *State age size.*
Sizes: 8, 10, 12, 14 and 16 years.
27 E 5105—White with Red....... **95¢**
Not Prepaid. Shpg. Wt., 8 oz.

The Blouse
Ⓑ Isn't this a sweetheart! Made of good quality, washfast Percale. Attractive white yoke of Cotton Broadcloth with dainty ruffle trim. Elastic held puffed sleeves. *State age size.*
Sizes: 8, 10, 12, 14 and 16 years.
27 E 5120—Blue Print.
27 E 5121—Red Print............... **75¢**
Not Prepaid. Shpg. Wt., 8 oz.

The Skirt
Just the skirt to wear with these adorable blouses, and your sweaters. Tailored in "grown-up" fashion of good quality, long wearing Flannel (50% wool, balance fine cotton yarns). Attractive stitched pockets. A real bargain at this low price. *State size.*
Sizes: 8, 10, 12, 14 and 16 years.
Waist: 24, 25, 26, 27 and 28 inches.
Lengths: 21, 23, 25, 27 and 29 inches.
27 E 5103—Medium Green. **$1.59**
27 E 5104—Light Navy Blue.....
Not Prepaid. Shpg. Wt., 12 oz.

The Blouse
Ⓒ You'll love this dainty Dotted Voile Blouse. Sheer organdy collar with wide ruffle edge and perky bow. Washes beautifully. One of the prettiest blouses ever made for such a low price. Sizes: 8, 10, 12, 14 and 16 years. *State age size.*
27 E 5122—Red and White.
27 E 5123—White with Red Dot.... **98¢**
Not Prepaid. Shipping Weight, 6 oz.

The Skirt
Summer weather calls for this jaunty skirt of fine quality, washfast Cotton Pique. It always looks fresh and cool, and it's so fashion right! Best choice for sports!
Sizes: 8, 10, 12, 14 and 16 years.
Waist: 24, 25, 26, 27 and 28 inches.
Lengths: 21, 23, 25, 27 and 29 inches.
State age size.
27 E 5125—White.
27 E 5126—Maize................. **98¢**
Not Prepaid. Shipping Weight, 10 oz.

Colorful Blouse
Ⓓ It's plaid, washfast Percale and it's made into the popular "Schoolgirl" style. Pleated front frills are charming.
Sizes: 8, 10, 12, 14 and 16 years. *State age size.*
27 E 5153—Green Plaid.
27 E 5154—Light Blue Plaid....... **85¢**
Not Prepaid. Shpg. Wt., 6 oz.

Ⓔ Swanky, rollicking "Classmate" sports jacket! Made of fine quality All Wool Flannel in double breasted style. Deep patch pockets and button trim. Adds that last smart touch to your sports outfit.
Sizes: 8, 10, 12, 14 and 16 years. *State age size.*
31 E 5127—Light Navy. **$2.98**
31 E 5128—Bright Red.........
Sent direct from New York to you ... but you pay the postage only from our nearest Mail Order Store. Shpg. Wt., 14 oz.

Cotton Mesh Shirt
Sizes. 8 to 16 yrs. *State size.*
27 E 5110 — White only. Not Prepaid. Shipping Weight, 8 oz... **85¢**

Cotton Gabardine Sleeveless Riding Vest
Ages: 8 to 16. *State size.*
27 E 5115—Maize only. Not Prepaid. Shipping Weight, 10 oz. **$1.49**

Cotton Gabardine Jodhpurs
Self knee reinforcements and foot-strap. *State waist, and inseam from crotch to below ankle bone.*
Waist: 23, 24, 25, 26 in.
31 E 5112—Tan.. **$2.98**

Cotton Whipcord Riding Breeches
Leather knee reinforcements. *State size.*
Waist: 23, 24, 25, 26 in.
31 E 5117—Tan.. **$2.49**
Jodhpurs and Riding Breeches are sent direct from New York to you.. but you pay postage only from our nearest Mail Order Store. Shipping Weight, each garment, 1 lb. 9 oz.

Smart PLAID BLOUSE **85¢**

Just what you want for Sports

ALL WOOL FLANNEL **$2.98**

BLOUSE **75¢** SKIRT **$1.59**

BLOUSE **98¢** SKIRT **98¢**

Genuine MICKEY MOUSE Watches

YOUR CHOICE $2.98 EACH

Watch Illustrations ¾ Actual Size

$1.39 IN GIFT BOX

Mickey Mouse Watch and Fob
Unbreakable Crystal

An Improved, Smaller Size, Better Model, Mickey Mouse Watch than the Regular Mickey Watches sold.

YOUR BOY is really a "do-er of things" when he owns a Mickey Mouse watch. Genuine thin model Ingersoll. On the dial is Mickey Mouse in gay colors telling you the time with his hands. For a second-hand there are three little Mickeys chasing each other in a circle. Mickey's on the back of the watch, too. And when the watch is in his pocket, Mickey's there, chipper as you please, dangling at the end of the "grown-up" looking fob. Nickel plated case. **4 F 1650** Shpg. wt., 6 oz...... **$1.39**

Mickey Mouse Wrist Watch
Regular $3.75 Value
Big Saving When You Buy at Sears.

Mickey Mouse on a wrist watch! Can you think of anything to please a child more? On the dial is Mickey Mouse in all his glory telling you the time with his hands. For a second hand, three Junior Mickeys chase around in a circle. Two Mickey Mouse characters in enameled colors on the wrist band. Genuine Ingersoll. Chromium plated case, unbreakable crystal. White dial with black figures. Shpg. wt., 6 oz.

| Metal Band. 4 F 950..$2.98 | Leather Band 4 F 951...$2.98 |

Mickey Mouse Alarm Clock

No trick getting up mornings with Mickey Mouse on the job to waken you. Mickey Mouse with his head wagging tells time with his hands. Genuine Ingersoll clock, 30-hour movement. Attractive red or green finish. State color wanted. 4⅝ in. high. Has 3⅝ in. dial. Shpg. wt., 1 lb. 8 oz.
5 F 8518...**$1.39**

Official Boy Scout Watches

...Around the dial are inscribed the 12 scout laws, while the minute hand points to them with this inscription: "A Scout Is." On the hour hand is the scout motto: "Be Prepared." Chromium plated cases and non-breakable crystals. Made by Ingersoll. Shpg. wt., each, 6 oz.

$1.89

Pocket Watch	Wrist Watch
Official colors on dial and hands.	Official colors on dial and hands. Leather Strap.
4 F 1652	Plain Dial 4 F 912........$3.39
Thin model...**$1.89**	Luminous dial 4 F 913........3.89

WHO'S AFRAID OF THE BIG BAD WOLF

Big Bad Wolf Wrist Watch—*$3.75 Value*

With each tick of the watch the Bad Wolf's evil eye is winking at the three little pigs on a bright colored dial. Center opening metal wrist band; decorated with Bad Wolf and Little Pigs. Thin model Chromium plated case. Nonbreakable crystal. Stem wind and stem set. Made by Ingersoll. Shpg. wt., 6 oz.

| Metal Band 4 F 952 $2.98 | Leather Band 4 F 953 $2.98 |

Big Bad Wolf Watch and Fob

With each tick of the watch the Bad Wolf winks at Three Little Pigs on bright colored dial. Dangling from black leather strap is a nickel plated fob with Three Pigs in bright colors. Message from Walt Disney on back of watch. Ingersoll, thin model nickel-plated case. Unbreakable crystal. Shpg. wt., 6 oz.
4 F 1651...........**$1.39**

Big Bad Wolf Alarm Clock

Three Little Pigs Alarm Clock. Ferocious jaws of Bad Wolf open and close with each tick of the clock. Bright red case and dial; little pigs and bad wolf in lifelike colors. Genuine Ingersoll 30-hour movement model. Case 4⅝ in. high with 3⅝-in. dial. Shpg. wt., 1 lb. 8 oz.
5 F 8519........**$1.39**

American Made Popular Size Laddie Wrist Watches

$2.79

Regular $3.50 Laddie Watch. Extremely popular; artistic in shape. Chromium plated case, plain dial. Made exclusively for Sears. A good timekeeper. Shpg. wt., 8 oz. Open link Chromium plated band.

| Metal Band 4 F 1702 $2.79 | Leather wristband 4 F 1703... $2.79 |
For above with luminous dial add 40c.

Genuine Ingraham Popular Priced Wrist Watch

$2.39

Handsome watches in stunning Chromium plated cases. Good timekeeper, too. Ingraham American made. Neat, plain pattern case and band. Raise gilt numerals. Shpg. wt., ea., 8 oz.

| Open Link Metal Band 4 F 1700 $2.39 | Leather Strap 4 F 1701 $2.39 |

Great News for the Youngster
Orphan Annie and Dick Tracy Wrist Watches
Made to Sell for $3.95

All the boys and girls are wearing them ... prize them beyond words. American movement. A fully guaranteed timekeeper. Chromium plated cases. Genuine leather strap. Shpg. wt., each, 8 oz.

| Orphan Annie | Dick Tracy |
| Annie's picture in colors on the dial. The ideal watch for the young American Miss who wants the latest. In attractive Orphan Annie box. **4F1715**...**$3.59** | Sears is right up to the minute with this genuine American Dick Tracy Wrist Watch. Has an official reproduction of Dick Tracy himself in colors on the dial. **4 F 1714**...**$3.59** |

WALDEMAR WATCH CHAINS ... *authentically styled*

Your watch deserves a fine chain. Sears Waldemar watch chains, styled for wear across the chest, are distinctive in appearance. Soldered Links. Expertly made with an eye for practical long wear. Length about, 12½ inches. Shpg. wt., each, 2 oz.

Popular Curb Link Chains—Very Attractive
4 F 1920—10-Karat solid natural gold light-weight about 12½ in. Soldered links.... **$5.98**
4 F 1910—Same as above, but heavier.. **$6.95**
4 F 1914—Same as above, but gold filled.. .89

Simple, Yet Rich-looking
White gold filled Waldemar watch chain. Soldered links. **$1.98**
4 F 1916
Combination white and natural color gold filled Waldemar watch chain. Soldered links. **$1.98**
4 F 1906

Smart Long Wear
Soldered Links. Waldemar chain, nickel, white gold color finish. You'll like it!
4 F 1900..........**69c**

Lots of Style
One of the very latest designs. White gold filled. Copied from a solid gold pattern. 4 F 1918 **$2.98**
Natural and white gold filled combination. 4 F 1908 **$2.98**

Style and Strength. White gold filled Waldemar fancy link. 4 F 1915 **$1.00**
Natural color gold filled. 4 F 1903 1.00

Pretty 10-kt. Solid Gold Chain White Gold. Substantial weight, fancy link. An attractive up to date design. 4 F 1922 **$6.95**
Same pattern as above but natural color gold. 4 F 1912 **$6.95**

Contrasting Color Gold Filled White and Natural gold filled Waldemar watch chain. With carefully soldered links. 4 F 1904... **$1.59**

Vest Chains
Natural color 12-kt gold filled. About 10 in. long. Shpg. wt., 2 oz. 4 F 1952 **$1.98**
14-kt. gold filled. 4 F 1960...**$4.50**

Belt Chains
Natural color gold filled soldered links. Length, 8½ in. Will fit belts up to 1¾ in. wide. Shpg. wt., 2 oz. 4 F 1956 **$1.19**

Dickens' Style
Length, 12 in. Shpg. wt., 2 oz. 4 F 1954 Natural color or rolled gold **$1.79**
4 F 1962—Natural color gold filled.......... **$2.98**

Vest Chain
11 in. long, charm attachment. Shpg. wt., 4 oz. 4 F 1950—Natural color rolled gold plated.. **$1.59**
4 F 1951—Natural color gold filled........ **$2.98**

QUALITY First—QUALITY Always—at *Sears*

Sears NEW Play-Costume Outfits

The Genuine Buck Rogers
A Six-Piece Outfit
- Toy Rocket Pistol. (Harmless.)
- Tan cotton suede cloth helmet with celluloid visor.
- Tan cotton twill breeches, cotton suede cloth puttees.
- Holster for rocket pistol.
- Orange, knit cotton shirt.
- Black cotton sweater with Buck Rogers insignia.

Here he is in his 25th Century outfit! You've heard him on the radio . . . seen him in the comic strip. Now you can join the fun! The Genuine outfit is sold only by Sears at this low price!

EVEN SIZES: 4 to 14 yrs. State age-size. Shpg. wt., 3 lbs. 3 oz.

40 H 4364 Outfit $3.89

A 8-Piece Outfit $1.98

B Outfit With Vest $1.00

C Bargain Special $1.35 8 Pieces

D 8-Piece Outfit $2.59

4-Piece Outfit $1.39

The Big Leaguer
- Striped gray cotton crash.
- Outfit consists of shirt, knickers, belt and cap.

Batter up! Looks just like a big leaguer's outfit! WASHABLE. Wears well and is inexpensive. Bat not included.

EVEN SIZES: 4 to 14 yrs. State age-size. Shipping weight, 1 pound, 5 ounces.

40 H 4382 $1.39
Baseball Suit ....

EVERY REAL BOY Deserves a Play Suit

A "Rodeo Rider"
—Washable cotton flannel plaid shirt; chap style khaki drill pants, side trimmings; pockets and belt.
—Belt with imitation cartridges, extra large pistol and holster. Rope lasso, bandana, cowboy hat.

Ride 'em cowboy! All the woolly western atmosphere you want in this cowboy outfit! Better quality and more elaborate than 40 H 4377.
EVEN SIZES: 4 to 14 years. State age-size. Shpg. wt., 2 lbs. 12 oz.
40 H 4379—8-Pc. Outfit ...$1.98

C "Broncho Buster"
—Checked cotton flannel shirt.
—Long wearing, elastic top khaki pants with genuine leather side trimmings, and showy metal studs.
—Bandana, lasso, belt, holster, toy pistol. Real looking "Cowboy" hat.

It's more fun to play "cowboy" when you've got a regular "broncho-buster" outfit! Our lowest priced complete outfit, and best seller!
EVEN SIZES: 4 to 10 years. State age-size. Shpg. wt., 1 lb. 12 oz.
40 H 4377—Outfit $1.35

B "Dude Rancher"
—Khaki cotton drill, regular style chaps with bright colored belt, side trimmings and metal studs.
—Vest with bright colored trimming.
—Fancy holster, belt and toy pistol.

Take to the trail in your own back yard! Includes all the trappings you need to be a first rate cattleman. Shirt not included.
EVEN SIZES: 4 to 10 years. State age-size. Shpg. wt., 1 lb. 5 oz. $1.00
40 H 4373—Cowboy outfit...

D "Stage Coach Dan"
—Real Western style corduroy front chaps—side trimmings "Doggy" designs.
—Big Western style corduroy topped hat, big toy "Six-Shooter" pistol, real looking holster and belt.
—Brightly colored plaid cotton flannel shirt, rope lasso, and bandana.

Bang! Bang! Now you can be a real Wild West hero. A very elaborate outfit for the price. It's some bargain!
EVEN SIZES: 4 to 14 years. State age-size. Shpg. wt., 2 lbs. 14 oz.
40 H 4352—8-Pc. Outfit... $2.59

10-Gallon Western Style Hat
Black cotton suede cloth. Neat trim. State Size.
SIZES: 6⅝, 6¾, 6⅞, 7, 7⅛.
Shpg.wt., 1 lb.
40 H 4387 59c

Outfit $1.59

6 Piece Outfit $1.98

Flying Ace — Was $2.59
—Coat, and lace-bottom breeches of sturdy cotton khaki drill. Washable.
—Artificial leather belt and puttees. Aviator's helmet and goggles.
EVEN SIZES: 4 to 14 yrs. State age-size. Shpg. wt., 2 lbs. 3 oz.
40 H 4353—Outfit $1.98

Heap Big Chief
—WASHABLE Outfit. Lace front khaki drill coat with bright colored trimming, imitation jewels, metal studs.
—Large headdress, colored feathers.
—Khaki drill pants, colored trimmings.
EVEN SIZES: 4 to 14 yrs. State age-size. Shpg. wt., 1 lb. 8 oz.
40 H 4386—Chief's Outfit $1.59

The Brave's Outfit
Similar to above, but lighter weight drill; smaller headdress, less trim.
EVEN SIZES: 2 to 10 years. State age-size. Shpg. wt., 1 lb. 1 oz.
40 H 4372—Brave's Outfit. $1.00

Juvenile Suits
for Ages 3 to 10 Yrs.

A Five-Piece Outfit

4-Pc. Longie Outfit $1.29

—Tannish brown tweed long pants; about ¼ wool.
—Button-on style tan cotton broadcloth waist. Closed cuff; shirt-style collar and necktie.
—Pants have side openings, side pockets, self-belt and buckle.

Stylish for spring. ALL SIZES: 3 to 9 years. State age-size. Read "How to Order" below. Shpg. wt., 9 oz.
40 H 3106 4-Pc. Longie Outfit $1.29

"Shorts" Outfit

—Brown tweed shorts; side openings. Abt. ½ wool and silk, full lined.
—Button on style tan cotton broadcloth blouse—shirt style collar, and necktie.
—Self belt—buckle.
ALL SIZES: 3 to 9 years. State age-size. Read "How to Order" below. Shpg. wt., 9 oz.
40 H 2515 4-Piece "Shorts" Suit. $1.09
40 H 2516 — Gray shorts, blue waist outfit... $1.09

← 5-Piece Cheviot Suit

—Navy blue twill weave cheviot, about ½ wool.
—Full lined shorts with side pockets. Self-belt with buckle.
—Eton style jacket to match; two patch pockets.
—White cotton broadcloth, button-on style blouse with Eton collar.
—Scarlet four-in-hand tie.

Strong cheviot, about ½ wool, balance cotton. When he wears an Eton Suit . . . he's as well-dressed as a little boy can be.
ALL SIZES: 3 to 10 years. State age-size. Read "How to Order" at left. Shipping weight, 1 pound 7 ounces.
40 H 3300—Navy Blue ½ wool cheviot $1.98

Was $2.45

Now
Was ~~$1.94~~ $1.69

—Navy blue cheviot longies, about one-half wool.
—Self belt, buckle and side pockets in pants.
—Blue cotton broadcloth blouse, button-on style, with rayon necktie.
—Slip-over, navy blue, all wool jersey jacket with neat, classy emblem.
Here's just the thing for early Spring! Bargain Priced. ALL SIZES: 3 to 10 yrs. State age-size. Read "How to Order," below. Shipping weight, 15 ounces.
40 H 2490 5-Piece Outfit $1.69

$4.95 and up

—Brown or navy blue.
—Two-button, single breasted full lined coat; three pockets.
—Single-breasted vest with pockets.
—Cuff bottom longies. Fly front; inside waistband.
ALL SIZES: 4 to 9 yrs. State age-size. Shpg. wt., 2 lbs. 11 oz.
40 H 3120—Brown, about ⁹⁄₁₀ wool and silk cassimere $5.25
40 H 3125—Navy blue half wool cheviot; balance rayon and cotton......$4.95

HOW TO ORDER FOR BOYS OF 3 TO 10 YEARS

Take chest and waist measurements. ORDER AGE-SIZE that corresponds to measurements below:

Age-Size To Order	3	4	5	6	7	8	9	10
Boy's Chest Measure, In.	22	23	24	24½	25	26	26½	27
Waist Measure, Inches	23	23	23½	24	24½	24½	25	25½

← Smart Jaunty RUGBY STYLE SUIT

—Durable Navy blue cheviot Rugby suit; about half wool.
—Full lined shorts; side openings, side pockets.
—Unlined Rugby style jacket. Notched lapels; two, strongly sewed, patch pockets.
—Blue cotton broadcloth button-on style blouse.
—Matching four-in-hand tie.
Rugby . . . the right suit for a boy! He can "treat it rough" . . . it's sturdy cheviot. ALL SIZES: 3 to 8 years. State age-size. Read "How to Order" at left. Shipping weight, 1 pound 5 ounces.
40 H 347 4-Pc. outfit...... $1.89

Bargain Leader for Junior's Wear
79c Cotton Suiting

Sturdy, black and white check cotton suiting or navy blue ½ wool cheviot.
• Dressy cuff bottoms.
• Two side pockets.
• Buttonholes in waistband.
• Self belt and buckle.
• Fly front with buttons.
He can have long pants . . . just like Dad's! Cool, sturdy weight cotton suiting or long-wearing cheviot. Cut to fit . . . well tailored. Low priced.
ALL SIZES. 4 to 9 years. Be sure to state age-size. Read "How to Order," above.
40 H 4468—Black and white check cotton suiting. Shpg. wt., 11 oz......79c
40 H 4467—Navy blue ½ wool cheviot. Shpg. wt., 14 oz.......$1.29

$1.00

Half Wool Shorts

—Navy blue cheviot or medium brown cassimere about one-half wool.
—Full lined shorts with fly front; regular pockets; self belt, buckle.
Have inside waistbands with buttonholes. Full cut and roomy.
ALL SIZES: 3 to 10 years. State age-size. Read "How to Order" above. Shpg. wt., 11 oz.
40 H 4439—Navy Cheviot $1.00
40 H 4440—Med. Brown Cassimere 1.00

75c
Last Spring ~~89c~~

Summer Shorts

—Genuine imported tan check linen or good quality gray cotton covert.
—Unlined. Four pockets. Self belt; buckle.
ALL SIZES: 4 to 15. State age-size. Read "How to Order" above. Shpg. wt., 10 oz.
40 H 4444—Tan Check Linen....75c
40 H 4469—Gray Covert 59c

Shirley Temple FASHIONS

All Wool Fleece Outfit One-Piece Snow Suit with Hat

(A) Hollywood style — at its best! Notice all its brand new fashion points . . . the wide plaid lapels, the ascot-tie, the pocket pipings, the swanky little hat! See how cunning Shirley looks in it! One-piece outdoor suit of heavy weight All Wool Fleece, the fine quality that takes those rich lovely colorings. Expertly tailored.
Ages: 2-3-4-5-6 yrs.
State age-size.
38 K 7932—Blue.
38 K 7933—Green.
Shipping weight, 2 lbs. 12 oz.

$5.95

All Wool Fleece Herringbone Coat, Legging and Hat Set

(B) Of course, Shirley's three-piece coat set had to be the very finest quality! It's so soft it feels like velvet, so closely woven it will wear extra long. Beautifully made in every detail. Coat is warmly interlined and lined with Rayon Taffeta. Hat has snap-on earmuffs. Talon slide fastened leggings.
Ages: 2-3-4-5-6 yrs.
State age-size.
38 K 6373—Blue.
38 K 6374—Red.
Shipping weight, 3 lbs. 14 oz.

$10.95

A whole page of cunning Shirley Temple Fashions! In big city stores they're going like wildfire! Shirley and her cute clothes have stolen everyone's heart; no wonder every little girl wants to wear the same styles!

Shirley Temple Dolls

Without Panties

With Panties

These dresses exemplify the beautiful costumes worn by Shirley Temple. The materials are of the finest wash fabrics available. The workmanship is exquisite. The trim is in keeping with the quality of the dresses, and the beautiful styles designed for Shirley. We will send you the dresses shown or equal values developed from Shirley's costumes in her latest pictures.
Ages: 3, 4, 5, 6 and 6½ years. *State age.*
38 K 5942—Blue.
38 K 5943—Red.
Shipping weight, 8 oz.

$1.89 each

38 K 5944—Red.
38 K 5945—Blue.
Shipping weight, 10 oz.

Shirley Temple Hats →

This favorite is made of fine all wool body felt. Stitched brim and fine ribbon bow! Shipping weight, 1 lb.
78 K 6485—Fits 20 to 20½ inch.
78 K 6486—Fits 20¾ to 21¼ inch headsize.

$1.79

Colors: Sand with Brown ribbon or Brown with Sand, Solid Navy or Solid Red. *Measure and state color.*

All Wool Three-Piece Suit —Coat, Hat and Pants

One of Shirley's favorites! Zip closing. *State age-size.*
Shipping wt., 3 lbs. 6 oz.
Ages: 7-8-9-10 Years
31 K 2960—Navy with Red and Blue Check.
31 K 2961—Brown with Orange and Brown Check **$7.95**
Ages: 3-4-5-6 Years
31 K 2963—Navy with Blue and Red Check.
31 K 2964—Brown with Orange and Brown Check **$6.95**

All Wool . . . Extra Warm Coat and Hat Outfit

Wide turn-back collar is silky-soft Beaver-Dyed Coney Fur! Coat is warm wool, interlined with deep-napped cotton flannel. Has four-button closing with two ornamental buttons. Rayon and cotton taffeta lined. Belted back.
Ages: 7-8-9-10 years. *State size.*
17 K 4665—Rust.
17 K 4666—Medium Blue.
17 K 4667—Medium Brown.
Shipping wt., 3 lbs. 6 oz.

$10.95

Shirley's Bolero-Dress! A 7 to 12 Year Style

America's First Lady of Fashion certainly knows a cunning style when she sees it! This "ensemble" would be the prize possession of any lucky little girl who owned it! Washfast percale check dress, pleated at back, too. Vat dyed jacket.
Ages: 7-8-10 and 12 years. *State age-size.*
27 K 4296—Red and Navy.
27 K 4297—Copen Blue and Navy.
Shpg. wt., 12 oz.

$1.89

Hair Bow

On band Cameo Center Elastic back.
Colors: Maize, Pink, Lt. Blue, White, Red or Nile. *State Color.*
Shpg. wt., 2 oz.
25 K 1217—Satin
25 K 1218—Rayon Moire.

14¢ each. 2 for 27¢

A complete Shirley Temple wardrobe for the little miss

Husky Well Made
PLAY SUITS
39c

(A) Dirt and rough-and-tumble play won't hurt this suit! Made of a good quality washable Chambray. Long legs; drop seat. Buttons down front. Red piping. Ages: 1, 2, 3, 4, 5, 6 yrs. State age-size. Shipping weight, 6 ounces.
38 H 6115—Blue

Chambray

45c EACH

(B) **Choice of Two Serviceable Materials.** Stoutly made, well-sewed, playsuits. Double needle seams throughout. Drop seat. Open down front. Ages: 2, 3, 4, 5, 6, 7 yrs. State age. Shpg. wt., 8 oz.
38 H 6154—Blue Pinstripe
38 H 6155 Hickory Stripe **45c**

(C) **Chambray—Serviceable** Strong Peg Top play suit. Good quality chambray that will stand soap and water and come out looking fresh and new! Opens down back. Five-button drop seat. Ages: 2, 3, 4, 5, 6, 7 yrs. State age. Shpg. wt., 7 oz.
38 H 6152—Blue
38 H 6153—Green **45c**

Self Help Drop Seat

98c

Covert

(D) **A New Play Suit** Choice of two serviceable, better quality, heavyweight cotton fabrics. Gay Turkey Red piping on collar and cuffs and fancy pockets. Buttons down front. "Self-Help" drop seat. Suits will wear and wear. Ages: 1, 2, 3, 4, 5, 6 years. State age. Shpg. wt., 7 oz.
38 H 6120—Blue Chambray
38 H 6121 Blue Covert **59c**

(E) **2-Piece Overall Style Play Suit.** Good quality cotton covert cloth. Tailored overalls with blouse that can be worn inside or out, with Talon hookless fastener and wide elastic at waist to prevent riding up. Adjustable straps on overall. Ages: 2, 3, 4, 5, 6 yrs. State age. Shpg. wt., 9 oz.
38 H 6104—Tan
38 H 6105—Blue
38 H 6106—Green **98c**

Gay ~SUNSHINE~ Clothes! So Healthful!

Cotton Broadcloth

Checked Cotton Print Little girls will adore this "ruffly" type of romper suit! Just the thing to wear on warm sunshiny days! Low back. Drop seat. Elastic at legs. Ages: 2, 4, and 6 years. State age-size. Shpg. wt., 4 oz.
38 H 6118—Blue
38 H 6119 Red **49c**

Backless Style Little boys like the freedom of action and the comfort of this healthful Sun Suit of good quality Cotton Broadcloth. Suspender back. Ages: 2, 3, 4, 5, 6 yrs. State age. Shpg. wt., 4 oz.
38 H 5456—White with Red
38 H 5457 Navy with White **59c**

Striped Printed Madras For Sister's sun tan—this Nautical one-piece suit with pleated shorts is perfect! It's backless and has a smart pique embroidered sailor collar. Elastic at sides of waist to make it fit snugly. Ages: 2, 3, 4, 5, 6 yrs. State age. Shpg. wt., 5 oz.
38 H 6128—Blue
38 H 6129 Red **79c**

Cotton Linene

Well Made Two-Piece Suit Dapper well cut little suit with cotton linene pants, novelty belt and cotton broadcloth waist. Ages: 1, 2, 3, 4 yrs. State age-size. Shpg. wt., 6 oz.
38 H 5452—Brown with yellow
38 H 5453 Blue with white **49c**

3-Piece Eton Suit **A dandy boys' suit— and a big value** The jacket and pants are of cotton linene. Sleeveless waist is of good quality broadcloth. Ages: 1, 2, 3, 4 years. State age-size. Shpg. wt., 8 oz.
38 H 5451 Oyster white **79c**

2-Piece Polo Suit Sporty—and what every boy likes! A cotton mesh polo style shirt with V-neck. Can be worn inside or out. Applique trim. Cotton broadcloth pants with wide elastic at back. Ages: 1, 2, 3, 4, 5, 6 yrs. State age. Shpg. wt., 5 oz.
38 H 5454—Blue w white top
38 H 5455 All Yellow **59c**

CHAMBRAY OR COVERT
↑ **59c**

39c EACH

Good Cotton Broadcloth Carefully made. Two-piece, sleeveless summer suit at a bargain price. All around belt. Ages: 1, 2, 3, 4, 5, 6 yrs. State age. Shpg. wt., 5 oz.
38 H 5496—White
38 H 5495—Yellow
38 H 5497—Blue

Sturdy Cotton Seersucker **Reduced from 59c** Two piece suit of such good quality it can be washed again and again! No ironing required! Ages: 1, 2, 3, 4, 5, 6 yrs. State age. Shpg. wt., 6 oz.
38H5407—Blue
38H5408—Tan

Service Weight Chambray Well fitting, overalls with strong seams. Will wear and wear. Adjustable shoulder straps. Buy several at this bargain price. Ages: 2, 4, and 6 years. State age-size. Shipping weight, 6 oz.
38 H 6171 Blue **29c**

Sears for QUALITY
at its LOWEST PRICE
Back-less for Healthful Sun-rays!

59c

2-piece Cotton Seersucker with Pleated Shorts Healthful to play in—easy to wash! No ironing necessary. Separate pleated shorts button on to backless waist. Let "Sis" play in them all day long—they are practical, sturdy and inexpensive. Seams all strongly stitched. Ages: 2, 3, 4, 5, 6 years. State age-size. Shpg. wt., 6 oz.
38 H 6122—Blue
38 H 6123—Red

Novel Overalls with Knitted Mesh Top

A crackerjack of a play outfit! Overalls of sturdy cotton linene have the tailored, well fitting appearance of high priced garments. The sweater style waist is of knitted cotton mesh. Ages: 2, 3, 4, 5, 6 yrs. State age-size. Shpg. wt., 6 oz.
38 H 6124 Blue and white **$1.00**

Sears BARGAIN SPECIAL

All 3 for 89c
- Fine Quality Nainsook. The quality of this set of 3 beautiful hand-embroidered dresses will appeal to you more than the low price. Soft fine material, colorful hand trim, careful stitching, deep hems. **New reduced price!** Ages: 6 mos., 1 and 2 years. State age. Shpg. wt., 5 oz.
38 H 5241—White

All 3 for 85c
- Soft Nainsook Bishop Slips. For every new baby. Keep a supply of these good quality Bishop Slips handy. They are carefully made and daintily finished with lace edging at neck and sleeves. Sold as a set only at a new lowered price. Full size, about 21 in. long. Infants' Size only. Shipping weight, 5 oz.
38 H 5001—White.

You'll Adore These Baby Clothes!
ALL HAND MADE
HAND EMBROIDERED from the Philippines

DRESS 49c — (A)
DRESS 79c — (B)
DRESS 95c — (C)
CREEPER 59c — (D)
SUNSUIT 49c — (E)
DRESS 59c — (F)
SLIP 29c — (G)
Complete Set $1.25 — (H)

EXQUISITE NEEDLEWORK!
Every one of these lovely garments completely made by hand in the Philippines. All beautifully embroidered on fine materials! All inexpensively priced for the excellent quality they are!

Three Charming Dresses and Slips
Soft, snowy white cotton Batiste, lavishly hand worked with tiny stitches, scallops, tucks! Every stitch by hand! Ages—6 mos., 1 and 2 yrs. State age. Shpg. wt., ea., 3 oz.
(A) Batiste Dress and Slip—Good Quality! 38 H 5244—Dress..49c 38 H 5245—Slip...39c
(B) Batiste Dress and Slip—Generously Embroidered 38 H 5246—Dress..79c 38 H 5247—Slip..49c
(C) Batiste Dress and Slip—Our Finest Quality 38 H 5268—Dress..95c 38 H 5269—Slip..69c

(D) **Creeper—Better Quality Cotton Broadcloth** All handmade. Buttons across bottom. Ages—6 mos., 1 and 2 yrs. State age size. Shpg. wt., 4 oz.
38 H 6001—White 38 H 6002—Blue
38 H 6003—Yellow 59c

(E) **Suspender Sun Suit! Fine Cotton Broadcloth!** Cunning! Assorted hand applique and embroidery trim. Buttons at side for easy laundering. Ages—1, 2 and 3 years. State age size. Shpg. wt., 3 oz.
38 H 6032—Blue 38 H 6033—Yellow
38 H 6034—White. Each 49c

(F) **Toddler Dress in Pretty Colors** Very lovely! Soft sheer cotton Batiste. Daintily hand embroidered. Pin-tucks! Deep hem. Pastel colors! Ages—6 mos., 1 and 2 yrs. State age size. Shipping weight, 3 oz.
38 H 5236—Pink 38 H 5237—Blue
38 H 5238—Yellow. Each 59c

(G) **Cotton Batiste Gertrude Slip** Hand scalloped hem, neck and armholes. Buttons over shoulder! A special value! Unusual low price for all hand-made slip. Ages—6 mos., 1 and 2 yrs. State age size. Shipping weight, 2 ounces.
38 H 5212—White 29c

(H) **Long Christening Set** Sheer white cotton Batiste Dress and Gertrude Slip to match. Dress exquisitely hand embroidered in front from top to bottom. Tiny tucks. Scalloped hems! About 21 in. long. Infants' Size only. Shipping weight, set, 3 oz.
38 H 5216 Dress......79c 38 H 5217 Slip......49c 38 H 5218 Set......$1.25

New Low Price

CHAMBRAY A FAVORITE OVERALL
Sears have reduced the price on these Baby's overalls, in spite of increased costs! Here it is—the same good quality Chambray, the same careful workmanship. Fast color good quality Chambray with Turkey red trim. Ages—1, 2, 3, and 4 years. State age-size. Shpg. wt., 4 oz.
38 H 6014 Blue Chambray.......25c

SOLD AS A SET 3 Creepers
Isn't this a value? Three well made hand embroidered good quality Cotton Broadcloth Creepers—full cut. Open leg style. Button across bottom. Ages—6 mos., 1, 2 yrs. State age-size. Shipping weight, set, 7 ounces.
38 H 6035—Three creepers in assorted colors; Blue, Pink and Yellow........3 for 95c

Hand Embroidered Cotton Broadcloth Creeper
Little ones are filled with pride when mother dresses them up in this better quality Puerto Rican made creeper! Hand smocked and embroidered. All around belt. Open leg style. Buttons across bottom. Ages—6 mos., 1, 2 yrs. State age-size. Shpg. wt., 4 oz.
38 H 6023—Blue 38 H 6024—Pink 49c

2-Piece Dimity and Cotton Broadcloth
Toddler Suit. Pants are plain color cotton broadcloth and button onto pleated waist of sheer white, shadow striped dimity. Ruffle on collar. Applique embroidery at cap sleeve. Pants button across bottom. Ages—1, 2, 3 years. State age-size. Shipping weight, 4 ounces.
38 H 6012—Blue 38 H 6013—Yellow 79c

Our Best Quality Cotton Broadcloth Creepers
Sears "Best" means better material, longer wear, better workmanship. You'll find all three features in these darling creepers. Front smocked and embroidered. Belt. Open leg style. Buttons across bottom. Ages—6 mo., 1, 2 yrs. State age-size. Shpg. wt., 4 oz.
38 H 6036—White 38 H 6037—Pink 38 H 6038—Blue....69c

Hand Smocked and Embroidered Easy to Tub and Iron
A price reduction worthy of note! The most stylish little girl will be delighted when she sees this pretty silk dress of weighted Crepe. Really a simple sweet style, hand embroidered and smocked. Makes a lovely gift. Ages—6 mo., 1, 2 yrs. State age size. Shpg. wt., 4 oz.
38 H 5239—White 38 H 5240—Pink....79c

A $6⁹⁵
Wool and Silk

B $7⁷⁵
Two-Tone Vest Suit

From Maine to California, the Choice of Best-Dressed Boys

2-Piece Suit $4³⁹
3-Piece **E** $5⁴⁹

2-Piece Suit $4⁹⁵
3-Piece $5⁹⁵ **F**

1935's Style SENSATION
NEW SPORT BACK

C
One-Trouser Suit
$8⁹⁵
Two-Trouser Suit $11⁴⁵

Today's Value $10⁴⁵
One Pants Suit

- Center Bellows Pleat; Yoke and Half Belt With Tuck Pleats
- Fine ALL WOOL Suiting in Popular Check Pattern
- Pleated, Cuff-Bottom Trousers

D $7⁹⁸ "Free Swing"

"Free Swing" Action Back
H $7⁹⁸

Last Fall $8⁴⁵

Wool and Silk

IT'S NEW
Hollywood's Own Style!

- Pleated, Sport Back Hollywood Jacket With Yoke and Half Belt
- Pleated Slacks, Slide Fastener Fly. Wide Cuff Bottoms

2-Piece Outfit
$5⁴⁵ **G**

Pleated Slacks
Slide Fastener Front

$1⁸⁹ **$1**⁷⁹

Junior Police Coat

-Strong cotton sheeting coated with a heavy layer of pure black rubber.
—Metal buckle fasteners.

Guaranteed 100% waterproof! Seams are cemented and steam vulcanized to keep out rain or sleet. Two big side pockets with flaps. Thousands sold each year!

SIZES: 6, 8, 10, 12, 14, 16, and 18 years. State age-size. Shpg. wt., 2 lbs. 14 oz. Read "How to Order" below.

40 D 3358—Black Rubber **$1.89**
Storm Coat.......................

40 D 3961—Sou'wester hat to match. ALL SIZES: 6½ to 7⅜. State size. Shipping weight, 8 oz...............**49c**

Our Lowest Price!

—Heavyweight waterproof **embossed black artificial leather.**
—Cotton suede cloth lining.

Here's the way to keep him warm and dry . . . inexpensively! Heavy artificial leather protects him from showers. The cotton suede cloth lining helps to keep him warm. Roomy raglan shoulders. Belt all around with ring buckle. Two deep slanting pockets. Take it from us, it's a real raincoat "buy"!

ALL SIZES: 6 to 16 years. State age-size. Read "How to Order" below. Shipping weight, 3 lbs. 14 oz.

40 D 3373—Black Artificial **$1.79**
Leather Raincoat................

INSIST ON THE ORIGINAL
BUCKSKEIN
TRADE MARK   REG. U.S. PAT. OFF.

WATERPROOF   WINDPROOF

$3⁹⁸

—Soft, leather-like, cotton suede cloth —never cracks or wrinkles.
—Withstood 40 pounds of water pressure.
—A 60-mile per hour wind can't penetrate.
—Washable fast color material.
—Double texture for extra warmth.

"Buckskein" double texture suede cloth with handsome fast color check cotton lining and interlining of rubber. Double breasted with raglan shoulders. Wide convertible collar. All-around belt with buckle. Genuine leather buttons and buckles. Adjustable storm tabs on sleeves keep out the wind and dampness. Seams are double stitched throughout for extra strength and wear. Can be worn as a topcoat or a raincoat. Smart and serviceable, rain or shine.

SIZES: 8, 10, 12, 14, 16, and 18 yrs. State age-size. Shpg. wt., 4 lbs. 2 oz.

40 D 3375—Honey **$3.98**
Brown Buckskein Coat....

40 D 3376—Navy Blue
Buckskein Coat.............**$3.98**

HOW TO ORDER

Take chest measure close up under arms snug but not tight over shirt or blouse. Be sure the tape is over shoulder blades at back. Our coats are cut extra large; therefore it is not necessary to make allowance for other clothing. Order corresponding age-size below.

Chest size, in..	24½	25½	26	27	27½	28½
Age-size	6	7	8	9	10	11

Chest size, in....	29	30	30½	31½	32	33	34
Age-size	12	13	14	15	16	17	18

BE A G-MAN
- RAINPROOF
- WINDPROOF
- MADE OF RUBBERIZED COTTON TWILL GABARDINE

G MEN

$3⁷⁹

Choice of Navy Blue or Chocolate Brown

Here it is, fellows! The nationally known "G-Men" raincoat sold exclusively by mail thru Sears. Heavy weight, double texture, water-proof cotton twill gabardine with a cotton plaid lining. Swagger raglan shoulders with detachable metal "G-Men" insignia on the epaulets. Shoulder seams are strapped and cemented for extra protection against leakage. Two deep slash open through pockets, piped on the inside. Regulation trench flap at neck to keep out rain and wind. High grade metal buttons—look like leather. It's just the coat for a real American boy to wear. Keeps him dry—keeps him warm—and there isn't a better looking raincoat to be had.

SIZES: 6, 8, 10, 12, 14, 16, 18 yrs. State age-size. Read "How to Order" below at left. Shpg. wt., 3 lbs. 11 oz.

40 D 3362—Navy Blue G-Man Raincoat........
40 D 3363—Chocolate Brown G-Man Coat. **$3.79**

Boyville
RAINCOAT DRYNESS
TOPCOAT WARMTH

$2⁹⁸

—**Waterproof** brown check cotton tweed.
—Brown plaid lining with interlining of rubber.
—Double breasted style with raglan shoulders.
—All around belt and buckle.
—Two big slash pockets.

He'll wear this coat rain or shine! When it rains, it's a weather-beating storm coat! When it shines, it's one of the smartest topcoats you'll see anywhere! Buttons snugly across the chest to keep out wind and rain. Convertible collar can be worn up or down. Genuine leather buttons. Adjustable storm tabs on sleeves. Double stitched throughout. You know the quality is exceptional because it's a Boyville! Priced to give you an out-of-the-ordinary value!

ALL SIZES: 6 to 18 years. State age-size. Read "How to Order" at left. Shipping weight, 3 pounds 10 ounces.

40 D 3377—Brown Check Tweed Coat......**$2.98**

▲ **SEARS-ROEBUCK** ▪

Berets (Bless 'em!) *are always becoming!*

25¢ B **29¢** C **33¢** D **39¢** E

THE *Sailor-Mate* **SHIPS ANCHOR!**

59¢ (A) Ahoy there, my lass! Here's an anchor beret in bright all wool felt cloth. Stand up ribbons. **COLORS:** Rust 609, Navy 214, Red 511, Green 313, Royal Blue 211. *Measure and state color.* 78 D 9410—Fits 21¾ to 22½ in. Shipping weight, 10 ozs.

(B) A regular Highland Tam! Bonnie Tweed, closely knit of fine Cotton Boucle. Fluffy rayon pompon! **COLORS:** Brown 614, Royal 211, Wine 514, Rust 609, Green 313. *Measure and state color.* 78 D 9690—Fits up to 22½-inch headsize. Shipping weight, 4 ounces........ **25¢**

(C) Jaunty, feather-spiked tam with a stiffened visor brim, knit of warm brushed rayon in fluffy finish. Looks and feels like wool. **COLORS:** Brown 614, Navy 214, Wine 514, Green 313, Royal Blue 211. *Measure and state color.* 78 D 9200—Fits up to 22½-inch headsize. Shipping weight, 4 ounces......... **29¢**

(D) All wool felt cloth with brightly piped crown and a smart composition ornament. Elastic in back. A smart "buy!" **COLORS:** Brown 614, Navy 214, Red 511, Royal Blue 211, Green 313, Rust 609. *Measure and state color.* 78 D 9705—Fits up to 22½ inch headsize. Shipping weight, 4 ounces......... **33¢**

(E) All wool! Hand crocheted of full, fluffy yarns in close stitch. Topped with bright yarn pompon. Elastic at edge. **COLORS:** White, Brown 614, Royal Blue 211, Red 511, Green 313, Rust 609. *Measure and state color.* 78 D 9700—Fits up to 23-inch headsize. Shipping weight, 3 ounces......... **39¢**

She'll be SO PROUD! You'll be SO PLEASED! with her new *"Class-mate"* HAT!
REG. U. S. PAT. OFF.

Shirley Temple's **FAVORITE**

1 79 The same hat — the same quality that Shirley Temple wears! And to prove it — there's a Shirley Temple label inside! Fine soft all wool body felt. Rayon cord ties. Ages: 6 to 12 years. **COLORS:** Brown 614, Navy 214, Red 511. *Measure and state color.* 78 D 9710—Fits 20⅛ to 20¾-inch headsize. 78 D 9711—Fits 21 to 21⅝-inch headsize. Shipping wt., 1 lb.

Be Sure to MEASURE! Little Heads Grow Rapidly!

Jane Withers **WEARS IT!**

1 00 Lively, loveable Jane Withers wears this hat of fine all wool body felt! Banded with ribbon to match rayon pompon. An elastic slips under her curls. Jane Withers label in each hat. Ages 10 to 16 years. **COLORS:** Sand 604, Navy 214, Red 511, Brown 614, Green 313. *State color.* 78 D 9715—Fits 21¼ to 21¾-inch headsize. Shipping wt., 1 lb.

59¢ The tam is good *all* wool felt cloth. Bright ribbons! **COLORS:** Brown 614, Royal Blue 211, Red 511. *State color.* 78 D 9730—Fits 21 to 21½-inch head. Ages 6 to 10. Shipping wt., 4 ounces.

A clever, perky little hat and a *good* one! Made of fine, all wool body felt with ribbon laced crown and 2-tone ribbon top-knot! Elastic slips under her curls. **COLORS:** Brown 614, Navy 214, Red 511, Green 313. *Measure and state color.* 78 D 9370—Fits 21¼ to 21¾-inch headsize. Ages 10 to 15 years. Shipping weight, 1 pound.

59¢ All the dash of the Highlander's cap in this warm, all wool felt cloth hat. Multi-colored ribbon and bright feathers. Ages 7 to 12 years. **COLORS:** Brown 614, Navy 214, Red 511. *Measure and state color.* 78 D 9535—Fits 21 to 21¾-inch heads. Shipping weight, 4 ounces.

89¢ Ages 9 to 13. It's the Homburg! Same care-free rolled brim, same jaunty dented crown. All wool body felt with ribbon and feathers. **COLORS:** Brown 614, Navy 214, Red 511. *State color.* 78 D 9540—Fits 21 to 21½-inch head. Shipping wt., 1 lb.

59¢ All wool felt cloth. For ages 6 to 12 years. **COLORS:** Brown with Orange, Navy with Red, Dk. Green with Light Green, or Red with Navy. *State color.* 78 D 9735—Fits 20¼ to 20¾-in. headsize. 78 D 9736—Fits 21 to 21½. Shipping wt., 1 pound.

Color-Numbers refer to "Color-Graph" facing first Index page.

89¢ Made popular by America's best loved little girl. All wool body felt with bright flat felt flowers in front, and ribbon ties. **COLORS:** Brown 614, Red 511, or Royal Blue 211. *State color.* 78 D 9415—Fits 20⅛ to 21¼-inch head. Ages 7 to 10. Shipping weight, 1 pound.

77¢ All wool "body" felt with "up-ordown" brim. Fits ages 8 to 15 years. **COLORS:** Brown 614, Navy 214, Red 511, or Sand 604. *State color.* 78 D 9545—Fits 20½ to 21-inch headsize. 78 D 9546—Fits 21¼ to 21¾. Shipping wt. one pound.

"Look! The Bag Matches My Hat!"

95¢ For ages 8 to 12. Lacings and bright pompons in knitted half wool and cotton. Matching bag. **COLORS:** Brown 614, Red 511, Navy 214. *State color.* 78 D 9205—Fits 21 to 21¾-in. Shipping wt., 1 lb.

"And My Scarf Matches Mine!"

49¢ Hat and scarf made of soft, wooly-finished brushed cotton. Predominating **COLORS:** Brown, Navy, Green or Red Plaids. *State color.* 78 D 9685—Fits up to 21½-inch heads. Ages 6 to 12. Shipping weight, 8 ounces.

95¢ The "big girls" will envy this smart off-the-face hat. Made of good all wool body felt, gathered at the front with 2-tone ribbons and shiny metal buttons. Ages 10 to 15. **COLORS:** Brown 614, Red 511, Navy 214. *State color.* 78 D 9230—Fits 21¼ to 21¾-inch headsizes. Shipping wt., 1 lb.

Color-Numbers refer to "Color-Graph" facing first Index page.

SEARS-ROEBUCK

TUNNEL COLLAR
Swagger!

Ages 10 to 14
6⁴⁸

Ⓐ

Ages 6 to 9
5⁴⁸

Remember Last Winter!
Class-mate
COATS

**ARE EXTRA-WARM
FOR ZERO WEATHER**

Ⓒ
**COAT, HAT,
SCARF, MUFF!**
6⁷⁵ SET

Ⓓ
Fur Trimmed
COAT, MUFF
6⁹⁸ SET

Ⓑ
Glorious **PLAID
FISHTAIL**
Ages 10 to 16
5⁹⁸

Fur Trimmed **COAT WITH BERET**

Ages 6 to 9   6⁹⁸ SET

Ages 10 to 14   7⁹⁸ SET

Fur Muff   1²⁹

Our Warmest **COAT**

✦ **4-STAR** ✦
**FEATURE
VALUE**

Ages 6 to 9
3⁴⁸

Age 10 to 14
4⁴⁸

Ⓔ

Ages 6 to 9
5⁴⁸

Ages 10 to 16
6⁴⁸

Ⓕ

Ⓖ

• **SEARS-ROEBUCK** •

YOUNG AMERICA SHOP

NEAT ZIP FRONT

Better Quality All Wool Worsted $1.39

A splendid value—most sweaters of this fine quality would cost you more. All wool worsted in better "links" knitting, firmer, more even stitches. Practical style with Byron collar, two pockets and contrasting trim. Medium serviceable weight. Nicely made.

Sizes: 4, 5–6, 7–8 years. State age-size. Shipping weight, 8 ounces.
38 K 7732—Legion Blue 212
38 K 7733—Red 508
38 K 7734—Gypsy Brown 623

Zip Slipover for Boys or Girls $1.19

Record breaking value! We sold similar quality for as much as $1.35 last year! Every thread All Wool Worsted—a warm, sturdy sweater, ideal for school! Zip style too—easy to slip into, neat-looking. Smart contrasting striped trim. Medium weight.

Sizes: 4, 5–6, 7–8 years. State age-size. Shipping weight, 7 ounces.
38 K 7735—Red 508
38 K 7736—Legion Blue 212
38 K 7737—Gypsy Brown 623

HEIGH-HO! THE 7 DWARFS And Ole Friend MICKEY MOUSE!

ALL SEVEN . . .
Sneezy, Grumpy, Happy, Bashful, Sleepy, Doc, Dopey, too!

Slipovers Made for Wear—and FUN!

Your young movie fan will want both styles—Mickey's such an old friend and now we have those jolly Seven Dwarfs too!—every last one of them, even darling Dopey! Sweaters that are "tops" for stout wear—sturdy *tubfast* cotton knit, medium heavy weight. Fleeced inside for extra warmth. (Designs printed on; doll not included.)
Sizes: 2, 3–4, 5–6, 7–8 years. State age-size. Shipping wt., each, 8 oz.

YOUNG AMERICA SHOP

DOUBLE FABRIC THROUGHOUT

ALL WOOL

SEARS Super Quality

$1.69 Set ©

$2.39 Set ©

$1.98 Set Ⓐ

$2.98 Set Ⓑ

SCHOOL GIRLS' FAVORITE — ALL WOOL TWIN SETS — FOR SCHOOL SPORTS, DRESS-UP

Ⓐ *Smart Medium Weight Set*
Grand serviceable twin set for all around wear. Good quality wool worsted. Crew neck cardigan has smart wooden buttons, fancy front. Short sleeve slip-on.
Sizes: 7–8, 9–10, 11–12, 13–14 years. State age-size. Shipping weight, 1 pound.
38 K 7518—Royal Blue 218
38 K 7519—Rust 609
38 K 7520—Bright Red 511..............$1.98

© *Brushed All Wool Set*
Sears dependable quality—low priced! Medium weight twin set in soft richly brushed all wool. Ribbed knit details. Crew neck. Slipover has short sleeves and is pretty worn alone too!

Ⓑ *New Two-Tone Zephyr Set*
"Tops" in style and quality! Newest details . . . grosgrain ribbon button band and smart buttons on cardigan. Allover fancy design, short sleeve slipover, 4-button opening. Fine soft all wool Zephyr.
Sizes: 7–8, 9–10, 11–12, 13–14 years. State age-size. Shipping weight, 1 pound 3 ounces.
38 K 7523—Light Brown 611 and Gold 709
38 K 7524—Navy Blue 214 and Red 508 ...$2.98

© *Links Knit Wool Worsted*
Here's a "gem" of an all wool worsted twin set. Looks lots higher priced! Both sweaters are *links knit in fancy allover design*. Cardigan has smart student collar. Short sleeve pullover with Brooks neck.

LATEST THING OUT!

Sonja Henie SWEATERS AND CAPS
SOLD ONLY AT SEARS BY MAIL

Pullover	Cap	Pullover	Toque
$1.59	59c	$1.89	59c

Every girl will be proud of her Sonja Henie sweater! Sporty wide ribbed knit pullover with smart contrasting color trim. Good quality softer, warmer all wool Zephyr.
Sizes: 7–8, 9–10, 11–12, 13–14 years. State age-size. Shipping weight, 13 ounces.
38 K 7514—Royal Blue 212
38 K 7515—Red 512.....$1.59
Hockey Cap—DOUBLE FABRIC Wool worsted. One size only. Shipping weight, 5 ounces.
38 K 8336—Royal Blue 212
38 K 8337—Red 512 ......59c

Dandy sweater . . . endorsed by Sonja Henie too! Warm as toast . . . it's *double fabric* throughout, even the sleeves. 54% wool worsted, balance cotton for added strength. Medium weight.
Sizes: 7–8, 9–10, 11–12, 13–14 yrs. State age-size. Shipping weight, 1 lb. 2 oz.
38 K 7516—Red 508
38 K 7517—White......$1.89
All Wool Toque—Shaker knit; vari-colored tassels. One size only. Shipping weight, 5 oz.
38 K 8334—Red 508
38 K 8335—White.........59c

For You!

FROM HOLLYWOOD'S
ADORABLE
GIRL STAR

Judy Garland
FASHIONS

FOR 10 TO 16's

LASTEX
WAIST
BLOUSE **98c**

ALL WOOL
PLAID
SKIRT **$1.95**

PLAIN
ALL WOOL
SKIRT

$1.95

CHARMING STYLES FOR GIRLS OF 10 TO 16

Accordion Pleats ... Plaid Trim $2.98

Everybody's in love with the crisp accordion-pleated skirt ... the button-front shirtwaist blouse with its trim collar, full puff sleeves, swanky pockets. In fine-quality all Rayon Pebble Crepe with bright Plaid Rayon Taffeta trim ... it's a dress you'll enjoy for school or dress-up. Well-tailored ... Sears best quality ... *excellent* value!

Sizes: 10, 12, 14, 16 years. **State age-size.** Shpg. wt., 1 lb. 6 oz.

27 K 4648—Royal Blue 218
27 K 4649—Zinnia Rust 609.$2.98

Stud-Effect "Jewel" Buttons $1.98

The Gaucho-Girl fashion for 10 to 16's with style details galore! Fine quality All Rayon Pebble Crepe in two-tone design ... shirtwaist with sparkly stud effect jewel buttons and perky bow is in lighter tone. Gaucho belt, gaily laced, and full, 12-gored skirt is deep-toned for effective contrast.

Sizes: 10, 12, 14, 16 years. **State age-size.** Shpg. wt., 1 lb. 6 oz.
27 K 4646—Capri Blue 220 Blouse; Navy 214 Skirt
27 K 4647—Dusty Pink 535 Blouse; Wine 514 Skirt...$1.98

Three-Piece Suspender Frock $1.98

Stunning! Two dresses in one, and a skirt, blouse or bolero to wear separately! The very chic Suspender skirt with 2-inch hem in fine quality All Rayon Pebble Crepe with crisp blouse of Plaid All Rayon Taffeta! Charming Bolero jacket too ... a style you'll adore for its pretty puff sleeves, wide revers faced with matching plaid.

Sizes: 10, 12, 14, 16 years. **State age-size.** Shpg. wt., 1 lb. 6 oz.

27 K 4650—Navy; Plaid Trim

27 K 4651—Wine; Plaid Trim. .$1.98

COLOR NUMBERS REFER TO COLOR-GRAPH IN BACK OF CATALOG ...

Judy Garland *swank, girls!* And prices are *low!* Blouse in fine-quality Slub yarn Cotton Broadcloth. *Choice of two skirts* in our finest-quality All Wool fabrics, expertly tailored ... 10-gore Kiltie Plaid or plain Flannel, 15-button-front style with zip pocket. Sizes: 10, 12, 14, 16.

Gypsy-Style Blouse
Shipping weight, 6 ounces.
Shirred Lastex band at waist. *Pearl buttons!*
27 K 4634—White, Powder Blue 225, Bittersweet 512.
State color and size.......98c

All Wool Plaid Skirt
Shipping weight, ea., 1 lb. 4 oz.
27 K 4637—Red and Navy Plaid. Sizes below.....$1.95
All Wool Flannel Skirt
Sizes below. **State size..$1.95**
27 K 4638—Navy 214
27 K 4639—Brown 614

Skirts, Age-size...	10	12	14	16	years
Waist Measure........	24	25	26	27	inches
Length........	24	26	28	30	inches

JIFFY ZIP AND SUSPENDER FROCKS

"Searspride" Zip Frock 98c

(A) All girls love Zip dresses! This one's a pretty deep-toned Floral Print ... a Searspride, too, which means *finest* quality Percale. Crisp white Lawn Peter Pan double collar, sleeve bands. Each side of blouse has a little piped pocket; and one flap that *looks* like a pocket. Inverted pleats at skirt front; 2-inch hem. Crown slide fastener.

Sizes: 10, 12, 14, 16 years. State age-size. Shpg. wt., 10 oz.
27 K 4642—Navy Blue Ground
27 K 4643—Wine Ground..98c

Tartan Plaid Suspender Dress $1.59

(B) Doesn't it look smart and becoming! Jumper skirt is a bright Tartan Plaid Cotton Suiting—*pre-shrunk* and tubfast. Pleated front and back; 2-inch hem. Tailored white Cotton Pique Blouse with big cavalier collar and full puffy sleeves, has stitching trim to harmonize with outfit. Skirt goes nicely with other outfits. Shipping weight, 15 oz.

Sizes: 10, 12, 14, 16 years. State age-size.
27 K 4640—Red and Blue Plaid Skirt with White Blouse................$1.59

10 to 16 SIZE SCALE

Age-size.....	10	12	14	16	years
Chest.....	29	31	32	34	inches
Length.....	33	37	41	44	inches
Measure fullest part of chest.					

Regular ~~$2.98~~ Value

TWO-IN-ONE FROCK

With Two Lovely DETACHABLE COLLARS

FOR 10
TO 16
GIRLS **$1.98**

One day, you can be sweet and pretty in a frilly, white lace collar! Next day, turn about and be tailored with a double collar of scalloped white pique! The dress itself is a beauty—blouse has rounded yoke, tucked front. Skirt has eight stitched-down pleats at front; 2-inch hem. Self-covered button trim. Nice puff sleeves. Fabric is a soft smooth Crown Tested Spun Rayon ...famous for durability, highly dependable quality.

Sizes: 10, 12, 14, 16 years. State age-size. Shpg. wt., 1 lb. 4 oz.

27 K 4644—Royal Blue 218
27 K 4645
Zinnia Rust 609.......$1.98

SEARS ⊕ ⊖

Ⓐ EMBROIDERED
and Plaid Lined
$2⁹⁸

Ⓑ ALL WOOL FLEECE
Coat and Skirt
$6⁹⁸
Coat Alone
$4⁹⁸

Ⓒ DOUBLE DUTY OUTFIT
Coat and Pants
$4⁹⁸
Coat Alone
$3⁷⁹

Ⓓ ALL WOOL FLEECE
Coat and Skirt
$5⁹⁸
Coat Alone
$3⁹⁸

We're 6 to 10 —

AND LOOK GROWNUP AS OUT-OF-DOORS WE GO

Ⓕ
THRILLS!
ALL WOOL
—REAL FUR
$6⁹⁸

Ⓔ
OUR BEST
DOUBLE
DUTY
OUTFIT
Coat
and Pants
$7⁹⁸
Coat
Alone
$5⁹⁸

◇ SEARS

Ⓐ A simply scrumptious little coat for such a tiny price! Bright candy-colored embroidery trimming on the collar and flap pockets—a pert swing in the back in grownup fashion. Fabric is just astonishing at this price; warm, durable Half Wool Fleece, balance Cotton. And it's *fully lined* with bright plaid Cotton Kasha—to keep you warm all winter long.
Colors: Navy, Burgundy Wine 514, or Laurel Green 313. **Age-Sizes:** 6, 7, 8, 9, 10. **State age-size, color;** see Size Scale on opposite page.
17 D 7000—Shpg. wt., 3 lbs. . .**$2.98**

Ⓒ GRAND BUY! Three-piece winter-warm outfit—double-breasted coat with Velveteen trimmed convertible collar and matching, adjustable suspender pants. Sturdy All Wool Fleece, Cotton Kasha lined throughout. Cotton Peasant scarf included. (Pants and scarf not sold separately).
Colors: Laurel Green, Burgundy Wine 514, or Navy Blue 214. **Age-Sizes:** 6, 7, 8, 9, 10. **State age-size, color;** see Size Scale on opposite page.
17 D 7004—**Coat, Pants, and Scarf**
Shpg. wt., 3 lbs. 8 oz. **$4.98**
17 D 7003—**Coat Only**
Shpg. wt., 2 lbs. 8 oz. **$3.79**

Ⓔ A $9.98 value. Double duty outfit in our finest extra-warm All Wool Fleece. New 12-button "Page Boy" swing-skirted coat with Laskinlamb Fur Collar. Plaid Cotton Kasha lined. Matching suspender pants, fully lined. (Pants not sold separately).
Colors: Skipper Blue, Laurel Green 313, or Burgundy Wine 514. **Age-Sizes:** 6, 7, 8, 9, 10. **State age-size, color;** Size Scale, opposite page.
17 D 7008—**Coat and Matching Pants.** Shpg. wt., 4 lbs. 14 oz. **$7.98**
17 D 7009—**Coat Only**
Shpg. wt., 3 lbs. 4 oz. **$5.98**

Ⓑ LOOK! Duplicate of an expensive Fifth Ave. two-piece outfit in soft, All Wool Fleece. Princess coat has a pretty Peter Pan collar of Gray Persian-Effect Fur Fabric; bow pockets. Matching swirling suspender-type wool skirt. (Skirt not sold separately).
Colors: Burgundy Wine, Teal Blue 238, Navy Blue 214. **Age-Sizes:** 6, 7, 8, 9, 10. **State age-size, color;** Size Scale on opposite page.
17 D 7002—**Coat and Matching Skirt.** Shpg. wt., 4 lbs. **$6.98**
17 D 7001—**Coat Only**
Shpg. wt., 3 lbs. 4 oz. **$4.98**

Ⓓ Plaid trims are new! Very colorful and saucy, too, on this adorable double-breasted coat of good, sturdy quality All Wool Fleece. Warm checked Cotton Kasha lining. Matching suspender swing skirt has cunning high waist and suspender straps. (Skirt not sold separately).
Colors: Navy Blue or Burgundy Wine 514. **Age-Sizes:** 6, 7, 8, 9, 10. **State age-size, color;** see Size Scale on opposite page.
17 D 7006—**Coat and Matching Skirt.** Shpg. wt., 3 lbs. **$5.98**
17 D 7005—**Coat Only**
Shpg. wt., 2 lbs. 8 oz. **$3.98**

Ⓕ The Pigtail Crowd loves it . . . because it's packed full of grownup fashion ideas! Just look at the real Beaver-dyed Coney Fur collar and pompons, the squared shoulders, the new bias cut flare that swings and swirls out when you skip along! Dressy All Wool coating, a smooth sturdy winter weight quality. Rayon Taffeta lining; warmly interlined. A $9.98 value.
Colors: Burgundy Wine, Skipper Blue 218, or Teal Blue 238. **Age-Sizes:** 6, 7, 8, 9, 10. **State age-size and color;** see Size Scale on opposite page.
17 D 7007—Shpg. wt., 3 lbs. . .**$6.98**

Two Detachable
Pique Collars →

Ⓖ
3-Piece
Bolero
Ensemble
$**1**98

Ⓗ
3-Way
Spun Rayon
Frock
$**1**79
In Plaid
$1.98

Paris "Copy Cat"
For Big and Little Sister
12 to 16   7 to 10
Ⓙ $**1**89 $**1**89

Ⓚ
2-Piece
Embroidered
Rayon Crepe
$**1**98

Ⓛ
My First Formal
in Swishy
Rayon Taffeta
$**2**98

Regular
Length $**1**98

We're In-Betweeners.. 10 to 16

AND WE LOVE THESE GROWNUP FASHIONS

Ⓖ Just look, will you? Three smart pieces: bolero and matching high-waisted suspender skirt in nubby fine quality All Spun Rayon, plus an adorable puffy-sleeved blouse in colorful All Rayon Plaid Taffeta. Wear the skirt with other blouses, the blouse with other skirts, the bolero with any dress. Well-tailored and a grand bargain!
Age-Sizes: 10, 12, 14, 16. State age-size; see Size Scale below, at right. Shipping weight, 1 pound 8 ounces.
7 D 4904—Burgundy with plaid blouse
7 D 4905—Navy with plaid blouse $1.98

Ⓗ Latest High School rave! Wear it three exciting ways: with cardigan neckline as is, or with either of the white cotton pique collars—Peter Pan or new Dutch Girl. Chic little Basic dress in our better quality All Spun Rayon. Age-Sizes: 10, 12, 14, 16. State age-size; see Size Scale below, at right. Shipping weight, 1 pound 6 oz.
In Plain Colors
7 D 4900—Hockey Green, Navy or Burgundy $1.79
Authentic Clan Royal Stewart Plaid
7 D 4903—Colorful Red Plaid $1.98

Ⓙ All the rage! A tight little bodice in plain color atop a swirling checked skirt with an adorable petticoat-effect ruffle peeping out. Crispy, rustling better quality All Rayon Taffeta. Petticoat ruffle and starch-white Cotton Pique collar are both easily removable. Nice details, too. Amazing Value!

Big Sister's Frock
Age-Sizes: 12, 14, 16. State age-size; Size Scale below. Shpg. wt., 1 lb.
7 D 4908—Navy Blue with Red and Navy Check $1.89

Little Sister's Frock
Age-Sizes: 7, 8, 10. State age-size; Size Scale on Page 256. Shpg. wt., 13 oz.
7 D 4912—Navy Blue with Red and Navy Check $1.89

Ⓚ Shake your dime bank, quick—In-Betweeners . . . and get this angelic two-piece Jacket dress for your very own! It's a $2.95 value in our very finest Crown Tested All Rayon Pebble Crepe in lovely new colors.
The cunning little jacket has scads of expensive colored embroidery, tiny covered buttons and loops, fine shirrings —and a perfectly adorable Little Girl double collar. Oh yes—the puff sleeves are pleated, too, in the very latest fashion. An eye-catcher for sure. Flare skirt has a bodice top—just wonderful to wear with other blouses, too.
Age-Sizes: 10, 12, 14, 16. State age-size; Size Scale at right. Shipping wt., 1 lb. 2 oz.
7 D 4916—Gold
7 D 4917—Navy
7 D 4918—Henna Rust $1.98

Ⓛ Glamorous! Romantic! and *so* grown up! The exciting tier-flounced dress that's all the rage, in shimmering better quality Celanese Rayon Taffeta (swish! swish!) with cording and shirring; velveteen bows, lace frilled sweetheart neck. Dress is easy to shorten. ·
Ankle-Length Formal
Colors: Lt. Blue, or Coral
Age-Sizes: 10—12—14—16
Chest: 29—31—32—34 in.
Length: 46—50—52—54 in.
State age-size and color. ·
7 D 4920—Shpg. wt., 1 lb. 2 oz. . . $2.98
Regular-Length Party Frock
Colors: Burgundy or Skipper Blue
Age-Sizes: 10, 12, 14, 16. Size Scale at right. Also comes in Age-size: 8. Size Scale, Pg. 256. State age-size and color.
7 D 4924—Shpg. wt., 1 lb $1.98

·Turn back the clock! Girls again are dressing like grownups.

Age-Size Scale for In-Betweeners—10 to 16
Sizes are correctly proportioned throughout for hard-to-fit figures of growing girls not yet developed enough to wear regular Juniors' sizes. Measure around chest over underwear at fullest part. Make no allowances. Will not fit adults.

Sizes:	10—12—14—16
Chest:	29—31—32—34 in.
Lengths:	33—37—40—42 in.

SEARS ◇

EXTRA ATTRACTIONS

Gym Suits . . . Robes . . . Jackets . . . The Important Extras
Every Well-Dressed Girl Should Have at Home or at School

Size Scale for Girls' Jackets, Gym Suits, Robes					
Age-Sizes:	7	8	10	12	14	16
Chest:	26	27	29	31	32	34

Size Scale for Girls' Shirts		
Size:	Small	Medium	Large
Age-Size:	7 to 8	10 to 12	14 to 16
Chest:	26 to 27	29 to 31	32 to 34

Numbers after color names refer to Color-Graph in back of book.

5% Discount for 6 or More

74c How this one-piece Gym Suit wears! Generously cut for action. Button shoulders, chest pocket. Elastic bloomer legs. Better washfast Cotton Linene.

Age-Sizes: 8, 10, 12, 14, 16. State age-size; Size Scale above. Misses' Size Range: 18, 20 only. State size; Size Scale, Page 80. Shpg. wt., 12 oz.

$1.00 One-piece Gym Suit with long, waist-length zip front, and action-pleated shorts. Takes hard wear! Breast pocket and hip pocket. Sturdily made in a better quality washfast Cotton Broadcloth.

Age-Sizes: 7, 8, 10, 12, 14, 16. State age-size; see Size Scale above. Shpg. wt., 10 oz.

Cotton Blanket Cloth
$1.00
Bright Indian pattern robe to keep you warm—with notched collar and shiny cord girdle to tie snug around your waist. Very useful, a bargain! Size Scale above.
Age-Sizes: . . . 8|10|12|14 only.
Length: . . . . . 35|38|41|44 in.
State age-size.Shpg.wt.,1 lb.6oz.
27 D 6444—Blue Grounds. $1.00

Half Wool Flannel
$1.98
Soft, cuddly-robe with convertible collar; piping trim. Half Wool Flannel, balance Cotton.
Age-Sizes: . . . 8|10|12|14 only.
Length: . . . . . 40|43|46|49 in.
State age-size, color. Shpg. wt., 1 lb. 9 oz. Size Scale above.
27 D 6442—Light Burgundy 514 or Royal Blue 218 . . . . . . $1.98

Gingham Girl
$1.00
Darling new gingham plaid house coat that buttons in a jiffy! Fluffy white cotton fringe. Washfast. A value! Size Scale above.
Age-Sizes: 7| 8|10|12|14|16.
Length: 38|40|43|48|52|54 in.
State age-size. Shpg. wt., 1 lb.
27 D 4693—Red Plaid
27 D 4694—Blue Plaid . . . $1.00

Classmate JACKETS AND PANTS

Classmates Are Selected for Sturdiness, Long Wear . . . in the 7 to 16 Size Range

Size Scale for Girls' Jackets, Shirts					
Age-Size:	7	8	10	12	14	16
Chest:	26	27	29	31	32	34 in.

Size Scale for Girls' Ski Pants, Overalls					
Age-Size:	7	8	10	12	14	16
Waist:	25	25	26	27	28	29 in
Outseam:	32	34	37	39	41	43 in.

Send your order to Sears nearest Mail Order House and allow postage from there. Items 17 D 4480, 17 D 4481, 17 D 4489, 17 D 4492, 17 D 4493, 17 D 4494, 17 D 4495, 17 D 4496 are shipped from New York. All other garments on this page sent from Sears Mail Order House nearest you.

Half Wool Ski Pants	All Wool Ski Pants	Hooded Sweat Shirt	Ski Pants	Checked Shirt	Bib Top Ski Pants	Sweat Shirt
$1.98	$2.98	98c	$1.79	$1.59	$1.98	59c

GROWING GIRLS LIKE SEARS
Sanforized-Shrunk
FLANNELETTE PAJAMAS

THESE ARE AUTHENTIC DORMITORY STYLES

- Beautifully tailored for long wear...double needle seams where needed.
- Sizes are carefully made to our full specifications... always neat, comfortable.
- Sanforized-Shrunk for lasting good fit...fabric will not shrink more than 1%.

THE PRETTIEST PAJAMAS EVER ... FOR ONLY **85¢** EAC

EASILY ~~$1.00~~ Values

OUR VERY BEST NEW STYLE PAJAMAS **$1.00** EACH

JIM DANDY is Classic

For girls with tailored tastes! Pretty plaid coat, plain trousers...smarter because the better quality Flannelette is in new "misty tone" colors, softer and richer. Wonderful value. Convertible collar. Sash. *Sanforized-Shrunk* Flannelette.

SWEETIE PIE is Swank

The ribbed Knit Cotton ski bottoms, waistband and cuffs make for warmth and style! There's a Peter Pan collar and trick pockets trimmed with deep-tone pipings! The Flannelette is a fluffy, warm good quality... *Sanforized-Shrunk* so the fit will last.

SONIA Goes Russian

The fashion both girls and grown-ups love! Dashing blouse has a snug, high Russian collar. The pocket boasts an emblem, richly embroidered. Deep-tone trim. Warm, cozy, good-quality Flannelette that's *Sanforized-Shrunk*. Strong, double-sewn seams.

Hello! The Jitterbug

No wonder it's a big fashion hit, girls! Cute loose boxy jacket with deep front and back yoke; pockets. Wide, flarey trousers with band front, elastic back. The fine quality Flannelette is the newest, sweet, posy-striped Print—*Sanforized-Shrunk* to fit like new always.

Colorful Print Trim

Handsome classic man-tailored coat style Pajamas, trimmed with beautiful print and piped in plain color, just like fine custom-mades. Fringed sash. Convertible collar. Lovely quality, warm, fluffy Flannelette—*Sanforized-Shrunk* for permanent good fit.

Striking Russian Style

$1.19 Suit   **2 for $2.29**

Bright colored pajamas made of good vat-dye cotton broadcloth. Lounge style coat with full belt. Elastic insert in trouser waists. Age-Sizes: 8, 10, 12, 14, 16, 18. State age-size. Shpg. wt., suit, 12 oz.; two, 1 lb. 8 oz.
33 D 1055—Black with Red Trim
33 D 1056—Red with Black Trim
33 D 1057—Blue with Red Trim

Flannelette Style Hit

98¢ Suit   **2 for $1.89**

He'll like the basque stripes with contrast color pleated trousers. Medium heavyweight flannelette pajamas with notch collar tops, elastic insert in trouser waists. Made large enough to fit comfortably after washing. Age-Sizes: 8, 10, 12, 14, 16, 18. State age-size. Shpg. wt., suit, 13 oz.; 2, 1 lb. 11 oz.
33 D 1096—Blue   33 D 1097—Maroon

New Ski-Type Pajamas

98¢ Suit   **2 for $1.89**

Warm, good-looking. Sturdy cotton yarns knit in the stretchy rib stitch. Napped slightly for softness. Heavyweight for real warmth. Pullover top has crew-neck and one pocket. Close-fitting cuffs on trousers and long sleeves. Full elastic trouser belt. A real cold weather garment that will be appreciated when the wind howls outdoors. Priced so low, you can afford TWO. Age-Sizes: 6, 8, 10, 12, 14, 16. State age-size.

SEARS 4-STAR FEATURE

Here's why! New Snap Fasteners On Trousers Can't Rip Off.. New Clear-Cut Patterns

$1.25 Suit

2 for $2.39

Sanforized to Keep Their Fit

Brightest—gayest pajamas we've ever offered! New plaids printed on medium heavyweight flannelette. Sanforized so fabric can't shrink over 1%. Tailored with a new wide waistband that never binds. Laundry-proof snap fasteners on trousers can't come off. Elastic inserts in waistband; adjustable tie at backs. No choice of color. Age-Sizes: 6, 8, 10, 12, 14, 16, 18. State age-size. See size scale below. Shpg. wt., a suit, 15 oz.; two, 1 lb. 13 oz.
33 D 1070—Notch Coat   33 D 1071—Notch Middy

Dress Them in CORDUROY

And Forget All About "Wear" and "Tear"

- As Smart as It Is Sturdy
- Grand for Active Youngsters
- Newest Play-Time Styles

We're all ready for the Corduroy vogue! Mothers are clamoring for play outfits in this splendid fabric which combines good looks with the sturdiest wear.

Did you ever see smarter styles at such modest prices? All in sturdy, good-quality Corduroy—tailored strongly and neatly. Order complete outfits or make your own play ensembles—with Bush jacket and overalls, or Bush jacket and jodhpurs. Above all, don't miss the peppy little "lumberjack" plaid shirt—perfect with Corduroys.

Corduroy "Jimmy" Overalls   **89c** Ea.

Smartly styled—with trouser cuffs. Two attractive shaped patch pockets. Adjustable suspenders have metal buckles. Well-made—bib top is lined for extra wear.
Age-Sizes: 1, 2, 3, 4, 5, 6. State age-size. Shipping weight, 13 ounces.
38 D 5482M—Navy 214
38 D 5483M—Brown 612
38 D 5484M—Wine 514

Cotton Flannel Shirt   **49c** Ea.

Jolly "lumberjack" plaid in bright colors! Neat collar; pocket. Long sleeves. Perfect shirt for corduroys; goes with overalls or jodhpurs.
Age-Sizes: 1-2, 3-4, 5-6. State age-size. Shipping weight, 6 ounces.
38 D 6869—Red Plaid

Trim Corduroy Jodhpurs   **$1.19** Ea.

Youngsters look darling in them! Smartly styled—with cuffs, belt with buckle. Two real set-in pockets. Well-made deep tearproof plackets.
Age-Size: 1, 2, 3, 4, 5, 6. State age-size. Shipping weight, 11 ounces.
38 D 5461M—Navy 214
38 D 5462M—Wine 514
38 D 5463M—Brown 612

Corduroy Bush Jacket   **$1.19** Ea.

Just like grownups—and just as smart for well-dressed little folks. 4 tailored pockets with button trim, all around belt, cute collar! Back is smartly fitted.
Age-Sizes: 1, 2, 3, 4, 5, 6. State age-size. Shipping weight, 10 ounces.
38 D 5458M—Navy 214
38 D 5459M—Wine 514
38 D 5460M—Brown 612

These Two Suits are ROLLIC BRAND Sanforized-Shrunk

Choice of 4 Fabrics   **59c**

Stout Cottons, sure to stand hard wear. Strong triple-stitched seams, bar tacked.
Age-Sizes: 1, 2, 3, 4, 5, 6. State age-size. Shpg. wt., 9 oz.
38 D 6107—Blue Chambray
38 D 6108—Pinstripe
38 D 6109—Hickory Stripe
38 D 6110—Blue Cotton Covert Cloth

39c Ea.   3 For **$1.12**

Real bargain! Rough-and-ready play suit for active youngsters. Choice of 2 good-quality fabrics. Drop seat.
Age-Sizes: 1, 2, 3, 4, 5, 6. State age-size. Shipping weight, 7 ounces.
38 D 6139—Blue Chambray
38 D 6140—Blue Cotton Covert

Pretty Styles Stout Fabrics   **49c** Each

Sears well made, sturdy play suits...grand bargains. Washing won't change fit! Choice of 2 fabrics. Sanforized-Shrunk (maximum fabric shrinkage 1%). Age-Sizes: 1, 2, 3, 4, 5, 6. State age-size. Shipping weight, each, 8 ounces.

Peg Top Style
Buttons down back. Drop seat. Contrasting print collar and trim.
38 D 6150—Blue Chambray
38 D 6151—Blue Cotton Covert Cloth

Two-Piece Style
Front opening Waist. Contrasting print trim. Pants button onto waist.
38 D 6152—Blue Chambray
38 D 6153—Blue Cotton Covert Cloth

How to Order Play Suits
Bring tape close up under arms for chest measure. Take length from center neck at back to point just below ankle. Order age-size nearest measurements.

Age-Size	1	2	3	4	5	6
To Fit Chest	19	20	21	22	23	24
Length	26	28	30	32	34	36

How to Order Jodhpurs
(1) Measure waist at normal waistline. (2) Measure inseam from crotch, inside leg, to point just below ankle. Order age-size nearest measurements.

Age-Size	1	2	3	4	5	6
To Fit Waist	19	20	21	22	22½	23
Inseam	11	12	13	14	15	16

COTTON TWILL

SPORT SET

Jacket or Jodhpurs **69c** Ea.
All Wool Sweater **69c** Ea.

Sturdy! Stands wear and tear of active play!
Age-Sizes: 1, 2, 3, 4, 5, 6. State age-size.

Cotton Twill Jacket
Notched collar; patch pockets. Pleated belted back. Shipping weight, 8 ounces.
38 D 5445M—Navy Blue 214
38 D 5446M—Wine 514

Cotton Twill Jodhpurs
Newest addition to children's sports togs! Set-in pockets. Adjustable belt. Shipping weight, 8 ounces.
38 D 5447M—Navy Blue 214
38 D 5448M—Wine 514

All Wool Sweater
Age-Sizes: 1-2, 3-4, 5-6. State age-size. Crew neck. Shipping weight, 5 ounces.
38 D 5943—Navy Blue 213

Fancy Play Suit   **59c**

Better quality checked Percale. Embroidery trim. Drop seat. Bow sash back.
Age-Sizes: 1, 2, 3, 4, 5, 6. State age-size. Shipping weight, 6 oz.
38 D 6143—Blue
38 D 6144—Red

Dress-up Play Suit   **59c**

Good-quality Cotton Broadcloth! Contrasting waist with juvenile embroidery trim. Opens down back.
Age-Sizes: 1, 2, 3, 4, 5, 6. State age-size. Shipping weight, 7 oz.
38 D 6141—Navy and Copen Blue
38 D 6142—Rust and Tan

Bib Overall and Shirt   **59c**

Serviceable, durable, good quality Blue Chambray "Jimmy" overalls with pretty applique and matching separate sports shirt. A grand "rough and tumble" 2-piece outfit that's equally nice for boys or girls.
Age-Sizes: 2, 3, 4, 5, 6. State age-size. Shipping weight, 8 ounces.
38 D 6122—Blue Chambray

Overall **69c**   Slipover **25c**

Corduroy Overall. Shpg. wt., 10 oz. Age-Sizes: 1, 2, 3, 4, 5, 6. State age-size.
38 D 6167—Navy Blue 214
38 D 6168—Wine 514
38 D 6169—Brown 612..69c

Combed Cotton Slipover.
Age-Sizes: 1-2, 3-4, 5-6. State age-size. Shipping wt., 4 oz.
38 D 5464—Navy Stripe
38 D 5465—Maroon Stripe..25c

ALL-AMERICAN FAVORITES
ROLLIC KNITS
REG. U. S. PAT. OFF.

- Strong Tearproof Seams
- Comfortable Safe Rubber Buttons
- Full Cut Roomy Drop Seat
- Double-Sole Feet for Double Wear

Rollics are Sears own famous warm knit cotton Sleepers—famous because they offer such excellent quality at economy prices. Year after year, mothers send back for them, they're so satisfactory! Knit from better-grade cotton to make them strong, serviceable; slightly fleeced inside as well as outside for cozy warmth. Each garment strongly and neatly made with flat-locked seams. Cut full and roomy for comfort and better wear.

Rollic One-Piece Sleeper—
Medium Weight
Drop seat at back. Pocket. State age-size.
Shipping weight, each, 14 ounces.
38 D 9322—Gray
38 D 9402—Blue
38 D 9403—Pink
Sizes 1, 2, 3 button down the back.

Age-Sizes	Each	Age-Sizes	Each
1	48c	6	73c
2	53c	7	78c
3	58c	8	83c
4	63c	9	88c
5	68c	10	93c

Rollic Extra-Pants Sleeper
Button-on pants—cut full and roomy to fit well over diapers. You'll find an extra pair wonderfully convenient—so easy to wash out in a jiffy. Pocket on waist. Age-Sizes: 1, 2, 3, 4. State age-size.
2-Piece Suit
Shipping weight, each, 12 ounces.
38 D 9372—Gray
38 D 9404—Blue
38 D 9405—Pink............79c
Extra Pants
Shipping weight, each, 6 ounces.
38 D 9373—Gray
38 D 9406—Blue
38 D 9407—Pink............39c

Thrift Priced
89c
When a cozy warm bathrobe costs so little, every little boy or girl should have one to make bedtime more comfortable and more fun. This one's soft cotton blanket cloth of good quality in pretty assorted jacquard designs. Smartly tailored with rayon cord trim. Pocket. Rayon cord tie.
Age-Sizes: 2, 4, 6. State age-size. Shipping weight, 12 ounces.
38 D 3276—Red
38 D 3277—Blue

Jolly Plaid
$1.25
The most popular robes this year are plaids! We've picked this one in lovely rich colors, and just the right-sized pattern for youngsters. Soft, fluffy genuine Beacon cotton blanket cloth. Lustrous rayon cord trim. Two big pockets. Tailored like a man's robe. Rayon cord tie.
Age-Sizes: 2, 4, 6. State age-size. Shipping weight, 1 lb. 3 oz.
38 D 3250—Blue
38 D 3251—Red

All Wool Flannel
$1.85
We can't think of a grander gift for a little boy or girl! It's a robe to be proud of! Adorable tailored style—in warm *All Wool Flannel* that's just as serviceable as it is fine. Pretty corduroy trim. True double-breasted front with pearl buttons. Self sash.
Age-Sizes: 2, 4, 6. State age-size. Shipping weight, 1 pound.
38 D 3280—Blue
38 D 3281—Wine

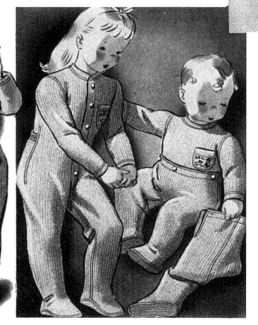

FAMOUS DR. DENTON'S
FINE KNIT SLEEP WEAR
These famous sleepers are also nationally advertised. Heavyweight, double-fleeced fabric, knit of high-grade cotton with 3% fine, natural color wool. Full cut. Unbreakable rubber buttons, extra-heavy feet. Quality Sleepers in every detail.

One-Piece Sleeper—1 to 10
Sizes 1 and 2 button down back and have no pocket. Sizes 3 to 10 with pocket. State age-size. Shpg. wt., ea., 13 oz.
38 D 9324—Natural Gray

Age-Sizes	Each	Age-Sizes	Each
1	90c	6	$1.35
2	$1.00	7	$1.45
3	$1.10	8	$1.55
4	$1.20	9	$1.65
5	$1.30	10	$1.75

Extra-Pants Sleeper—1 to 3
Button-on pants, cut full to fit easily over diapers. State age-size.

2-Piece Suit		Extra Pants	
Shpg. wt., 10 oz.		Shpg. wt., 6 oz.	
38 D 9376—Natural Gray		38 D 9377—Natural Gray	
Age-Size 1	$1.00	Age-Size 1	50c
Age-Size 2	$1.10	Age-Size 2	55c
Age-Size 3	$1.20	Age-Size 3	60c

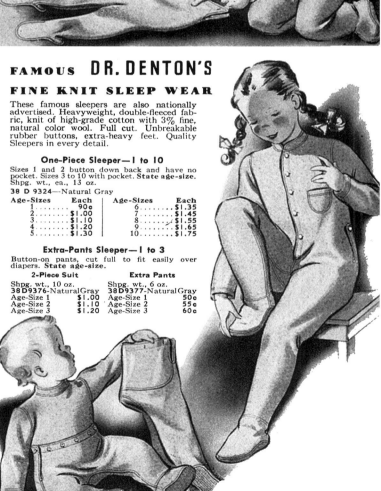

Lowest Priced
43c Ea. 3 for $1.25
Our economy flat knit cotton Sleeper! Sturdy, good quality at lowest price! Year after year, mothers send back for it! They like the medium weight knit cotton, lightly fleeced. Well made with roomy feet, convenient drop seat, handy pocket.
Sizes full cut; strongly sewed seams. Sizes 1, 2, and 3 button down the back. Sizes 4, 5, and 6 button down the front.
Age-Sizes: 1, 2, 3, 4, 5, 6. State age-size. Shipping weight, each, 10 ounces.
38 D 9323—Light Gray

One-piece Style
59c Ea. 3 for $1.73
Medium weight ribbed knit cotton, slightly fleeced. Instead of buttons, seat has Lastex band top which fits snugly, but stretches conveniently. Unbreakable rubber buttons down front. Strong, flat-locked seams. Convenient pocket.
Sizes 1, 2, and 3 button down the back. Sizes 4, 5, 6, 7 button down the front.
Age-Sizes: 1, 2, 3, 4, 5, 6, 7. State age-size. Shipping weight, ea., 11 oz.
38 D 9400—Pink
38 D 9401—White
38 D 9420—Blue

Extra Pants Sleeper
59c 2-Pc. Suit   29c Extra Pants
Two-piece Sleeper; button-on pants . . . extra pair at small cost! Medium weight ribbed knit cotton, slightly fleeced. Unbreakable rubber buttons.
Age-Sizes: 1, 2, 3, 4. State age-size.
2-Piece Suit
Shipping weight, 11 ounces.
38 D 9380—Blue
38 D 9381—Pink
Each, 59c........3 for $1.73
Extra Pants
Shipping weight, 6 ounces.
38 D 9325—Blue
38 D 9326—Pink
Each, 29c........2 for 55c

THE "LITTLE WOMEN" COME TO LIFE

C *Jo*
$**1**98
2 for $3.88

D *Amy*
95c
2 for $1.85

F *Beth*
59c

95c
2 for $1.85

Jo Again

All Dresses on This Page in Sizes 10 to 16 Years

Age-Size	Chest	Length
10 yrs.	29 in.	33 in.
12 yrs.	31 in.	37 in.
14 yrs.	32 in.	41 in.
16 yrs.	34 in.	44 in.

A *Meg*
$**1**98

B *Amy Again*
$**1**98

Dresses A, B, and C, shipped directly from New York to you...you pay postage only from nearest Mail Order House.

Jo's Princess

E You Teen-agers will rave about this dress! It has smooth princess lines and oodles of snowy white fine cotton "Jitter-Bug" lace! Kick pleats for swing! Side placket for a snug waist! 2-inch hem. Sears finest percale... Luxable colors. Shipping weight, 12 ounces.
27 L 4050—Green Jade 307.
27 L 4051—Skipper Blue 212.
27 L 4052—Rose Pink 523.
Each..95c;.....2 for $1.85

Jo's "Beau Catcher"

C Here's our version of a $7.95 Fifth Avenue printed dress-up frock for so much less! The pert puffed sleeves and new heart-shaped neck, flaunt a gay facing! Lastex shirred waist. **State color.** Shpg. wt., ea., 1 lb.

7 L 5369—Rayon Taffeta—Lt. Blue, Pink, or White.
7 L 5372—Rayon French-type Crepe—Lt. Blue, Pink, or White.
Each..$1.98;....2 for $3.88

Amy's Pet

B All your girl friends will envy you in this smart tailored dress with its precious heart-shaped pockets, white piping, and stitched-down pleated skirt. Sail-Along fabric—a fine quality, all spun rayon in exclusive Wedgewood print. Shipping weight, 1 pound 2 oz.
7 L 5366—Crushed Strawberry
7 L 5367—Copen Blue 220.
7 L 5368—White Ground, Red Print. Each............$1.98

Beth Loves It!

F You'll be simply mad about this miser pocket dress—and Mother will say "What a bargain!" Beautifully made of our good quality cotton Percale print in Luxable, washfast colors. The shirred pocket emphasizes the Lastex shirred waistline, and there's a two-inch hem in the skirt so Beth can grow. Shipping wt., 11 ounces.
27 L 4046—Wine.
27 L 4047—Copen Blue...59c

Amy's Dirndl

D Simply precious—with its gay print peasant scarf, and bright embroidery at ruffled neck and sleeves! Quaint laced one-piece suspender-effect tops a snug Lastex shirred waist—for that dainty, fragile look! Sheer dimity top and our finest percale. Luxable, washfast colors. 2-in. hem. Shpg.wt., each, 12 oz.
27 L 4048—Lt. Navy Blue.
27 L 4049—Wine.
Each..95c; . . . 2 for $1.85

Meg's Favorite

A Sixteen tucks of swing in this umbrella stitched skirt! Swirls wide from detachable Gaucho laced belt that ties in back. Hand embroidery at new squared neck; two-tone, self covered buttons. In lovely All Rayon Crepe—it's a perfect Sunday Best! Shipping weight, 15 ounces.
7 L 5363—Royal Blue 917.
7 L 5364—Dusty Rose 534.
7 L 5365—All White. ..$1.98

For sizes see size scale above. State size.

FOR A MODERN CINDERELLA

For Budgets That Haven't Quite Grown Up!
All Dresses on This Page Are Priced at $1.00 **EACH**

Each Dress Is LUXABLE and Wrapped in Cellophane

(A) Rayon Taffeta

(B) French Type Rayon Crepe

(C) Fine Poplin

(D) Shantung Effect Poplin

(E) Organdy and Finest Percale

(F) Fine Poplin

(G) Fine Poplin

(H) Organdy With Rayon Slip

(J) Lovely Organdy

WE LOVE TO *Change-About*
Just like the grownups do

Adorable Four-Piece Outfit. 7 to 14-ers will cut a pretty figure in this chic outfit, looking just like a dancing Ballerina, with skirt and pigtails flying and silver color "Jingle Bell" buttons tinkling merrily. So smart, so very grownup! The long sleeved little jacket is gay with bell buttons and thick confetti-colored wool fringe. The wide circular skirt is full lined with good quality Red Rayon Taffeta, and has the same expensive thick wool fringe all around the bottom. The elastic-back panties are bright Red Sateen, cotton fleece-lined. Cute Navy Blue peaked hood is lined with bright Red. Both suit and hood of warm better quality Half Wool Flannel, balance Cotton; tailored and detailed like an outfit many times as costly.

$4⁴⁸

Colors: Navy Blue with Red. **Age-Sizes:** 7, 8, 10, 12, 14 only. **State age-size;** see Size Scale below. Shipping weight of four-piece outfit, 3 pounds.
7 D 4952—4-Piece Outfit—Jacket, Skirt, Hood, Panties........................$4.48
7 D 4954—2-Piece Outfit—Jacket and Skirt only. Shpg. wt., 2 lbs. 2 oz...........$2.98

RED SATEEN PANTIES

Size Scale For Girls' Skirts	7	8	10	12	14	16 in.
Age-Size:	7	8	10	12	14	16 in.
Waist:		25	25	26	27	28	29 in.
Length of Waistband Skirts including waistband:			16	17	20	24	26	28 in.
Length of Bodice-Top Skirts including bodice			26	27	30	34	38

Size Scale For Girls' Blouses, Shirts and Jackets
Age-Size: 7, 8, 10, 12, 14, 16 in.
Chest....26, 27, 29, 31, 32, 34 in. Measure every time you order; *don't guess.* Read how to measure on Page F in back of book.

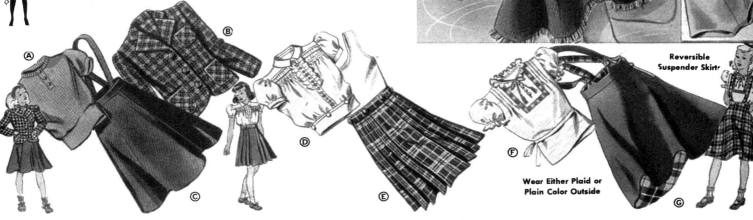

Reversible Suspender Skirt

Wear Either Plaid or Plain Color Outside

Three adorable Change-Abouts, in better quality fabrics.
Age-Size: 7, 8, 10, 12, 14 only. **State age-size and color;** see Size Scale above.

(A) Cotton Knit Blouse. Removable imitation pearl studs, crew neck; snug little waistband. A Big Value!
Colors: Copen Blue 215, or Bittersweet 512.
27 D 4656—Shipping weight, 6 ounces.............**59c**

(B) Tweed or Plaid Jacket. 25% Wool, balance Cotton and Rayon. Patch pockets. Unlined. **Colors:** Colorful Blue, or Brown Tweed; also Red Plaid.
7 D 4653—Shipping weight, 2 lbs. 6 oz..........**$1.98**

(C) All Wool Flannel Suspender Skirt. Thrifty value! New umbrella stitched flared skirt. Detachable suspenders.
Colors: Navy Blue, or Burgundy 514.
27 D 4650—Shipping weight, 12 ounces........**$1.29**

Age-Sizes: 7, 8, 10, 12, 14 only. **State age-size and color;** see Size Scale above.

(D) Button-On Cotton Broadcloth Blouse. Adorably frilled; smocked, embroidered. Large pearl buttons on waist. Little Girl collar; pert puff sleeves with double cuffs. Better quality, nice and smooth.
White with colorful embroidery.
27 D 4658—Shipping weight, 5 ounces.............**79c**

(E) All-Around Pleated Bodice-Top Skirt. Pleats dance out when you walk. Skirt buttons onto both detachable bodice and cute blouse described above. Two inch hem.
7 D 4167—All Wool, in colorful Red Plaid or Plain Navy Blue. Shipping weight, 14 ounces.........**$1.59**
27 D 4165—Half Wool, balance Cotton; in colorful Red Plaid. Shipping weight, 6 ounces..........**$1.00**

Age-Sizes: 7, 8, 10, 12, 14 only. **State age-size and color;** See Size Scale above.

(F) Embroidered Cotton Slub Broadcloth Blouse—Fine Quality. Pretty as a doll! Gay and ruffly; can be worn in or outside of skirt. Pearl buttons, loops, lots of tucks.
27 D 4659—White with colorful trim and piping. Shipping weight, 7 ounces.......................**98c**

(G) New Reversible Plain-and-Plaid Swing Skirt. Suspenders button onto skirt, reversible zip side closing.
7 D 4661—Plain Navy, Half Wool Flannel, (balance Cotton) on one side with Red Plaid Cotton Suiting on reverse side. Shipping weight, 1 pound 6 ounces.........**$1.98**
27 D 4663—Plain Navy, finest 80-sq. Percale on one side with Red Plaid gingham on reverse side. Shipping weight, 1 pound..........................**$1.00**

Three Change-Abouts! The cunning little Classic Jacket, wide skating skirt and a sweet blouse make an adorable suit together, each piece just grand to mix with other outfits.
Age-Sizes: 8, 10, 12, 14, 16. **State age-size and color;** see Size Scale above.

(H) Fine Cotton Slub Broadcloth Blouse. Sweet as a posy! Embroidered; ragooted, with tinkling bell at neck. Tuck it inside skirt, or wear outside.
27 D 4669—White. Shipping weight, 6 ounces.....**98c**

(J) The new Dutch Girl Skirt in All Wool Flannel. Wide flare, Dutch pockets; zip placket; embroidered belt. **Colors:** Navy or American Beauty 537.
7 D 4664—Shipping weight, 1 pound...........**$1.98**

(K) Buttoned-Up Jacket in All Wool Shetland. Two patch pockets; two simulated flap pockets. Unlined.
7 D 4667—Navy Blue. Shpg. wt., 1 lb. 8 oz.....**$2.98**

It's a Sears idea—and very grownup! Buy both the Plaid and Plain Jackets, Plaid and Plain Skirts and change about to your heart's content. Makes 4 exciting change-about ensembles. Well tailored, and all fine quality.
Age-Sizes: 8, 10, 12, 14, 16. **State age-size;** see Size Scale above. Shipping weight, each, 13 ounces.

(L) New All Wool Flannel "Shortie" Jacket. Adorable little girl collar, puff sleeves and buttons and buttonholes. Tailored slash pockets.
7 D 4671—Colorful Blue and Green Plaid
7 D 4672—Plain Navy Blue...................**$1.59**

(M) All Wool Stitched Gored Skirt. 8 stitched gores give a swirling fullness. Detachable suspenders button on.
7 D 4674—Colorful Blue with Green Plaid
7 D 4675—Plain Navy Blue.............Each, **$1.59**
Any two of the above pieces for................**$2.98**

A darling of a two-piece *Change-About* suit! Cute enough to turn your friends double-green with envy. The short fitted jacket has pockets abloom with gay felt flowers. Opens down front with six merry Jingle Bell buttons and buttonholes. Skirt has stitched down front and back pleats. Detachable suspenders. Fine quality All Wool Flannel.

Age-Sizes: 8, 10, 12, 14, 16. **State age-size and color;** see Size Scale above. Shipping weight, each, 1 lb. 10 oz.

Colors: Teal Blue 238 or Burgundy 514
7 D 4676—Long Sleeves......................**$3.29**
7 D 4678—Short Sleeves.....................**$2.98**

Dresses for 10 to 16's

New eye-catching styles Teens love for Parties, School or Sunday best...all at penny-wise prices

Peggy says:

"I salute you in my 'Little Corporal' dress!"

"Don't you love the nice square shoulders and the novelty button-effect trim?" Broad patent leather-like belt, graceful flared skirt with two slash pockets and side placket. Fine detailing plus choice of 2 better quality fabrics make this an exceptional value! *Teen Girls' Sizes*: 10, 12, 14, 16. *State size*; see Size Scale below. Shpg. wt., 1 lb. 3 oz.

Alpaca-Type All Spun Rayon
7F6633—Cadet Blue 575.
7F6634—Light Burgundy 415. $1.98
20% Wool, balance Spun Rayon
Pastel Colors
7 F 6635—Dusty Blue 577.
7 F 6636—Dusty Rose...... $2.98

Spun Rayon $1.98

20% Wool $2.98

Turban Included

3-Piece Outfit $1.98

(A) Thrilling bolero jacket, skirt and blouse! Cute boxy jacket has metal nautical buttons; waistband skirt has adjustable suspenders, side placket. Better quality nubby All Spun Rayon. Finest Percale blouse has back neck closing. (Beanie not included.) *Teen Girls' Sizes*: 10, 12, 14, 16. *State size*; Scale below. Shpg. wt., 1 lb. 8 oz.
7 F 6643—Scarlet 311 jacket, Skipper Blue 569 skirt, Blue Check Blouse.
7 F 6644 — Skipper 569 jacket, Burgundy 415 skirt, Wine Check Blouse. 3 Pieces........... $1.98

$2.49 Plaid Top $1.98 Plain

(B) Our New Turban Dress. You 'Teen-agers will adore the new bishop sleeves, saddle pockets, fitted waistband with leather-like belt, metal buttons! The matching wrap-around turban makes this a complete outfit! Side placket. Better quality Spun Rayon.
Teen Girls' Sizes: 10, 12, 14, 16. *State size*; Scale below. Shpg. wt., 1 lb. 6 oz.
7 F 6650—Red Clan Plaid top; Light Royal 565 skirt, turban. 2 pcs. **$2.49**
7 F 6651–All Burgundy 415
7 F 6652–All Navy
2 pieces....... **$1.98**

Hood Attached $2.98

(C) New Hood Dress. The 'Teen age crowd is crazy about this darling "hood-winker"! See the novelty pockets on the shirred front skirt . . . and the eye-catching lustrous Rayon Taffeta plaid lining of the attached hood and sash! In lovely All Rayon Pebble Crepe. Side placket, 2-in. hem. Beautiful detailing you usually find in much higher priced dresses.
Teen Girls' Sizes: 10, 12, 14, 16. *State size*; see Size Scale below. Shipping weight, 1 pound 3 ounces.
7 F 6649—Burgundy 415.
7 F 6648—Navy... $2.98

Printed Spun Rayon $1.98

(D) Double breasted shirt waist dress — every school-girl's favorite! Look at the cute pockets and flared skirt with front box pleats. Pointed self-collar with detachable Cotton Pique collar. Side placket. 2-in. hem. Better quality All Spun Rayon.
Teen Girls' Sizes: 10, 12, 14, 16. *State size*; Scale below. Shpg. wt., 1 lb. 2 oz.
7 F 6637—Light Wine Ground Print.
7 F 6639—Deep Copen Ground Print. Each $1.98

Trapunto Trim $1.98

(E) Swishy All Rayon Taffeta. Imagine how pretty you'll look in this slim fitted waist and wide flaring skirt! Trapunto trim on front waistband, slash pockets. Tie-back sash. Pastel colors for parties, too!
Teen Girls' Sizes: 10, 12, 14, 16. *State size*; see Size Scale, below. Shipping wt., 1 lb. 1 oz.
7 F 6645–Light Aqua 657
7 F 6646–Party Pink 453
7 F 6647–Light Navy Blue. Each...... $1.98

$1.98 2-Piece Dress

(F) Gay, Colorful Wool Embroidery trims this darling 2-piece frock. Cute fitted jacket has self-covered buttons, self loops. Tie-back belt. Bodice top, gored skirt has side placket. Better quality All Rayon Pebble Crepe.
Colors: Navy Blue, Henna Rust 265, American Beauty 463. *'Teen Girls' Sizes*: 10, 12, 14, 16. *State size, color*; Size Scale at left. Shipping weight, 1 lb., 2 oz.
7 F 6640—2 pcs.. $1.98

Teen Girls' Size Scale for Dress, Jacket, Blouse and Skirt

Measure to get a Good Fit

Sizes:	10	12	14	16	
Chest:	30	31½	33	34½	inches
Height:	56	61	63	65	inches
Waist:	25	26	27	28	inches
Hips:	33	34½	36	37½	inches
Dress Length:	34	37	40	42	inches
Skirt Length:	24	26	27	28	inches
(Includes Waistband)					

COTTON
100% AMERICAN
MADE IN U·S·A

A 2-Piece Pinafore Dress

B Snip 'n Fit Coat Dress

C Dress With Separate Bolero

D Choice of Fabrics

E New Wide Skirt

$1.00 EACH

H 3-Piece Playsuit Set

F Knit Shirt.....29c

G Sanforized Overalls..$1.00

J Cotton Crash Suit

K 2-Piece Dress

L Snip 'n Fit Sailor Dress

Happiness Ahead for You Who Wear These Slick Clothes...Startling Values! 10 to 16'ers!

SEARS New Sportswear
JUST FOR 10 TO 16'ers

Features This 4-Pc. Outfit

$1.98 Change-around the 4 Pieces in Many Ways

2-Piece Set $1.00 Separate Slacks 69c

Super-value 4-piece slacks outfit . . . skirt, slacks, shirt, and shorts with metal ring belt. 3-complete outfits. Better Woven Cotton Suiting.

In-or-out striped shirt; Sports collar, patch pocket, 4-button front closing.

Plain color fitted waistband slacks; belt loops, front pleat for extra fullness; 3-button side closing.

Plain color flared, waistband skirt buttons down the front, belt loops.

Striped shorts have action pleat, 3-button side closing and belt loops.

Plain color belt, self-fabric; adjustable metal rings.

Teen Girls' Sizes: 10, 12, 14, 16. State size; Scale, opposite page. Shipping wt., 1 lb. 11 oz.
27H5245—Blue combined with Blue, White pin stripe.
27H5246—Rose combined with Rose, White pin stripe.
4-Pieces........................$1.98

2-Piece set—Shirt, slacks with belt (description above).
27H5220—Plain Blue Slacks; Blue, White pin stripe shirt.
27H5221—Plain Rose Slacks; Rose, White pin stripe shirt.
2-Pcs—Shpg. wt., 14 oz..$1.00

Separate Slacks with Belt. (for description see above).
27H5222—Plain color Blue
27H5223—Plain color Rose
Each—Shpg. wt., 10 oz...69c

Two-Pc. Outfit For Play or School $1.00

A marvelous 2-piecer with saucy striped waistband skirt that buttons down the front. Separate 1-piece playsuit has action-pleated shorts. Stripe trim on collar, tie-belt and pocket matches skirt. Better washfast Percale.
Teen Girls' Sizes: 10, 12, 14, 16. State size; see Size Scale, opposite page. Shipping weight, 10 ounces.
27H5241—Green-Tan-White Stripe Skirt with Apple Green 711.
27H5242—Blue-Gray-White Stripe Skirt with Sailor Blue 559.2 Pcs.,$1.00

Pinafore Playsuit; 3-Pc. Change-arounds $1.49

Peppermint stripe pinafore with matching kerchief. Bib top, fitted waistband; buttons down back. Built-up to wear as separate sun-back dress. Complete 1-piece playsuit has action pleated shorts, tie belt. Better washfast Percale Pinafore, kerchief; better washfast Cotton Broadcloth White Playsuit.
Teen Girl's Sizes: 10, 12, 14, 16. State size; Size Scale, opposite page.
27 H 5247—Red-and-White Stripe
27 H 5248—Blue-and-White Stripe
Shpg. wt., 12 oz........3 Pcs.,$1.49

OVERALLS
Sanforized-Suiting Corduroy JACKET Corduroy
$1.00 $1.98 $1.98

Overalls done to a "T" for you Teens! Carefully designed to fit the Teen girls' figure. Built-up back with 3-button closing to wear without shirt; adjustable metal ring suspenders. Fitted front waistband with darts for a good fit. Two patch pockets. Choice of two durable fabrics. Marvelous values!
Teen Girls' Sizes: 10, 12, 14, 16. State size; Size Scale, opposite page.

Better Quality Sanforized-Shrunk All Cotton Denim Suiting
(max. shrinkage 1%). Shpg. wt., 12 oz.
27 H 5228—Light Denim Blue
27 H 5229—Denim Rose.......$1.00

Better Quality Wide Wale All Cotton Corduroy
Cotton lined top. Shpg. wt., 1 lb. 6 oz.
◆ H 4210—Aqua Blue
◆ 7 H 4211—Sunset Rose
◆ 7 H 4212—Navy Blue.......$1.98

Corduroy Jacket can take it! Smartly loafer jacket—single breasted boxy style. Pointed collar; buttons down the front. 2 Patch pockets. Made of better quality Corduroy. Sizes as above. State size. Shipping weight, 1 lb. 2 oz.
◆ 7 H 4215—Scarlet
◆ 7 H 4216—Aqua Blue.......$1.98

Garments marked with diamonds ◆ on these two pages are shipped from New York City. Send your order to nearest Mail Order House, or for these garments alone, you may send directly to New York. Pay postage only from nearest Mail Order House. Color numbers refer to Color-Graph preceding first Index Page in back of book.

"Crown Tested" Rayon Slacks Suit $1.98

Ⓐ Slacks are comfy, carefree for all year round . . so it pays to buy a quality suit like this. Two-tone, 2-pc. slacks suit for Teens. Loose boxy jacket, saddle stitching trim. Pearl-like buttons down front and on patch pockets. Hi-waist slacks have belt loops, adjustable metal rings on self belt; Crown zip placket. Better Crown Tested All Spun Rayon Poplin.
Teen Girls' Sizes: 10, 12, 14, 16. State size; Size Scale on opposite page. Shpg. wt., 1 lb. 4 oz.
◆7H4213—Sunset Rose 429 top, Sky Blue 555 slacks.
◆7H4214—Princess Yellow 157 top, Aqua 675 slacks.2 Pcs. $1.98

Glen Plaid or All Wool Flannel
$2.49 Jacket $1.98 Skirt

Ⓑ Suit yourself with this single breasted 3-button classic jacket, Rayon Taffeta yoke lined, and fitted waistband skirt with Crown zip. Choice of 2 fabrics.
Teen Girls' Sizes: 10, 12, 14, 16. State size; Scale, opposite page. Shpg. wt., for jacket, 1 lb. 8 oz.; for skirt, 1 lb. 1 oz.

Half Wool, Balance Rayon Glen Plaid Tweed—Color: Navy and Copen Blue Glen Plaid.
◆ 7 H 4200 M—Jacket....$2.49
◆ 7 H 4203 M—Skirt....$1.98

Better Quality All Wool Flannel.
◆7H4201 M—Jacket—Navy
◆7H4202—Jacket—Cardinal 313.
Each...................$2.49
◆7H4204 M—Skirt—Navy. $1.98

CLASSIC BLOUSE
Better quality Cotton Broadcloth. **Colors:** White, Copen 607. Sizes above. State size, color.
27H5044—Shpg.wt., 7 oz....79c

Separate Blouse 79c

GOOD MIXERS

For sizes 7 to 14

You've heard about good mixers before. What makes them good? Girls love them for their color, their casual comfort—mothers find these jumpers and two pieces the easiest and most inexpensive way to a wardrobe of many changes, to give varied service for school and after school hours. Blouses not included.

Jumpers, 2-piecers mix with blouses

A—Fine-ribbed corduroy, fashion's number one fabric, is used for our heart-necked jumper. Skirt flares, is smartly gathered in front. Buttons down the back. Neatly finished at the armholes. *Colors:* Red or blue. *Sizes:* 7, 8, 10, 12, 14. See size scale, page 258A. *State size, color.*
◆ 77 F 7774—Shipping weight, 1 pound $3.49

B—Fine quality chambray in many-colored stripes. Bib-topped jumper with your favorite set-in waistband above a gathered dirndl skirt. Large, handy pockets. Banding detail. Buttons down back. Washable, simple to keep neat and fresh. Not in stock until Sept. 1. Do not order before that date. *Sizes:* 7, 8, 10, 12, 14.
47 F 7776—   *State size.* Shpg. wt., 10 oz $1.49

C—Warm wool and rayon (50% reused wool, 50% rayon) in a gay red plaid . . wonderful with white blouses. See the square neck, the set-in waistline, full gathered skirt below. It buttons in back. Dry clean. *Sizes:* 7, 8, 10, 12, 14. Not in stock until August 15. Do not order before that date.
◆ 77 F 7775—   *State size.* Shipping wt. 1 lb $3.49

D—Classic suit in wonderful, pinwale corduroy. Faultless tailoring in the jacket . . the smooth dart-fit through waistline. Patch pockets, crisply notched lapels. The skirt is gored front and back, buttoned at the side. *Colors:* Green or red. *Sizes:* 7, 8, 10, 12. See size scale on page 238.
◆ 77 F 7941—*State size, color.* Shpg. wt., 1 lb. 10 oz $5.49

E—Newest of two-piecers in a favorite plaid . . (25% new wool, 20% reused, 55% rayon). Fitted jerkin, buttons at side. Gored skirt has trouser tucks. Dry clean. *Color:* Red-white-navy plaid. *Sizes:* 7, 8, 10, 12, 14.
◆ 77 F 7773—   *State size.* Shpg. wt., 1 lb. 8 oz . . . $3.98

Quality Coats for girls .. sizes 7 to 10

Specially designed for these sizes by a famous maker. His best workmanship is in them.

$10.98 Each, cash ⅓ down, Easy Terms

A—All wool fleece, soft, sturdy 100% reprocessed wool. Fitted reefer with dainty velveteen touches and neckline that buttons up snugly. Deep pockets under those cute hip flaps. Fully lined and warmly interlined. 2 in. hem. *Colors:* Brown or oatmeal tan. *Sizes:* 7, 8, 9, 10. Size scale below. *State size, color.* Shipping wt., 4 lbs.
◆ 77 F 7341......$10.98

B—Coachman coat in fine quality knit back fleece .. 30% new, 20% reused wools, 50% cotton. Velveteen for collar and pocket flaps, nicely stitched. Deep lapover for warmth, panel back. Fully lined, interlined. 2-in. hem. *Colors:* Honey brown or polo tan. *Sizes:* 7, 8, 9, 10. Scale below. *State size, color.* Shipping wt., 4 lbs.
◆ 77 F 7344......$10.98

C—All wool wrap (40% reprocessed, 60% reused) dressed up with a coney fur collar. Nice touches like the button-yoke, gathers above a set-in back waistband, detachable belt. Flap pockets. 2-in. hem Rayon lining, warm interlining. *Colors:* Teal blue or wine. *Sizes:* 7, 8, 9, 10. Scale below. *State size, color.* Shpg. wt., 4 lbs.
◆ 77 F 7346......$10.98

Rain-or-shine Reversibles for sizes 7 to 10 $9.98 Each, cash ⅓ down, Easy Terms

E—Fly-front fleece (soft, sturdy 37% new, 15% reused wools, 48% rayon) in a bright red. Nice stitching detail. Reverses to natural tan cotton gabardine treated to shed water. *Sizes:* 7, 8, 9, 10. Scale below. *State size.*
◆ 77 F 7343—Shpg. wt., 3 lbs.... $9.98

D—Colorful plaid (20% new, 20% reused wools, 60% rayon) for this fly front reversible's sunny side. Full boxy cut. Reverses to natural tan cotton gabardine, treated to repel rain. *Sizes:* 7, 8, 9, 10. Scale below. *State size.*
◆ 77 F 7342—Shpg. wt., 3 lbs..... $9.98

Size Scale for 7 to 14	Size	7	8	9	10	12	14
	Chest:	26	27	28	29	30½	32 in.
	Waist:	23½	24	24½	25	26	27 in.
	Coat length:	27	28½	30½	32	34	36 in.

C Built-up overall
   in washable cotton $1.39

D Tuck-in slack suit
   in washable denim $1.98

E Sanforized slack suit
   in cotton chambray $2.79

F Dress-up slack suit
   in Luxable rayon $3.98

K Sanforized playsuit
   in two cottons $1.98

L Sanforized shorts
   in sturdy denim   89c

N Pullover knit shirt 98c
   Sanforized shorts $1.89 and $1.39

P Cotton knit shirt $1.49
   Cotton twill shorts $1.98

[A] STRIPED PERCALE..... $1.69	[B] UNBLEACHED MUSLIN $2.98	[C] EVERGLAZE CHINTZ. $2.98	[D] CHECKED COTTON.... $1.98

Pinafores, Blouses, Skirts

Teens' washable cottons, sizes 10 to 16

[A] STRIPED PERCALE pinafore. Built-up front, criss-cross straps in back. Set-in waistband, patch pockets, dirndl skirt buttons at back. Blouse not included. Washable. *Colors:* Red or blue. *Sizes:* 10, 12, 14, 16; scale, pg. 212. *State size, color.* Shpg. wt., 10 oz.
47 H 7872.........$1.69

[B] UNBLEACHED MUSLIN pinafore with full gathered skirt. Dashing bright red bandana cloth pockets with matching trim at neck. Button opening all down the back. Washable. *Color:* Cream with red. *Sizes:* 10, 12, 14, 16; scale, page 212. *State size* Shpg. wt., 10 oz.
♦ 77 H 7874.......$2.98

[C] EVERGLAZE CHINTZ pinafore with suspender front, solid back. Ric-rac trim. Patch pockets. Dirndl skirt, button side placket. Blouse not included. Washable. *Colors:* Maize or copen. *Sizes:* 10, 12. 14, 16; size scale on page 212. *State size, color.* Shipping wt., 10 oz.
♦ 77 H 7873.......$2.98

[D] CHECKED COTTON pinafore with embroidered ruffle, red lacing trim. Slash pockets on dirndl skirt. Blouse not included. *Colors:* Blue or red with white. Washable. *Sizes:* 10, 12, 14, 16; size scale on page 212. *State size and color.* Shpg. wt., 12 oz.
♦ 77 H 7871.......$1.98

[E] WHITE PEASANT BLOUSE in sheer cotton. Gay embroidered square neck. Shpg. wt., 8 oz. Sizes below.
47 H 7961.........$1.19
DIRNDL SKIRT in blue and white checked cotton. Red band, applique apple trim. Shpg. wt., 10 oz. Sizes below.
♦ 77 H 7960.......$1.98
Available after Feb. 1st.
Sizes: 10, 12, 14, 16; size scale, page 210. *State size.*

[F] RHUMBA BLOUSE in white cotton sheer. Shpg. wt., 8 oz. Sizes below.
47 H 7963.........$1.49
DIRNDL SKIRT in sunny yellow Sanforized percale (max. shrink, 1%). Embroidery, ric-rac trim. Shpg. wt., 10 oz. Sizes below.
47 H 7962.........$1.69
Sizes: 10, 12, 14, 16; size scale, page 210. *State size.*

[E] BLOUSE $1.19 SKIRT $1.98

[F] BLOUSE $1.49 SKIRT $1.69

Boyville Jr.
OUR OWN TRADE MARK
Swim Trunks

[A] **Wool Swim Trunks** . . . 100% virgin wool worsted in 2-tone combination with knit-in patterns. Adjustable drawstring waist. **$1.49**
Sizes: 4, 6, 8, 10. Colors: royal (bright) blue combination or maroon (wine red) combination. State size and color.
43 L 7635—Shipping weight, 6 oz $1.49

[B] **Fine cotton and rayon satin twill.** (38% cotton, 62% rayon.) Boxer model with full elastic waist. Adjustable drawstring; handy, button down flap coin pocket. **$1.98**
Sizes: 4, 6, 8, 10. Colors: light blue, light tan and maize (yellow). State size, color.
43 L 7637—Shipping weight, 7 oz $1.98

Boyville
REG. U.S. PAT OFF.
Swim Trunks

[C] **100% pure zephyr wool.** Handsome knit-in pattern; adjustable drawstring waist. Knit cotton built-in supporter. Shipping weight, 7 ounces. **$1.64**
Sizes: 8, 10, 12, 14, 16. Colors: royal (bright) blue, maroon (wine red). State size and color.
43 L 7638 . . . .$1.64

[D] **Sanforized cotton twill Swim Trunks.** Popular boxer model with full elastic waist. Adjustable drawstring; knit cotton built-in supporter. Button-down flap coin pocket. Sanforized-Shrunk—maximum fabric shrinkage 1%. Shpg. wt., 8 oz. **$1.98**
Sizes: 8, 10, 12, 14, 16. Color: tan only.
43 L 7639—State size $1.98

Boyville
REG. U.S. PAT OFF.
Sweatshirts

[E] **Cotton Sweatshirt, good quality.** Low-priced for a sturdy flat knit cotton sweatshirt. Warm cotton fleecing inside. Double ribbed cuffs, neck and bottom. Washable. **74c**
Color: silver (pale) gray. Sizes: small (6–8); medium (10–12); large (14–16). State size wanted.
43 L 7211—Shipping weight, 11 ounces 74c

[F] **Junior Commandos colorful Sweatshirt.** Thrilling action scene on front. Sturdy, long wearing flat knit cotton with heavy cotton fleecing inside. Double ribbed cuffs, neck and bottom. Easily laundered. Washable separately. Shipping weight, 14 ounces. **83c**
Colors: medium blue or red. Sizes: 4, 6, 8, 10. 12, 14, 16. State size and color wanted.
43 L 7223 . . . . .83c

[G] **Heavyweight Sweatshirt, our finest.** Strongest and longest wearing because it's made of heavyweight flat knit cotton with thick absorbent cotton fleecing. Sleeve construction allows full freedom, easy action. Double ribbed cuffs, neck, bottom. Wash separately. **99c**
Color: Dark gray, bright blue trim. Sizes: small (6-8); medium (10-12); large (14-16). State size.
43 L 7218—Shipping weight, 1 pound 99c

SIZE SCALE FOR SWIM TRUNKS						
If weight is between	35–42	43–52	53–65	66–77	78–96	97–115	116–130 lbs.
Order size..	4	6	8	10	12	14	16

SIZE SCALE FOR SWEATSHIRTS						
Measure chest over shirt and under armpits. Order size corresponding to chest measure. If boy is taller or shorter than average, a size larger or smaller will fit better.						
If height is....	41	45	49	54	59	64	68-in.
If chest measures.	22	24	26	28	30	32	34-in.
Order size....	4	6	8	10	12	14	16
Order size....	(Small)		(Medium)		(Large)	

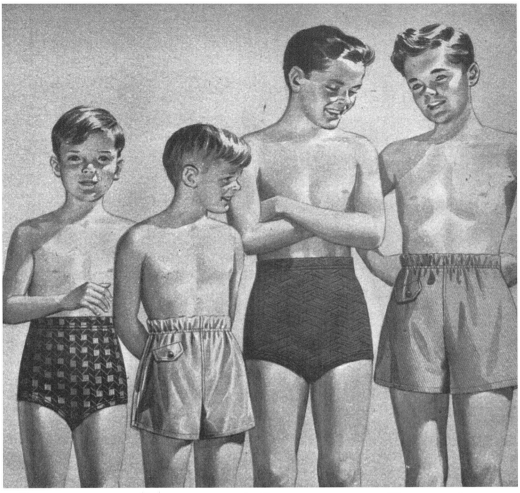

[A] Wool Trunks $1.49   [B] Satin twill . . $1.98   [C] All wool . . .$1.64   [D] Cotton twill . $1.98

[E] Sweatshirt . . . . .74c   [F] Commando Sweatshirt 83c   [G] Heavyweight Sweatshirt. 99c

Boyville
REG. U.S. PAT. OFF.

Raincoats

Boyville capeskin leather Jackets

Good quality zip style . . . fully lined

- Genuine capeskin leather
- Full cotton plaid lining

$8⁹⁵

Available after Sept. 1. Smart, serviceable jacket—good looking and warmly lined for chilly days. Convertible collar may be worn up or down. Half belted back. Adjustable side straps and cuffs. Two deep muff pockets, handy chest pocket.

Please state size: 8, 10, 12, 14, 16, 18. See page 238.
40 D 3484—Tan (medium). Shpg. wt., 2 lbs. 4 oz. . . $8.95

Our best quality capeskin, rayon lined

- Lustrous full rayon lining
- Zipper front and 5 pockets.

$12³⁵

Available after Sept. 15. Sturdy leather jacket that's smart for school, dress or play. Well fitting half belted back. Adjustable side straps. Two lower flap pockets for all your valuables and deep muff pockets. Button-flap chest pocket.

Please state size: 8, 10, 12, 14, 16, 18. See page 238.
40 D 3412—Tan (medium). Shpg. wt., 2 lbs. 6 oz. $12.35

Zipper surcoat style, extra long

- Extra fine quality capeskin
- Fully lined with rayon

$12⁹⁵

Available after Sept. 15. 2 to 3 inches longer than regular jackets. Has convertible collar, chest pocket, 2 muff pockets, half belted back. Shipping weight, 2 pounds 10 ounces.

State size: 8, 10, 12, 14, 16, 18. See page 238.
40 D 3438—Tan (medium). $12.95

Our finest Aviator style sheepskin Jacket

- Tough horsehide leather sleeves
- Warm sheepskin leather body

$15⁷⁵

Available after Sept. 15. About 2 in. longer than most jackets. Sheepskin leather . . . wooly side turned in, smooth side out. Lambskin collar, warm red sleeve lining. 25% wool, 75% rayon. Zip front. Adjustable side and cuff straps. 3 pockets.

Please state size: 8, 10, 12, 14, 16, 18. See page 238.
40 D 3504—Dark brown. Shpg. wt., 3 lbs. 4 oz. $15.75

Lined gabardine Raincoat

$6⁵⁴

Three-quarter length raincoat that's "tops" with every young fellow. Cotton gabardine is heavyweight, moisture resistant, in an attractive oyster tan color. Styled with concealed button fly front, railroad stitching trim on collar and bottom, two large patch pockets, small change pocket. Plaid cotton flannel lining in body; rayon lining in sleeves.

State size: 10, 12, 14, 16, 18, 20.
See page 372. Shpg. wt., 2 lbs. 8 oz.
40 L 7620—Oyster (light) tan . . . $6.54

— HOW TO ORDER BOYS' —
KNICKERS AND BREECHES

Measure boy's height without shoes. Measure waist over trousers or pants.

If height is		If waist is		Order size
42	to 44	22	to 24	6
45	to 46	22½	to 24½	7
47	to 49	23	to 25	8
50	to 51	23½	to 25½	9
52	to 53	24	to 26	10
54	to 55	24½	to 26½	11
56	to 57	25	to 27	12
58	to 59	25½	to 27½	13
60	to 61	26	to 28	14
62	to 63	26½	to 28½	15
64	to 65	27	to 29	16
65½	to 66½	27½	to 29½	17
67	to 68	28	to 30	18

Style-Right Swim Suits .. a colorful parade of the gay, flattering fashions girls like for swimming or sunning .. in sizes 4 to 16

[A] $2.98
Rayon Sharkskin

[B] $2.98
Rayon and Cotton Knit

[C] $2.98
Rayon and Cotton Knit

[D] Wool Jersey
$1.69
Sizes 4, 6, 8
$1.98
Sizes 7, 8, 10

[E] $3.98
Rayon Jersey

[A] PRINTED RAYON SHARKSKIN in a flattering 1-piece princess style .. is first choice of this season's beach beauties. Has softly gathered bodice, gracefully flared skirt. The stunning multi-print on white ground adds to its beauty. Buttons at back. Knit cotton lined. *Sizes* 8, 10, 12, 14, 16. *State size.* Shipping weight 7 oz.
98 H 4820—Multi-color print.....$2.98

[B] ONE-PIECE SUIT knit of rayon and cotton in a velvet-like texture. Snowy daisy-chain braid trims neck and shoulder straps. Half skirt style .. the ideal suit for swimming. Tie straps. Knit cotton lining.
Sizes 8, 10, 12, 14, 16; scale below. *Please state size.* Shipping wt. 9 oz.
98 H 4818—Bright red.........$2.98
98 H 4819—Royal (bright blue)... 2.98

[C] 2-PIECE STYLE knit of rayon and cotton in attractive velvet-like jacquard pattern. Center strap bra top has contrasting braid shoulder straps and tie back. Trunks have half skirt, drawstring waist. Knit cotton lined front.
Sizes 8, 10, 12, 14, 16; size scale below. *State size.* Shipping weight 7 oz.
98 H 4815—Bright red.........$2.98
98 H 4816—Medium blue........ 2.98
98 H 4817—Yellow............. 2.98

[D] ALL WOOL JERSEY SWIM SUITS. 1-piece style; applique trim. Braided shoulder straps tie in back. *Children's sizes* 4, 6, 8. *State size.* Shpg. wt. 5 oz.
29 H 3810—Bright red. ,........$1.69
29 H 3811—Royal (bright blue)... 1.69
Style as above, except with gathered bodice; knit cotton lining. *Girls' sizes* 7, 8, 10. *State size.* Shpg. wt. 6 oz.
29 H 3812—Bright red.........$1.98
29 H 3813—Royal (bright blue)... 1.98

[E] PRINTED RAYON JERSEY in gorgeous color combinations, fashions one of our loveliest beach suits. 2-piece style has graceful loop-knot bra top, ties at neck and in back. Trunks have elastic shirred, print rayon jersey front .. with solid color rayon satin lastex back. All-around elastic waistband for snug, trim fit.
Sizes 8, 10, 12, 14, 16; see size scale below. *State size.* Shpg. wt. 7 oz.
98 H 4821—Pink; light lime green   98 H 4822—Med. blue; yellow
98 H 4823—Yellow; American beauty (deep rose).................Each $3.98

Size Scale for Bathing Suits, Sizes 4 to 16

Order size:	4	6	7	8	10	12	14	16
If height is:	36-40	40½-46	46½-50	50½-52	52½-56	56½-58½	59-61	61½-63
If weight is:	32-37	38-48	49-58	59-64	65-80	81-92	93-104	105-115

N $6.45
Top Quality
P $3.98
Good Quality

R $5.45
Top Quality
T $3.98
Good Quality

For buzzin' around to class or date
"Little boy" saddles, moc-type smarties
With Kerrybrooke 100% Teen-age styling

Brown 'n' White moc-style . . . two qualities

N TOP QUALITY . . . two-color moc-type oxford. Fine quality brown 'n' white leather upper. Leather insole. Goodyear welt construction. Leather sole, rubber heel. Shipping wt. 1 lb. 14 oz.
• A (very narrow) girls', women's sizes 5, 5½, 6, 6½, 7, 7½, 8, 8½, 9. C (med.) girls', women's sizes 3½, 4, 4½, 5, 5½, 6, 6½, 7, 7½, 8, 8½, 9. *Please state size and width wanted.*
15 H 2818—Brown, white . . Pair $6.45

P GOOD QUALITY . . . brown 'n' white moc-style oxford . . . the light of your Teen-age life. Favored kick-off back seam. Supple leather upper. Moc-type last. . . roomier at the toe. Extra-flexible construction. Sturdy, long-wearing synthetic sole, leather heel.
• C (med.) girls', women's sizes 4, 4½, 5, 5½, 6, 6½, 7, 7½, 8, 8½, 9. *State size.* Shpg. wt. 1 lb. 8 oz.
15 H 2218—Brown, white . . Pair $3.98

Favorite Brown 'n' White Saddles . . . two qualities

R TOP QUALITY . . . "little boy" saddles; wider toe, broader saddle. Fine quality brown and white leather upper. Goodyear welt. Non-marking red rubber sole, heel. Shpg. wt. 1 lb. 14 oz.
• A (very narrow) girls', women's sizes 5, 5½, 6, 6½, 7, 7½, 8, 8½, 9. C (med.) girls', women's sizes 3½, 4, 4½, 5, 5½, 6, 6½, 7, 7½, 8, 8½, 9. *Please state size and width.*
15 H 2797—Brown, white . . Pair $5.45

T GOOD QUALITY . . . sparky saddles so dear to teen-age hearts. Pin-money priced for extra value. Extremely flexible construction. Pliant, easy-on-your-feet leather upper. Sturdy red rubber sole and heel are non-marking, outwear leather.
• C (med.) girls', women's sizes 4, 4½, 5, 5½, 6, 6½, 7, 7½, 8, 8½, 9. *State size.* Shpg. wt. 1 lb. 10 oz.
15 H 2297—Brown, white . . Pair $3.98

SIZES 7 TO 14
THE GRADE SCHOOL CROWD

A $4.98
Part Wool

B $4.98
Part Wool

C $5.98
All Wool Flannel

2-pc. all wool Suits take top honors

$9.98   **$10.98**

DOUBLE BREASTED CLASSIC, smartly tailored in 60% new wool, 40% reused wool. The jacket has silver color metal buttons, new half belt in back. Fully rayon lined. Zipper placket skirt has tucks and pleats in front, kick pleat in back. *Sizes 7, 8, 10, 12, 14; see size scale on page 1363. State size. Shipping wt. 2 lbs.*

77 K 5027—Bright red . $9.98
77 K 5028—Med. blue. 9.98

ALL WOOL CARDIGAN SUIT has a smart solid color blazer jacket, fully lined . . . trimmed with gay plaid to match skirt. Plaid skirt is pleated all around; zipper placket. *Sizes 7, 8, 10, 12, 14; see size scale on page 1363. Please state size.* Shipping weight 2 lbs.

77 K 5030—Green jacket; navy blue and green skirt....$10.98
77 K 5031—Red jacket; navy blue and green skirt....$10.98

These school girls' Suits team with fashion news . .
all the cute styles for classroom or dress

A CLASSIC JERKIN SUIT . . . perfect for dress-up and school wear. The all wool jacket has bright silver-color metal buttons. The skirt has a zipper placket, pleats and tucks for smooth fit in front and a kick pleat in back. The skirt is 31% new wool, 14% reprocessed wool, 55% rayon. (For shirt, see page 83.) *Sizes 7, 8, 10, 12, 14; see size scale on page 1363. State size.* Shpg. wt. 2 lbs.

77 K 5032—Green jacket; navy blue and green plaid skirt............$4.98

77 K 5033—Navy blue jacket; navy blue and green plaid skirt........$4.98

B TWO-TONE JACKET SUIT is styled for action . . . lots of fullness in the jacket, plenty of pleats in the skirt. Smartly bloused all wool jacket has breast pocket. Part wool skirt (25% new wool, 20% reused wool, 55% rayon) has box and side pleats in front, kick pleat in back; concealed placket. (For shirt, see page 83.) *Sizes 7, 8, 10, 12, 14; see size scale on page 1363. State size.* Shpg. wt. 2 lbs.

77 K 5036—Red jacket; black and white checked skirt.............$4.98

77 K 5037—Brown jacket; brown and white checked skirt.............$4.98

C ALL WOOL FLANNEL BOLERO SUIT has pert little bows appliqued on the jacket and skirt . . . a flattering young style the school crowd adores. Its smart long-sleeve bolero jacket is warm, practical and can be worn with other skirts. The full dirndl skirt goes well with every blouse. Has a concealed zipper placket. (For blouse see page 83.) *Sizes 7, 8, 10, 12, 14; see page 1363. State size.* Shpg. wt. 2 lbs.

77 K 5034—Bright red $5.98

GRADE SCHOOL CROWD
SIZES 7 to 14

HONEYLANE
THE RIGHT WAY
TO SAY
GIRLS' WEAR

A **$8.45**
Part Wool

B **$9.95**
All Wool

C **$9.95**
All Wool Jacket
Part Wool Skirt

E
$3.98
Rayon

F
$3.98
Corduroy

D **$6.95**
All Wool

G **$3.98**
Part Wool

SUITS .. Sears famous Honeylane values

Well made, full cut, newest details

A **CLASSIC PLAID SUIT** in fine 35% new wool, 20% reprocessed wool, 15% reused wool, 30% rayon. Rayon yoke lined jacket has flap pockets, skirt has box pleats front, back; side zipper. Dry clean. *Sizes 7, 8, 10, 12, 14; see page 1309. State size.* Shpg. wt. 1 lb. 14 oz.
077 D 5050—Gray background plaid . . .$8.45

B **ALL WOOL SUIT** is up-to-the-minute with its cute short cut jacket, swing-wide skirt. Rayon yoke lining, rich looking silver-color buttons, trim decorative tabs. Side zipper. Dry clean. *Sizes 7, 8, 10, 12, 14; see page 1309. State size.* Shpg. wt. 1 lb. 12 oz.
077 D 5051—Copen (medium blue) $9.95
077 D 5052—Bright red 9.95

C **SMART SWINGSTER** has an all wool, unlined jacket, silver-color buttons, nipped waist, flip-out peplum effect back. Collar trimmed in plaid of skirt (60% new wool, 40% rayon). Side zipper. Dry clean. *Sizes 7, 8, 10, 12, 14; see page 1309. State size.* Shpg. wt. 2 lbs.
077 D 5057—Green top; plaid skirt $9.95
077 D 5058—Navy blue top; plaid skirt . 9.95

D **ALL WOOL BOLERO SUIT**. Unlined jacket has cheery red lapels, cuffs, buttons. New-look swing skirt has smart cummerbund effect in red, too. Side button placket. Dry clean. (Blouse not included.) *Sizes 7, 8, 10, 12, 14; see page 1309. Please state size.* Shipping weight 1 pound 11 ounces.
077 D 5054—Light navy blue $6.95
077 D 5055—Kelly (bright green) 6.95

JUMPERS swing skirts

in newest fashion

E **SWEETHEART JUMPER** in rich rayon is smocked and shirred at waist, has flouncy ruffle hemline with petticoat insert of rayon taffeta. Built-up, buttoned back. Dry clean. (Blouse not included.) *Sizes 7, 8, 10, 12, 14; see page 1309. State size.* Shpg. wt. 1 lb. 1 oz.
77 D 5146–Dark green $3.98
77 D 5147–Gray 3.98

F **FINE PINWALE CORDU-ROY** jumper studs its waistband with glittery gold-color nailheads. Your pet dirndl skirt made full by billowy gathers. Side button placket; built-up back. Dry clean. (Blouse not included.) *Sizes 7, 8, 10, 12, 14; see page 1309. Please state size.* Shpg. wt. 1 lb. 2 oz.
77 D 5143–Bright red . . $3.98
77 D 5144–Bright blue. 3.98

G **PRETTY PLAID JUMPER** in fine part wool, (60% new wool, 40% rayon) has smart shoulder tabs. A swirly skirt with deep full-gathered self ruffle. Buttons in back, tie sash. Dry clean. (Blouse not included.) *Sizes 7, 8, 10, 12, 14; see page 1309. Please state size.* Shipping weight 1 pound 3 ounces.
77 D 5145—Scotch plaid on white ground. $3.98

SIZES 10 TO 16
FOR THE HIGH SCHOOL CROWD

[A] [B]

Rugged Sports Separates . . built to stand the gaff of
Teens' outdoor doings . . and they can really take it

Teens have fun in their own boy fashions of warm, hefty woolens

$9.98   **$5.98**

[A] ALL WOOL PEA JACKET, (90% reprocessed wool, 10% reused wool), styled like the real "McCoy," cut like a gob's. Wear it for sports or school with the wide convertible collar pushed up; your hands poked deep into sturdy pockets. Nautical buttons. Plaid cotton lining. Dry clean. *Sizes* 10, 12, 14, 16; see page 1363. *State size.* Shpg. wt. 3 lbs. 5 oz.
98 K 6906–Navy blue..$9.98

[B] 100% VIRGIN WOOL Shirt, in the big bold Buffalo plaid you've been borrowing from your brother or your best beau. Now you can have your own . . cut just like a boy's. Collar is reinforced in back to keep it in shape; adjustable button cuffs. Dry clean. *Sizes* 10, 12, 14, 16; see page 1363. *Please state size.* Shipping weight 1 pound 1 ounce.
98 K 6903–Red, black..$5.98

$1.98	$1.98	$2.98	$1.79	$3.98	$7.98
Dungarees	Shirt	Slacks	Shirt	Corduroy Slacks	Jacket

ZIPPED DENIM DUNGAREE with all the hoop-la of red stitching, copper rivets. They're as tough as good fabric can make them. Two deep pockets; reinforced back yoke; concealed zipper. Wash separately. (Belt not included.) *Sizes* 10, 12, 14, 16; see size scale on page 1363. *Please state size.* Shipping weight 13 ounces.
98 K 6326—Navy blue $1.98

PLAID COTTON FLANNEL SHIRT. Hand wash separately. *Sizes above.* Shpg. wt. 8 oz.
98 K 6750 — Colorful plaid Each................$1.98

GOOD-WEARING SLACKS with lots of price appeal and the trim lines Teens go for. Part wool (50% reused wool, 30% cotton, 20% rayon). Pleated for a sleek fit; side pocket; concealed placket. Dry clean. (Belt not included.) *Sizes* 10, 12, 14, 16; see page 1363. *State size.* Shipping wt. 1 lb. 2 oz.
98 K 6300—Gray.....$2.98
98 K 6301—Dk. brown 2.98
98 K 6302—Navy blue. 2.98

CLASSIC COTTON SHIRT. Washable. *Sizes above.* State size. Shpg. wt. 8 oz.
98 K 6733—White.... $1.79

PIN WALE CORDUROY SLACKS, well tailored; wash separately. Pleated front; side pocket. Zipper. (Shirt and belt not included.) *Sizes* 10, 12, 14, 16; see page 1363. *State size.* Shpg. wt. 1 lb. 2 oz.
98 K 6322—Lt. navy...$3.98
98 K 6323—Brown.... 3.98
98 K 6324—Green..... 3.98

CORDUROY JACKET, mannish cut; leather-like buttons. Rayon lined. Dry clean. *Sizes* 10, 12, 14, 16; see page 1363. *State size.* Shpg. wt. 2 lbs.
98 K 6900—Bright red.$7.98
98 K 6901—Green..... 7.98
98 K 6902—Lt. tan.... 7.98

HONEYLANE
THE RIGHT WAY
TO SAY
GIRLS' WEAR

C
$3.49
Jumper

D
$3.69
Jacket
$2.69
Skirt

B
$2.69
Slacks
$1.98
Shirt

A
$2.29
Slacks

E
$1.98
Shorts

F
$2.98
2-Piece Set
$2.29
Jeans Only

"BLU SURF Sport Denim". . Joshua L. Baily famous fabric
Sanforized (max. fabric shrinkage 1%) and extra sturdy

A DUDE RANCH DENIMS, dungaree-style slacks brought up to date with colorful printing of the "Wild West" all over front. Action-cut and carefully fitted with pleated front, darts in back. Red-button placket. Red stitching finish, double needle strength at all points of strain. Back patch pocket. Wash separately. Will take plenty of hard wear. Sears low-priced. (Shirt sold on page 66.) Sizes 10, 12, 14, 16; size scale on page 67. State size. Shpg. wt. 13 oz.
98 L 6332—Navy blue $2.29

C DENIM JUMPER has a built-up front so it can be worn without a shirt. Shoulder straps button to a low sun-tan back. Sleek set-in waistband has wonderful side buckles that adjust to perfect fit. Two carry-all pockets on a swingy skirt. Buttons down back to below waist . . . easy to get into. Wash separately, takes plenty of hard wear. Low priced at Sears. Try teaming it with polo shirts and blouses. Sizes 10, 12, 14, 16; size scale, page 67. State size. Shpg. wt. 12 oz.
98 L 6100—Light blue $3.49
98 L 6101—Barn red 3.49

E DENIM SHORTS are fully cut, take smart tailoring touches from the boys'. Looped for belts, cuffed bottoms, speedy side zipper closing. Added attractions are the red and white checks of woven cotton gingham on handy pockets. Team with all your shirts and halters. Wash separately; wears beautifully. (For shirt, see page 67.) Sizes 10,12,14, 16; size scale, page 67. Shpg. wt. 7 oz.
98 L 6624—Light blue $1.98
98 L 6625—Barn red 1.98

B DENIM SLACKS are well cut . . . pleated in front, dart-fitted in back, looped for your pet belts. Side pocket and zipper closing. Wash separately. Sizes 10, 12, 14, 16; scale, page 67. State size. Shpg. wt. 13 oz.
98 L 6333—Light blue $2.69
98 L 6334—Barn red 2.69
CHECKED CLASSIC SHIRT of woven cotton gingham. Yoke back. Washable. Sizes 10, 12, 14, 16. State size. Shipping weight 8 oz.
98 L 6780—Blue and white $1.98
98 L 6781—Red and white 1.98

D BOXY DENIM JACKET trimmed with red and white woven gingham checks. Convertible collar; 2 pockets. Wash separately. (For shirt, see above.) Sizes 10, 12, 14, 16; scale, page 67. State size. Shpg. wt. 14 oz.
98 L 6964—Light blue $3.69
98 L 6965—Barn red 3.69
DENIM GORED SKIRT has adjustable side buckles, two patch pockets. Wide, full sweep. Zipper back. Wash separately. Sizes 10,12,14,16. State size. Shpg. wt. 12 oz.
98 L 6102—Light blue $2.69
98 L 6103—Barn red 2.69

F DENIM TWO-PIECER has well-fitted built-up bra with button back. Pedal jeans are trimmed with red and white checks of woven gingham. Zipper closing, belt loops, cuffs. Wash separately. Sizes 10,12,14,16; scale, page 67. State size. Shpg. wt. 1 lb.
98 L 6435—Light blue $2.98
98 L 6436—Barn red 2.98
PEDAL JEANS ONLY. Shipping weight 10 oz.
98 L 6335—Light blue $2.29
98 L 6336—Barn red 2.29

PARTYTIME PALS

for the little miss . . Biltwels in shining black patent, crisp white, gay red or rich brown leather . . flexible construction for easy-wearing, fine-fitting

YOUNG MISSES' SIZES
12½ TO 3, 3½ TO 7

M $2.98

Bonny little Two-strap . . just like the newest style for Mom

---

Sturdy Searolite or leather soles, wrinkle-resistant leather insoles

F A, C widths . . : woven vamp, strap adjusts. Leather insole; durably sewed; Searolite sole, rubber heel.
• A (very narrow), C (med.) girls' 12½, 13, 13½, 1, 1½, 2, 2½, 3. *State size, width.* Shpg. wt. 1 lb. 4 oz.
15 E 1669—Brown   15 E 1670—Red . . . . .Pair $4.88
• A (very narrow), C (med.) jr. misses' 3½, 4, 4½, 5, 5½, 6, 6½, 7. *State size, width.* Shpg. wt. 1 lb. 6 oz.
15 E 1671—Brown   15 E 1672—Red . . . . .Pair $5.45

H B and D widths . . . black patent leather. Leather insole, quarter lining. Leather sole and low heel.
• B (narrow), D (medium wide) girls' 12½, 13, 13½, 1, 1½, 2, 2½, 3. *State size, width.* Shpg. wt. 1 lb.
15 E 1236—Black patent leather .Pair $4.88
• B (narrow), D (med. wide) jr. misses' 3½, 4, 4½, 5, 5½, 6, 6½, 7. *State size, width.* Shpg. wt. 1 lb. 6 oz.
15 E 1246—Black patent leather .Pair $5.45

G Dainty One-Strap . . . with party-going manners. Dressy cut-outs. Shining black patent or smooth white leather. Flexible construction. Adjustable buckle. Leather insole. Leather sole with rubber heel lift.
• D (medium wide) girls' sizes 12½, 13, 13½, 1, 1½, 2, 2½ and 3. *Please state size.* Shpg. wt. 1 lb. 2 oz.
15 E 1159—Black patent leather
15 E 1164—White leather . . . . .Pair $4.88

J Black Patent Ankle-Strap . . . smooth leather insole, quarter lining. Leather sole, rubber heel lift.
• D (medium wide) girls' sizes 12½, 13, 13½, 1, 1½, 2, 2½ and 3. *Please state size.* Shpg. wt. 1 lb. 2 oz.
15 E 1174—Black patent leather .Pair $3.98
• D (medium wide) jr. misses' sizes 3½, 4, 4½, 5, 5½, 6, 6½ and 7. *Please state size.* Shpg. wt. 1 lb. 6 oz.
15 E 1189—Black patent leather .Pair $4.35

K Sweep-Strap Party-Goer . . . with a new "grown-up" look. Glistening black patent leather. Leather insole, quarter lining . . . inner smoothness. Long-wearing sewed construction. Flexible leather sole, rubber heel.
• D (medium wide) girls' sizes 12½, 13, 13½, 1, 1½, 2, 2½, 3. *State size.* Shpg. wt. 1 lb. 4 oz.
15 E 1403—Black patent
15 E 1402—White leather . . . . .Pair $3.49

L Winsome T-Strap . . . cut-out, perforated for style-rightness. Soft leather made over good-fitting last. Flexible construction for easy wearing. Leather insole. Snug-fitting pear-shaped heel. Roomy toe. Leather sole, rubber heel lift.
• D (medium wide) girls' sizes 12½, 13, 13½, 1, 1½, 2, 2½, 3. *State size.* Shipping weight 1 lb. 2 oz.
15 E 1165—White leather
15 E 1166—Black patent . . . . . . .Pair $3.69

M Slipper Delight . . . in sparkling black patent or smooth white leather. Pretty perforated trim. Made over roomy foot-form last with broad toe, snug heel. Shape-retaining leather insole. Sturdy leather sole, heel lift.
• D (medium wide) girls' sizes 12½, 13, 13½, 1, 1½, 2, 2½, 3. *Please state size.* Shpg. wt. 1 lb.
15 E 1223—White leather
15 E 1235—Black patent. . . . . .Pair $2.98

N Done in black patent, red leather, as dainty as your little girl herself. Straps reinforced for wear, adjust for secure fit. Sweetheart vamp. Flexible welt construction. Cork and rubber midsole filler . . . cushiony for comfort wear. Smooth leather insole, quarter lining add to wear and comfort. Long-wearing leather sole, rubber heel lift.
• C (medium) girls' 12½, 13, 13½, 1, 1½, 2, 2½, 3. *State size.* Shpg. wt. 1 lb. 2 oz.
15 E 1404—Black patent leather
15 E 1412—Red leather . . . . .Pair $4.88

SUNDAY-BEST HATS for little girls and
the grade school crowd. darling

styles, pretty as can be . . . all sensibly priced

A DRESS-UP SET. Half bonnet of straw-like braid has adorable rippled brim faced with contrasting color shirred rayon taffeta, flowers. Matching bag abt. 6x9 in. *Colors* Copen blue with pink; natural with copen blue or pink: white with copen blue or pink. *State color.* Hat fits all sizes. Price incl. 24c. Fed. Ex. Tax on bag.
078E2740E—Set. Shpg. wt. 14 oz. $3.74
078E2735—Hat only. Wt. 13 oz. 2.29

B SCOTTY HAT AND BAG SET. Straw-like braid, rayon taffeta. Bag abt. 6 in. in diam. *Colors* Natural, white, red, copen blue. *State color.* Price includes 32c Fed. Ex. Tax on bag. *Hat, bag set.* Shipping weight 13 oz.
078 E 2720E—Fits 20 to 20¾ in. . . . $3.69
078 E 2721E—Fits 21 to 21½ in. . . . 3.69
Hat only. Shipping weight 11 oz.
078 E 2715—Fits 20 to 20¾ in. $1.79
078 E 2716—Fits 21 to 21½ in. 1.79

A $3.74 Set $2.29 Hat only

B $3.69 Set $1.79 Hat only

$1.48
ROLLER of strawlike braid. *Colors* Natural with navy; all pink, white or copen blue. *State color.* Shpg. wt. 1 lb. 5 oz.
078E2700—Fits 20¼ to 20¾ in.
078E2701—Fits 21 to 21½ in.
Each $1.48

$1.98
STRAW-LIKE BRAID with nosegay. *Colors* Natural with navy blue; natural with red; all white. *State color.* Shpg. wt. 11 oz.
078E2750—Fits 19½ to 20 in.
078E2751—Fits 20¼ to 20¾ in.
Each $1.98

$2.29
FLOWER HALO. Half bonnet of straw-like braid. *Colors* Natural with navy blue; all white, copen blue, pink, red. *Please state color.* Fits all headsizes. Shipping weight 12 ounces.
078 E 2710 . . . . $2.29

$2.19
POSEY BONNET. Rough straw. *Colors* Natural with black, navy blue or red. *State color, headsize.* Shipping weight 14 ounces.
078E2725—Fits 19¾ to 20½ in.
078E2726—Fits 20¾ to 21¼ in.
Each $2.19

$1.98
STRAW BRAID. *Colors* Copen blue, rose, natural or red with navy; white with black. *State color.* Shipping weight 1 lb.
078E2705—Fits 19¾ to 20¼ in.
078E2706—Fits 20½ to 21 in.
Each $1.98

$2.35
ROUGH STRAW, flowers, ribbon. *Colors* Natural with navy, red or copen blue. *State color.* Shipping weight 13 oz.
078E2810—Fits 20¾ to 21¼ in.
078E2811—Fits 21½ to 22 in.
Each $2.35

98c
BERET of 100% pure wool. Imported from France. *Colors* White, red, navy blue, copen blue, brown. *Please state color.* Shipping weight 2 oz.
078 E 2745—Fits 20 to 21½ in.
Each 98c

$1.94
OFF-THE-FACE brim with dainty flowers, open crown. Straw-like braid. *Colors* White, natural, red, copen blue. *State color.* Fits all headsizes. Shipping weight 1 lb.
078 E 2795 . . . . $1.94

$2.39
CLOCHE BRIM, straw braid, flowers. *Colors* Natural with red, navy blue or brown. *State color.* Shpg. wt. 1 lb.
078 E 2815—Fits 20¾ to 21¼ in.
078 E 2816—Fits 21½ to 22 in.
Each $2.39

$2.29
STRAW, RIBBON, flowers. *Colors* Natural with brown, navy or red; all white. *State color.* Shipping weight 1 lb. 1 oz.
078 E 2790—Fits 20½ to 21 in.
078 E 2791—Fits 21¼ to 22 in.
Each $2.29

BRACELETS, LOCKETS AND RINGS . . charming jewelry to captivate any child

**SIZES
7 TO 16**

Sears is famous for Dungaree Values

GUARANTEED DUNGAREES
Western-style in Sanforized blue denim

Two qualities with these super-features

- Sanforized blue denim won't shrink over 1%
- Copper rivets firmly anchored at front pockets
- Five belt loops at waistband . . . all bar-tacked
- Double-needle orange stitching throughout
- Tailored in flattering, slim-fitting western style
- Back yoke and back patch pocket are bar-tacked
- Two large, front inside "swing" pockets
- Inside seams neatly finished . . . no raw edges
- Laundry-proof metal Gripper Fastener at waist
- Convenient side zipper . . . opens, closes in a jiffy

PRICES SLASHED
to an all time low

Last Fall Price Was $2.59

Heaviest 8-oz.
$1.98 — Sizes 7 to 14
$2.19 — Sizes 10 to 16

Heaviest 8-oz. Denim

The same wonderful, long wearing dungarees that we've sold by the thousands at their regular higher price. (Please wash separately.)
Sizes 7, 8, 10, 12, 14; see size chart, page 57. *State size.* Shipping weight 1 lb. 2 oz.
77 E 5343—Navy blue...$1.98
Sizes 10, 12, 14, 16; see size chart, page 57. *State size.* Shipping weight 1 lb. 4 oz.
77 E 6343—Navy blue...$2.19

Good Quality Denim

$1.79 — Sizes 7 to 14
$1.89 — Sizes 10 to 16
Last Fall Price Was $1.94

Sizes 7, 8, 10, 12, 14; see size chart, page 57. *State size.* Shipping weight 1 lb.
77 E 5326—Navy blue...$1.79
Sizes 10, 12, 14, 16; see size chart, page 57. *State size.* Shipping weight 1 lb. 2 oz.
77 E 6326—Navy blue...$1.89

Cotton Plaid Shirt

Sanforized woven cotton plaid (won't shrink over 1%). Notch collar style with patch pocket, short sleeves, back yoke, double-needle stitched sleeves. Wash separately.
Sizes 7, 8, 10, 12, 14; see size chart on page 57. *State size.* Shipping weight 6 oz.
77 E 5794—Multi-plaid...$1.69
Sizes 10, 12, 14, 16; see size chart on page 57. *State size.* Shipping weight 7 oz.
77 E 6794—Multi-plaid...$1.79

SEARS

Denims
**SIZES
1 TO 4**

AT SEARS LOWEST PRICE

Sanforized, won't shrink more than 1%
.. copper rivets, buttons.. double-needle
stitched .. detachable suspenders

Only $1.29 Each
2 for $2.54

REGULAR DUNGAREES with button-side closing . . . for boys and girls. Yoke back for better fit. 2 front pockets, 1 back pocket. Wash separately. *Sizes* 1, 2, 3, 4. *State size.* Shpg. wt. each 8 oz.
29K6844—Navy blue.$1.29
2 for............. 2.54

Sanforized woven plaid cotton Shirt

98¢ Was $1.29

Fabric won't shrink more than 1%. Short sleeves. One pocket. Wash separately. *Sizes* 1, 2, 3, 4. *State size.* Shpg. wt. 5 oz.
29 K 6508—Multicolor plaid...............98¢

NEW! FLY-FRONT
**Blue Denim
DUNGAREES**

$1.29 Each   2 for $2.54

- Sanforized, won't shrink more than 1%
- Detachable suspenders
- Double-needle stitched
- Copper rivets, buttons
- Zipper-fly closing

The newest version of Sears famous blue denims. Buttoned waistband. Yoke back. 2 front pockets, 1 back pocket. (Shirt sold on opposite page.) Wash separately. *Sizes* 1, 2, 3, 4. *State size.* Shpg. wt. each 11 oz.
29 K 6803—Navy blue.$1.29
2 for............. 2.54

Measure to be sure

Order size	Size Chart for Sizes 1 to 4			
	1	2	3	4
If height is	29½–31	31½–34	34½–37	37½–40 in.
If chest is	20	21	22	23 in.
If weight is	22½–25	25½–29	29½–34	34½–38 lbs.
Coat length	16	17	18	19½ in.
Dress length	15½	16½	17½	19 in.

"YIPPEE"

Gold Bond Boots for children

Top notch values

Sizes 5½ to 8, 8½ to 4

M **$7.79**

N **$7.79**

Gold Bond
THE *RIGHT* WAY
TO SAY
**COWBOY
BOOTS**

P **$4.79**
5½ to 8

59c T

R **$6.79**

Texas-made . . . quality materials, construction,
wear-defying service at Sears low prices

M Just like the boot a real cowboy wears. Rough it up, scuff it up, it can take it, it's a stamina-built Gold Bond. Inlaid kidskin leg, sturdy leather vamp. Flexible Goodyear welt easy to resole. Smooth leather insole. Husky wear-defying leather sole, cowboy-type heel.
• Child's sizes 8½, 9, 9½, 10, 10½, 11, 11½, 12, 12½, 13, 13½, 1, 1½, 2, 2½, 3. Wide width. *Please state size.* Shipping weight 1 lb. 10 oz.
15K1251—Tan vamp, brown leg.Pair $7.79
15K1262—Red leg and vamp . . Pair 7.79

N Roy Rogers and his famous horse "Trigger" in raised design on leg. Fine saddle leather. Leather sole, rubber heel lift.
• Child's 8½, 9, 9½, 10, 10½, 11, 11½, 12, 12½, 13, 13½, 1, 1½, 2, 2½, 3, 4. Wide width. *Please state size.*
15 K 1292—Saddle leather leg, tan vamp. Shpg. wt. 1 lb. 2 oz. . . Pair $7.79

Last Spring Price Was **$9.85**
NOW
$779

P New. Genuine Texas Boot at a low, money-saving price. Rugged creamy tan kid leg, green underlay . . . brown leather vamp. Smooth leather insole. Strong "bend" leather sole, heel; rubber heel lift.
• Child's 5½, 6, 6½, 7, 7½, 8. Wide width. *State size.* Shpg. wt. 14 oz.
15K1299—Cream leg, tan vamp. Pr. $4.79
• Child's wide 8½, 9, 9½, 10, 10½, 11, 11½, 12, 12½, 13, 13½, 1, 1½, 2, 2½, 3. *State size.* Shipping weight 1 pound 2 ounces.
15 K 1298—Cream leg, brown vamp
Pair. $5.79

R For your little make-believe cowboy or cowgirl. Texas-built boot that takes plenty of hard wear, asks for more. Blond leg, red underlay. Rich wine-tone leather vamp. Welted side seams, lined leg; inner smoothness, Goodyear welt. Oak color rubber sole, leather heel, rubber lift.
• Child's sizes 8½, 9, 9½, 10, 10½, 11, 11½, 12, 12½, 13, 13½, 1, 1½, 2, 2½, 3. Wide width. *Please be sure to state size wanted.* Shipping weight 1 lb. 10 oz.
15 K 1250—Blond leg, winetone vamp. . . . . Pair $6.79

T Child's Spur. Safe leather rowell. Strap adjusts. Fits boots to size 3.
15 K 6005—Spur. Shipping weight 6 ounces. . . . . Pair 59c

Now! Improved Roy Rogers Jeans and Jacket . . new, heavier 9-oz. denim packs greater wear

JEANS
Zipper fly **$1.79**
Button fly **$1.69**

Smooth zipper or button fly front

Western-style yoke back for better fit

Roy Rogers
CONE *deeptone* DENIM

JEANS AND JACKET

Denim Jeans and Jacket "branded" by Roy Rogers

• New! Super-strong 9-ounce Roy Rogers denim
• Narrow cowboy-style legs; yoke-style back

Zipper fly **$1.79**
Button fly **$1.69**

Rein-in partner! Lasso these slick-fittin' Western jeans. They're Roy Rogers official jeans, made of new specially constructed 9-oz. denim for service. Sanforized for lasting fit. (fabric shrinkage 1%). Sunfast deep-tone blue. Strong copper rivets anchor front strain points; heavy thread bartacks in back. Extra-long cowboy-style legs; yoke-style back. Double-stitched seams, no raw edges to rip, fray or ravel. Sturdy drill front swing pockets, 2 hip pockets, plus watch pocket. Extra-heavy bartacked belt loops. Genuine leather patch on back. *State size* 4, 6, 8, 10, 12, 14, 16. See chart below. Shpg. wt. 1 lb. 7 oz. Belt not included. Wash separately.

50 K 9128M—Button fly, deeptone blue denim jeans $1.69
50 K 9129M—Zipper fly, deeptone blue denim jeans. 1.79

ROY ROGERS DENIM JACKET to match Jeans above. Heavy 9-oz. Sanforized denim (shrinkage 1%). Pleated front and back, copper riveted Snug-fitting waist. Leather patch on front. *State size* 4, 6, 8, 10, 12, 14, 16. Size scale jackets on page 93. Wash separately. Shpg. wt. 1 lb. 6 oz.

50 K 9131M—Deeptone blue Western-style jacket. $1.79

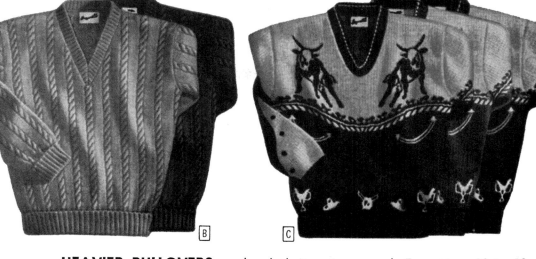

HEAVIER PULLOVERS . . closely knit, extra warm! Even sizes 10 to 18

[A] NEW WOOL WORSTED SKI SWEATER. Our best boys' pullover. Closely knit of extra fine, extra heavy wool yarns — tightly twisted for extra strength. Almost unbeatable for warmth, long wear. Shape-holding, double-ribbed neck; heavier knit cuffs, bottom. Jacquard-knit design on both front, back. Hand wash separately. *State size* 10, 12, 14, 16, 18. See the size chart below. Shpg. wt. 10 oz.
43 K 2370—Navy combination
43 K 2372—Brown combination.$4.77

[B] WORSTED PULLOVER **$3.87** IN CABLE STITCH. Fine, rich wool yarns knit in the sporty cable stitch . . exceptionally warm, handsome, comfortable. Firmly knit of tightly twisted yarns to keep its shape, take hard wear. Ribbed neck, cuffs, bottom. Hand wash separately. *State size* 10, 12, 14, 16, 18. See the size chart below. Shipping weight 10 ounces.
43 K 2345—Camel (light) tan
43 K 2342—Dark blue........$3.87

[C] WESTERN-STYLE, **$3.87** ALL WORSTED WOOL. Strong, closely knit 2-ply worsted yarns . . wonderfully warm, remarkably rugged. Jacquard-knit steerhead figures on both front, back. Smart Western-type cuffs. Hand wash separately. State size 10, 12, 14, 16, 18. See the size chart below. Shipping weight 10 ounces.
43 K 2363—Maroon combination
43 K 2364—Green combination
43 K 2362—Navy combination.$3.87

[A] **$4.77**

MEASURE . . . to be sure (see page 93)

HOW TO ORDER BOYS' SWEATERS AND KNIT SHIRTS—Measure chest around body under the arms and over the tips of the shoulder blades.

If chest is..	25	26½	28	29½	31½	33	34½ in.
Order size	6	8	10	12	14	16	18
	Extra Small	Small		Medium		Large	

THRIFTY, WARM PULLOVERS in shape-holding knits

[D] WORSTED SLEEVE- **$1.89** LESS, SOLID COLOR. English rib stitch . . firmly knit of rich, worsted wool. Ribbed V-neck, armholes, bottom. Hand wash separately. *State size* small (8–10); med. (12–14); large (16–18). See size chart above. Shipping weight 6 ounces.
43 K 2308—Medium blue
43 K 2309—Camel (light) tan.$1.89

[E] WOOL SLEEVELESS, 3- **$1.98** COLOR STYLE. Closely knit for wear, warmth. Ribbed V-neck; self-turned armholes. Continuous knit-on worsted and elastic form-fit bottom. Hand wash separately. *State size* small (8–10); med. (12–14); large (16–18). See size chart above. Shipping weight 6 ounces.
43K2330—Navy combination.$1.98

[F] SPORTY PULLOVER. **$2.59** Sturdy and warm sweater, 60% worsted wool and 40% cotton. Tightly knit. Knit-in Jacquard pattern on front. Knit-on cuffs, bottom. Hand wash alone.
State size 10, 12, 14, 16, 18. See size chart above. Shpg. wt. 11 oz.
43K2341—Brown combination
43K2340—Blue combination.. $2.59

[G] RUGGED PART WOOL. **$1.98** 20% worsted wool, 80% cotton. Jacquard-knit medieval pattern on front. Sporty panel-ribbed knit. Slightly brushed back, sleeves. Hand wash separately.
State size 8, 10, 12, 14, 16, 18. Size chart above. Shpg. wt. 11 oz.
43 K 2327—Maroon combination
43 K 2326—Royal blue comb..$1.98

[H] WORSTED PULLOVER. **$2.94** Fine virgin wool. Baby shaker stitch—sturdy, holds its shape. Takes plenty of rough treatment. Tightly ribbed cuffs, bottom and neck fit snugly. Hand wash separately.
State size 10, 12, 14, 16, 18. See size chart above. Shipping wt. 10 oz.
43 K 2358—Medium brown
43 K 2356—Maroon..........$2.94

[J] COTTON PULLOVER. **$1.94** Heavier combed cotton yarns—tightly twisted. Jacquard-knit deer heads on front and back. Allover snowflake pattern. Tightly ribbed cuffs, bottom. Hand wash separately.
State size 8, 10, 12, 14, 16, 18. See size chart above. Shipping weight 9 oz.
43 K 2306—Green combination
43 K 2305—Brown combination.$1.94

SIZES 7 TO 14

A $3.98
Nylon Fitted Cardigan

B $2.89
Nylon Fitted Pullover

Worsted Boxy Pullover
$1.98
Our Best Quality
$2.69
D

Worsted Fitted Pullover
$1.79
Our Best Quality
$1.98
C

E Worsted Boxy Cardigan $2.49
Our Best Quality 2.98

100% DUPONT
NYLON

Washes in a flash .. dries in a jiffy
Retains shape without blocking
Luxuriously soft .. wears longer

A NYLON LONG SLEEVE FITTED CARDIGAN. Ribbed knit crew neck, cuffs and wide bottom. Button front reinforced with matching nylon ribbon. Hand washable. *Girls' sizes* 7, 8, 10, 12, 14; size chart on page 1362. *State size.* Shpg. wt. 15 oz.
77 K 4772—Pink...........$3.98
77 K 4773—Light blue...... 3.98
77 K 4774—Yellow......... 3.98
77 K 4775—White.......... 3.98

B NYLON SHORT SLEEVE FITTED PULLOVER. Hand-looped ribbed-knit crew neck, cuffs and wide bottom. Hand washable. *Girls' sizes* 7, 8, 10, 12, 14; size chart on page 1362. *State size.* Shpg. wt. 13 oz.
77 K 4768—Pink...........$2.89
77 K 4769—Light blue...... 2.89
77 K 4770—Yellow......... 2.89
77 K 4771—White.......... 2.89

HONEYLANE CLASSICS

in two qualities of
100% virgin wool worsted

C SHORT SLEEVE FITTED PULLOVER. Ribbed crew neck, cuffs and bottom. Hand washable. *Girls' sizes* 7, 8, 10, 12, 14; see size chart on page 1362. *Please state size. Good Quality Worsted.* Shipping weight 9 ounces.
77 K 4739—White..........$1.79
77 K 4733—Copen blue..... 1.79
77 K 4734—Bright red...... 1.79
77 K 4735—Yellow......... 1.79
Our Best Quality Worsted. Shipping weight 10 ounces.
77 K 4654—White..........$1.98
77 K 4655—Pink........... 1.98
77 K 4656—Yellow......... 1.98
77 K 4657—Light blue...... 1.98

D LONG SLEEVE BOXY PULLOVER. Ribbed-knit crew neck, cuffs, and bottom. Hand washable. *Girls' sizes* 7, 8, 10, 12, 14; see size chart on page 1362. *Please state size.* GOOD QUALITY WORSTED. Shipping weight 7 ounces.
77 K 4692—Light blue......$1.98
77 K 4690—Yellow......... 1.98
77 K 4776—Kelly green..... 1.98
77 K 4689—Bright red...... 1.98
Our Best Quality Worsted. Hand-looped neck. Shpg. wt. 11 oz.
77 K 4778—Light blue......$2.69
77 K 4698—White.......... 2.69
77 K 4699—Pink........... 2.69
77 K 4777—Kelly green..... 2.69

E LONG SLEEVE BOXY CARDIGAN. Ribbed-knit crew neck, cuffs, bottom. Button-front reinforced with rayon ribbon. Hand washable. *Girls' sizes* 7, 8, 10, 12, 14; size chart on page 1362. *State size. Good Quality Worsted.* Shipping weight 11 ounces.
77 K 4695—Bright red......$2.49
77 K 4784—Kelly green..... 2.49
77 K 4696—Copen blue..... 2.49
77 K 4697—Light brown.... 2.49
Our Best Quality Worsted. Hand-looped neck. Shipping wt. 12 oz.
77 K 4617—Bright red......$2.98
77 K 4713—Kelly green..... 2.98
77 K 4620—Light brown.... 2.98
77 K 4786—Royal blue..... 2.98

WOOL WORSTED Twin·Set

Pullover $1.79   Cardigan $2.59

Ribbed-knit crew neck, cuffs and bottom. Hand washable. *Girls' sizes* 7, 8, 10, 12, 14; size chart on page 1362. *State size.*
Short Sleeve Pullover. Shpg. wt. 9 oz.
77 K 4733M—Copen blue 77 K 4734M—Red
77 K 4735M—Yellow   Each........$1.79
Long Sleeve Cardigan—button-front reinforced with rayon ribbon. Shpg. wt. 11 oz.
77 K 4736M—Copen blue 77 K 4737M—Red
77 K 4738M—Yellow   Each........$2.59

NOVELTY KNIT Worsted Twin Set

Pullover $1.98   Cardigan $2.98

Attractive pineapple weave with rows of cable stitch on front. Rib-knit crew neck, cuffs, bottom. Hand washable. *Girls' sizes* 8, 10, 12, 14; size chart on page 1362. *State size.*
Short Sleeve Fitted Pullover. Shpg. wt. 10 oz.
77 K 4680M—Yellow.................$1.98
77 K 4681M—Emerald green.......... 1.98
77 K 4682M—Pink.................. 1.98
Long Sleeve Fitted Cardigan. Button-front reinforced on reverse side with matching rayon ribbon. Shipping weight 11 ounces.
77 K 4683M—Yellow.................$2.98
77 K 4684M—Emerald green.......... 2.98
77 K 4685M—Pink................... 2.98

ETON SUITS for his Sunday best, 3 styles, durable fabrics   **SNAPPY LONGIE SUITS** all wool, or cotton gabardine

ECONOMY-PRICED 3-Pc. check'n' solid **$4.98** 3-pc. suit
Eton suit. 2 button check coat is 12% wool, 38% reused wool, 50% rayon. Flannel shorts: 5% wool, 17% reprocessed wool, 28% reused wool, 31% cotton, 19% rayon. White washable cotton button-on blouse, long sleeves. *State size 3, 4, 5, 6.* See chart, opposite page. Shipping weight 2 pounds.
40E3207–Brown 3-pc. suit.
40E3214–Blue 3-pc. $4.98

4-PC. FINE WALE CORDUROY SUIT . . . **$5.25** 4-pc. suit
smart looking, but rugged! Eton coat has lined sleeves; shorts have side openings, pleats. Self belt. Sanforized white cotton (fabric shrinkage 1%) button-on blouse, short sleeves. Eton collar, pocket. *State size 3, 4, 5, 6.* See How to measure chart on opposite page. Shipping weight 2 pounds.
40E3171–Navy blue
40E3172–Dk. brown. $5.25

100% ALL NEW WOOL FLANNEL . . . **$5.95** 3-pc. set
for his Sunday-best! Solid shades of navy blue or dark brown add to flannel richness. Eton coat with 2 pockets. Lined shorts with side openings. White cotton long sleeve button-on style blouse. *Please be sure to state size 3, 4, 5, 6.* See How to measure on opposite page. Shipping weight 2 pounds.
40E3148–Navy blue
40E3149–Dk. brown.$5.95

2-TONE CASUAL SUIT, Sanforized cotton **$4.49** 2-pc. suit
gabardine (shrinkage 1%). Coat sleeves, back, collar and pockets are dark brown; teal front coat has teal (greenish blue) longies. Tan front coat has brown longies. Self-lined bib pants. Wash separately. *Please be sure to state size 3, 4, 5, 6.* See chart on opposite page. Shipping weight 2 pounds 5 ounces.
40E3156–Teal, brown
40E3157–Tan, brn. $4.49

ALL WOOL 4-Pc. 2-tone cardigan longie **$8.95** 4-pc. suit
suit. Coat: all new blue check cassimere, rayonlined. Suspender longies: navy blue all wool flannel, imitation fly front, side openings. Cuffs. Self belt. Sanforized white cotton shirt, long sleeves. *State size 3, 4, 5, 6.* See How to measure chart on opposite page. Shipping weight 2 pounds 8 ounces.
40 E 3230–Blue 4-piece longie suit $8.95

100% NEW WOOL 2-Pc. CASUAL SUIT **$8.75** 2-pc. suit
. . . his eyes'll sparkle when he sees it! Sporty coat front of smart check; solid tone flannel back, sleeves, front yoke. Rayon body, cotton sleeve linings. Button fly suspender longies. 2 pockets; cuffs. *State size 3, 4, 5, 6.* See How to measure chart on opposite page. Shipping weight 2 pounds 8 ounces.
40E3154–Brown, 2-piece.
40E3155–Blue 2-pc. $8.75

JR. SPORT SHIRTS ..all.. **SANFORIZED** cottons .**WASHFAST** colors

LONG OR SHORT SLEEVE SPORT SHIRT. **$1.29** Short sleeves
Neatly tailored of good quality Sanforized cotton broadcloth—shrinkage 1%. In-or-out bottom; 2-way collar—may be worn open, closed, or with a tie. Tie not included. Strongly stitched seams. Shipping weight 7 ounces.
Color white. *State size 3, 4, 5, 6.* See chart on opposite page.
43 E 3070–Short sleeves. $1.29
43 E 3071–Long sleeves. 1.39

SMART SOLID COLOR SPORT SHIRT of **$1.39** Each
durable, Sanforized cotton broadcloth—shrinkage 1%. Short sleeve style with 2-way collar—wear it open or closed. Square-cut in-or-out sport bottom. Double-stitched at strain points. Clear, fast-to-washing colors stay bright.
State color blue, maize. *State size 3, 4, 5, 6.* See size chart on opposite page. Shipping weight 6 ounces.
43 E 3072 . . . .$1.39

NEAT TATTERSALL CHECK—looks **$1.49** Each
smart anywhere. Fine Sanforized 80x80 print —won't shrink over 1%. Made for summer comfort with short sleeves, 2-way collar, and in-or-out sport bottom. Fast-to-washing colors on white background. Double stitched.
State color gold and brown, blue and red. *State size 3, 4, 5, 6.* See size chart on opposite page. Shpg. wt. 6 oz.
43 E 3074 . . . .$1.49

COLORFUL WESTERN PRINT to delight **$1.59** Each
little lads. Carefully tailored of better quality Sanforized cotton fabric that takes lots of wear, keeps its fit—shrinkage 1%. Short sleeves, 2-way collar, in-or-out bottom. Fast-to-washing colors stay bright.
Please be sure to state color blue, tan. *State size 3, 4, 5, 6.* See size chart on opposite page. Shipping weight 7 oz.
43 E 3076 . . . .$1.59

HANDSOME WESTERN TYPE SHIRT styled like the ones **$1.69** Each
hard-ridin', bronco-bustin' cowboys wear. Distinctive red piping trim at collar, cuffs, and pocket. Well tailored of rich, fine quality cotton broadcloth. Sanforized—won't shrink over 1%. 2-way collar, long sleeves, in-or-out sport bottom. Sturdily stitched. Color is washfast.
State size 3, 4, 5, 6. See size chart on opposite page. Shpg. wt. 7 oz.
43 E 3078—Maize $1.69

HONEYSUCKLE
THE RIGHT WAY TO SAY CHILDREN'S WEAR

A $4.98

B $5.98

C $3.98

D 69c

E $1.59

SMARTLY TAILORED all-wool Suits

A All-Wool Flannel
classic. Gold color buttons on boxy unlined jacket, waistband and side closing of skirt. 2 box pleats front and back, adjustable suspenders. Dry clean. *Sizes 3, 4, 5, 6, 6x. State size.* Shpg. wt. 1 lb. 4 oz.
29 E 4045—Copen blue
29 E 4046—Coral rose
Each............$4.98

B All Wool Flannel
—plain and plaid. Solid color flared back unlined jacket with back shoulder yoke, cutaway front, gold color buttons. 4-gore plaid swing skirt. Adjustable suspenders. Dry clean. *Sizes 3, 4, 5, 6, 6x. State size.* Shpg. wt. 1 lb. 3 oz.
29 E 4048—Copen blue
29E4047—Red. Ea. $5.98

All-wool Cape

C All-Wool Flannel
cape enhanced by dainty bird and floral sprig embroidery on the collar and arm slits. Gold color metal button and link closing at the neck. Unlined. Simply tailored style. Dry clean. *Sizes 3, 4, 5, 6, 6x. State size.* Shpg. wt. 15 oz.
29 E 4049—Navy.. $3.98
29 E 4050—Red... 3.98

THRIFT-PRICED washable cotton Skirts

D Printed Check
Gingham has double row of rick-rack all around. Dirndl style billows out from the tiny elastic shirred waist. Adjustable suspenders. Blouse sold below. *Sizes 3, 4, 5, 6, 6x. State size.* Shpg. wt. 5 oz.
29E4100—Red and white
29E4101—Blue and white
Each............69c

E Washable Calico.
Colorfast floral print with a gay apron ruffle -trimmed with rick-rack going all around the front and sweeping up the back. Adjustable button-on suspenders. Blouse sold below. *Sizes 3, 4, 5, 6, 6x. State size.* Shpg. wt. 6 oz.
29 E 4102—Multicolor print............$1.59

F 79c

G Last Fall Price Was $1.59 $1.49

H $1.69

J $1.69

A PERFECT TEAM

Sheer Cotton Blouse
Cotton Poplin Skirt
both are washable

White Blouse $1.69

L Cool, sheer cotton with double row of rick-rack around the top at front and back. Red drawstring shirrs the neck and ends in bow. Elastic cuffs on short sleeves. Sizes 3, 4, 5, 6, 6x. State size. Shipping weight 5 oz.
29 E 4638—White. $1.69

Black Skirt $1.98

M Combed cotton mercerized poplin dirndl skirt with self ruffle popping up above the border flounce; five rows of white rick-rack (one edging the wide hemline). Adjustable button-on suspenders; side button placket. Sizes 3, 4, 5, 6, 6x. State size. Shpg. wt. 13 oz.
29 E 4114—Black.. $1.98

PLENTY OF DRESS-UP FRILLY STYLES in white washable cotton Blouses

F Cotton Broadcloth
Classic with notched collar, button front, patch pocket. Unusual value for this quality good count broadcloth. Washable. *Sizes 3, 4, 5, 6, 6x. State size.* Shipping wt 5 oz.
29 E 4635—White...79c

G Washable Cotton
broadcloth. Self ruffle on Peter Pan collar. Colorful embroidery, pleats and ruffle on concealed button front. Puff sleeves. *Sizes 3, 4, 5, 6, 6x. State size.* Shpg. wt. 5 oz.
29 E 4603—White. $1.49

H Washable Cotton
broadcloth. Ruffle on high neck and around tucked front yoke. String bow. Puff sleeves with cuff. Button back. *Sizes 3, 4, 5,6, 6x. State size.* Shipping weight 5 ounces.
29 E 4636—White. $1.69

J Washable Cotton
Broadcloth. Eyelet yoke trimmed with self ruffle edged with gold-color rick-rack. Rickrack on elastic cuff of puff sleeves. Button back. *Sizes 3, 4, 5, 6, 6x. State size.* Shpg. wt. 9 oz.
29 E 4637—White. $1.69

Size Chart, Sizes 3 to 6x for Skirts, blouses, Suits

Order size:...	3	4	5	6	6x
If chest is......	22	23	24	25	25½ in.
Skirt length.....	11	12	13	14	15 in.

K Washable Cotton Broadcloth
combination blouse and slip. Ruffle edge on Peter Pan collar. Multicolor embroidery on ruffle front. Buttons to waist. Full skirt with ruffle bottom. Sizes 3,4,5,6,6x. State size. Shpg. wt. 10 oz... $1.98

K $1.98
Blouseslip

Sears famous HONEYSUCKLE
CORDUROYS
Made to our rigid specifications for fabric..fit..fine workmanship

[A] $1.98 Overalls

[C] $1.39 Boxer Shorts

For Girls and Boys Sizes 1 to 4

[B] $4.98 set Overalls and Jacket

[D] $1.98 Boxer Longies

HONEYSUCKLE Overalls and 2-piece Jacket Set

- Fine pinwale corduroy .. soft, yet rugged and long-wearing
- Overalls have double-fabric bibs, adjustable suspenders, pocket
- Strongly stitched throughout

[A] OVERALLS, with embroidered design on bib-front. (Polo shirt sold at right.) State size 1, 2, 3, 4; size chart, opposite page. Shpg. wt. 8 oz.
29 K 6804—Copen blue ... $1.98
29 K 6800—Bright red 1.98

[B] JACKET AND OVERALL SET. Jacket has zipper front, elastic at sides, 2 pockets, cotton kasha lining. Adjustable suspenders on overalls. Hand wash separately. State size 1, 2, 3, 4; size chart, opposite page. Shpg. wt. 1 lb. 1 oz.
29 K 6813—Bright red. 2-pc.$4.98
29 K 6814—Copen blue. 2-pc. 4.98

HONEYSUCKLE boxer Shorts and Longies

- Wide elastic all around waist
- Long-wearing pinwale corduroy
- Fly-front, two handy pockets
- Double needle stitching at all points of extra strain

[C] BOXER SHORTS. (Polo shirt sold at right.) Hand wash separately. Sizes 1, 2, 3, 4; size chart, opposite page. State size. Shpg. wt. 5 oz.
29 K 6871—Gray $1.39
29 K 6870—Royal blue 1.39
29 K 6872—Medium brown... 1.39

[D] BOXER LONGIES. Full length, full cut. (Shirt sold at right.) Hand wash separately. Sizes 1, 2, 3, 4; size chart on opposite page. State size. Shipping weight 6 ounces.
29 K 6873—Brown
29 K 6874—Gray
29 K 6875—Royal blue
Each $1.98

WALT DISNEY Movie Stars in COLOR on Sanforized blue denim SIZES 1 to 4 © W. D. P.

$1.69

$1.09

$1.49

Cartoons hand screened .. won't run or crack off. Designed by Walt Disney studios. Denim won't shrink more than 1%. Wash separately. (Shirts sold separately.) Sizes 1, 2, 3, 4; size chart on opposite page. State size.

DONALD DUCK and playmates on overalls. Double fabric bib-top, back pocket. Shpg. wt. 7 oz.
29 K 6846—Colorful print on navy blue $1.69

PLUTO AND PUPS on boxer shorts. Elastic all around waist. For girls and boys. Shpg. wt. 5 oz.
29 K 6847—Colorful print on navy blue $1.09

MICKEY MOUSE and Minnie on boxer longies. Elastic around waist. Shpg. wt. 4 oz.
29 K 6848—Colorful print on navy blue $1.49

89c

69c Long Sleeves

59c Short Sleeves

59c Short Sleeves

69c Long Sleeves

COMBED COTTON KNIT POLO SHIRTS, 2-button shoulders

NURSERY DESIGN is screen-printed by hand. Long sleeves. Wash separately. Sizes 1, 2, 3, 4; see size chart on opposite page. State size. Shpg. wt. 5 oz.
29 K 6987—Yellow
29 K 6988—Med. blue
29 K 6989—White
Each 89c

STRIPED. Wash separately. Sizes 1, 2, 3, 4. State size. Shpg. wt. ea. 4 oz.
Long Sleeve Style.
29 K 6830—Red 69c
29 K 6831—Blue 69c
2 for $1.35
Short Sleeve Style.
29 K 6864—Red 59c
29 K 6865—Blue 59c
2 for $1.15

SOLID COLORS. Wash separately. Sizes 1, 2, 3, 4. State size.
Short Sleeve. Shpg. wt. 4 oz.
29 K 6834—Med. blue 59c
29 K 6833—White 59c
2 for $1.15
Long Sleeve. Shpg. wt. 4 oz.
29 K 6866—Med. blue 69c
29 K 6867—White 69c
29 K 6868—Yellow 69c
2 for $1.35

[E] 89c

[F] $1.39

[G] $1.69

Tots' Tailored Shirts

Washable cottons. State size 2,3,4; size chart, opposite page. Shpg. wt. 5 oz.

[E] CLASSIC white cotton short sleeve shirt. Double stitched seams.
29 K 6525—White 89c

[F] COTTON FLANNEL. Long sleeves. Sanforized, won't shrink over 1%.
29 K 6512—Red print $1.39
29 K 6513—Yellow print 1.39

[G] PLAID COTTON FLANNEL. Sanforized fabric, won't shrink more than 1%. Long sleeve style.
29 K 6514—Red and navy plaid .$1.69

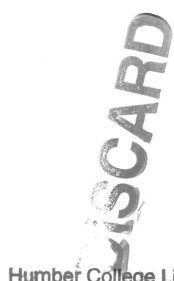